FOREVER YOUNG

MANCHESTER UNITED F.C.
CLIFF GROUND

'He was incredible'
Ryan Giggs

The Story of
ADRIAN DOHERTY
Football's
Lost Genius

FOREVER YOUNG

OLIVER KAY

FOREVER YOUNG

The Story of Adrian Doherty,
Football's Lost Genius

OLIVER KAY

Quercus

First published in Great Britain in 2016 by

Quercus Editions Ltd
Carmelite House
50 Victoria Embankment
London EC4Y 0DZ

An Hachette UK company

A CIP catalogue record for this book is available
from the British Library

HB ISBN 978 1 84866 994 9
TPB ISBN 978 1 78429 541 7
EBOOK ISBN 978 1 84866 986 4

10 9 8 7 6 5 4 3 2 1

Typeset by Jouve (UK), Milton Keynes

Printed and bound in the UK by Clays Ltd, St Ives plc

PROLOGUE

The busker lowers his head and moves towards the oncoming crowd. It fills his field of vision, but he pushes his way through the throng, shuffling away from the congestion and the noise and the edifice of Old Trafford. He carries on up Warwick Road, past the street vendors – 'Eighty pence, your programme', 'United scarf, only a pound' – and onto Chester Road, where the match-day smells of fish and chips, salt and vinegar, cigarettes, ale and horse dung fill the air. He reaches the bus stop, where he waits, leather guitar case in hand, trying not to catch anyone's eye. The bus pulls up and spews its passengers onto the pavement, chanting as they go. He gets on, hands over his fare and sits quietly, the stadium disappearing behind him, as the bus resumes its journey into Manchester.

He gets off at the bottom of Deansgate and encounters another crowd, this time the mass of Saturday afternoon shoppers. He hates being in a scrum, hates the hustle and bustle of the city, but he goes on, head down. He turns onto Market Street and walks along the front of the Arndale Centre. He pitches up in his usual place, unfastens the buckle, gets out his guitar, slings the case onto the floor, starts strumming – C major, D minor, E minor, F major, G major – and he is into his stride.

Most of the passers-by try to ignore him. A few offer a sympathetic smile. The odd one even chucks him a few pence. The busker smiles in gratitude, but he isn't doing it for the money. He has more money than a teenager of modest tastes knows what to do with. He just wants to play, he wants to sing, he wants to perform. He wants the sense of escapism that comes over him as he works his way towards the refrain, belting it out with an anguished sincerity that even the most blinkered, head-down shoppers cannot quite manage to shut out.

> *How does it feeeeeel*
> *To be on your own*
> *With no direction home*
> *Like a complete unknown*
> *Like a rolling stone?*

The busker loves Bob Dylan. He especially loves 'Like a Rolling Stone', the hobo's anthem. The lyrics have a barbed edge, as Dylan's vagrant seems at first to sneer at 'Miss Lonely', a society woman who has suffered a sharp fall from grace, but the confrontational tone gradually gives way to compassion and a glorification of life on the street. The howling is an assault on the busker's vocal cords – and, he would concede, on the eardrums of passers-by – but it feels therapeutic after a long, mind-numbing, physically exhausting week. He is letting out his emotions, just like those Manchester United supporters he passed earlier, who by now will be watching the action unfold from the terraces at Old Trafford.

As inconspicuous as he might look – pale, slight, scruffy,

dressed in what look suspiciously like second-hand clothes – the busker is not a complete unknown. Far from it, in fact. Adrian Doherty is a Manchester United footballer of outstanding promise, spending his Saturday mornings playing alongside another hot prospect named Ryan Giggs in the club's A team. Doherty and Giggs are United's rising stars. The expectation is that sooner or later both will be bringing their pace and trickery to the first team – Doherty on the right wing, Giggs on the left. Both players have been compared, dauntingly, to the great George Best, Doherty even more so because he hails from Northern Ireland. He has already travelled with the first team, narrowly missing out on the substitutes' bench at the age of sixteen, for a match at Southampton. Alex Ferguson believes Doherty has 'great potential and could go all the way'. 'I'm sure he'll make it,' the United manager says.

The mystery to Ferguson, Giggs and the rest of the coaches and players at United is why Adrian Doherty at times appears almost ambivalent about his wonderfully bright future. Music seems to excite him as much as football. Poetry, too, it is rumoured. When the club offered him an unprecedented five-year professional contract, to take effect from his seventeenth birthday, he stunned Ferguson by proposing a one-year deal before they settled on a compromise of three. His team-mates cannot work him out. The ritual among the apprentices and young professionals is that, after playing their Lancashire League fixtures on Saturday mornings, they head to Old Trafford to watch United's first team in the afternoon. But Doherty prefers to give his two complimentary tickets away. He cuts an incongruous figure outside the ground, the scruffy lad with his guitar case, itching to hand over the tickets to some lucky soul so he can get on with his business. His football ambitions are far more serious than his dreamy demeanour suggests, but for now his Saturday afternoons are about music. At 4.45 p.m. he might look into a shop window – Rumbelows, Tandy or the like – to check the United result on the BBC's videprinter. He might check the scores on Ceefax when he gets back to his digs later on. Or he might not. It is unlikely to be the first thing on his mind.

'I had never seen anything like him before,' says Ryan Giggs, sitting in an office at Manchester United's training ground. 'You would look at him the first couple of times in the changing room and think, "Well, he can't play . . .", because Doc didn't really look like a footballer if you know what I mean. He was unorthodox in the way he dressed and the way he acted. He wasn't like the rest of us. He played the guitar, he loved his music and he was obsessed with Bob Dylan. As a sixteen-year-old, I didn't have a clue who Bob Dylan was.

'But once he was out on the pitch, he was incredible. He was the quickest I had ever seen and he was so brave as well. He was an incredible talent. Incredible.'

Everyone knows the story of Ryan Giggs, the boy wonder who was always destined for the top and who stayed there, tormenting full-backs, winning trophies and breaking records, for what seemed an eternity. What has been lost in the mists of time is that the most successful player in United's fabled history was not always regarded as the best performer, or even the best winger, in the club's youth team. Opinion is divided among former team-mates, but there are plenty who, whatever their pride at having played alongside a living legend of British football, swear that at times even Giggs found himself in the shadow of Adrian Doherty.

'I wouldn't disagree with that,' Giggs says. 'It seemed like every time we went on the pitch, over a period of about six months, he was doing something special, whereas I at that time was a bit inconsistent. Doc always seemed to be able to handle any situation. He was off the cuff. Playing alongside him or training with him or watching him, he would do something that would make you smile – beating three or four men and sticking it in the top corner. But what really stays in my mind is how brave he was. He would have defenders kicking lumps out of him, because of the type of player he was, and he would just get up and demand the ball again and keep running at them again and again.

'I wouldn't say he had a "ping" like Scholesy [Paul Scholes] or a technical kind of cross like Becks [David Beckham], but at the same time, he could switch the play and cross it. He could go past people at will. He could ride tackles like you wouldn't believe. He could go inside, out-side, play one-twos, pass and move. He just seemed to have a picture in his head from a very early stage. You know in *The Matrix*, where everything clicks together, where it's all happening quickly, but in the character's head it's happening in slow motion? It was like that with Doc. It looked like it was all instinctive, but it's a bit like Wayne Rooney, where, yes, he's a street footballer, but you know he's also a real natural with a real football brain. Doc was the same.

'For the manager [Alex Ferguson], he was the ideal player. The manager loved fast, attacking players, especially wingers. He used to bollock me regularly, but he never used to give Doc a bollocking – partly because he was very good at managing people and knowing what made them tick, but mainly because Doc did the right things every time, whereas I would end up learning the hard way. Doc just didn't upset the manager. Being the type of player he was, a winger who was unpredictable and took risks, you would expect him to lose the ball from time to time, but honestly he would lose it very rarely. He was a freak. He was incredible.

'He was definitely at the same level as me. He had been involved with the first team before me and he had travelled with them a couple of times. He was definitely on the brink of making his first-team debut. Who knows what would have happened if things had gone differently? He definitely had the talent. You never know for certain whether players will adapt and do it in the first team, but my guess is that, mentality-wise, it would have been no problem for him.

'When I think about Doc, I feel a great sadness that he wasn't able to give the pleasure he would have given to his team-mates, the fans and himself. People would have loved watching him. But there's also a happy memory of the talent he had and the character he was – a freakish talent, a unique character, a boy who would just go out and play.'

CHAPTER I

Take a walk along the River Mourne on a mild spring morning and, as the buzz of the traffic fades into the distance, you find yourself looking at Strabane through the eyes of its most famous son. Brian O'Nolan, better known as Flann O'Brien, one of the great figures of Irish literature, called it 'that happy-go-lucky town at the confluence of two tumbling rivers'. His brother Ciarán wrote that their childhood days by the Mourne were 'the happiest of our lives, particularly the hours spent in the long grass of the riverbank while the sun seemed to stand still in the cloudless summer sky and we could hear the distant clang of moving machines and the faint hum of the turbines in the linen mill'.

Now, like a century ago, life in this corner of County Tyrone is quiet. The tourist board describes Strabane, the nearby Sperrin Mountains and the surrounding forests and glens as 'a truly unspoilt world of scenic beauty' and 'a place where stories are to be told, secrets are to be unlocked and where friends are to be found'.

This story begins in a very different Strabane, far from the rural idyll described by the O'Nolans. 'Happy-go-lucky' is certainly not the adjective one would apply to the Strabane in which Adrian Doherty was born on 10 June

1973. The decline of the textile and farming industries had caused the unemployment rate in the town to soar. By the time of the 1971 census, 20.5 per cent of Strabane's men of working age were unemployed, far beyond the UK average of 4 per cent at the time. The town was also a major pressure point in the Troubles, which were at their mindlessly destructive height as tension escalated between Northern Ireland's Nationalist/Republican (largely Catholic) minority, which sought to break away from the United Kingdom, and its Unionist/Loyalist (largely Protestant) majority. Strabane was not as severely affected as Belfast or Derry, or as volatile as the so-called 'Bandit Country' of South Armagh, but, as a Nationalist stronghold barely a mile from the border with the Republic of Ireland, it was a scene of frequent riots, bombings and gun battles. One frequent claim is that, between the end of World War Two and the start of the Balkan conflict of the early 1990s, it was, relative to size and population, the most bombed town in Europe.

The Troubles reached Strabane, like much of provincial Northern Ireland, on 9 August 1971. That was the day the British Army launched Operation Demetrius, involving dawn raids and the mass arrest and internment – imprisonment without trial – of 342 Irish Nationalists suspected of involvement with the Irish Republican Army (IRA). Operation Demetrius sparked four days of violence as British soldiers were attacked in towns across Northern Ireland. Shortly before midnight that evening Winston Donnell, a 22-year-old Ulster Defence Regiment (UDR) soldier, was shot dead by a gunman from a car at a vehicle checkpoint near Clady, five miles outside Strabane.

It was the first of seventy-eight deaths that occurred in the area through bombings, shootings and other violent incidents over the two decades in which the Troubles raged.

'Strabane was blown to pieces,' Jimmy Doherty says. 'There were explosions left, right and centre. Historic buildings were damaged or ruined. If you approached a car and there was no one inside, you were paranoid, worrying that a bomb was about to go off. If you went into a store, your bags would be searched in case you were carrying firebombs or anything else. Mothers would be made to take their babies out of their prams so the prams could be searched for explosives. You couldn't blame the soldiers for that. Young soldiers were getting shot at every day. It was a war zone. A lot of people moved away, to Australia, Canada and so on. There was a bit of an exodus.'

Jimmy and Geraldine Doherty did not consider joining the exodus. War zone or not, the north-west was their home. Jimmy had been brought up in the Brandywell area of Derry – near the stadium of the same name, where he played football for Derry City during the 1960s. As one of the few local players to be signed on a professional contract, he was a recognisable face in Derry and Strabane, but it was his long hair, flowery shirts, flared trousers, cheeky smile and quick wit that made more of an impression on Geraldine Barrett when, like so many couples across Ireland in that era, they met at a showband dance. 'Those nights were the highlight of the week,' Jimmy says. 'There wasn't much else for people to look forward to. We would go to the Palindrome, in Strabane, and it would be crammed every week.'

Jimmy and Geraldine hit it off immediately, to the

delight of her father, John Barrett, and the disapproval of her redoubtable mother, Rose, who had already seen one of their seven daughters, Nellie, marry a footballer (Willie Ferry, who played for Derry City before Jimmy). Geraldine had no interest in the sport, but she was warned by her mother that footballers had fewer brain cells than ordinary folk because of 'all that heading of the ball'. 'And when Geraldine's mother saw what I was wearing, with the flowery shirts and the long collars, she was even more horrified,' Jimmy says. 'But we ended up getting on very well.'

After a two-year courtship, Jimmy and Geraldine married at St Mary's Church in Strabane on 8 June 1970 – 'during the Mexico World Cup,' Jimmy helpfully points out – and moved into a rented house on the Ballycolman estate, just south of the town centre. It was a new-build, with two bedrooms and central heating. They were moving up in the world, but the Ballycolman was home to a large number of Strabane's unemployed and it had not escaped anyone's notice that so many Catholics were out of work while so many of the local businesses were run and positions filled by the town's small Protestant minority. This issue, reflecting a perceived trend through much of Northern Ireland, was at the heart of the unrest that had even spread to apolitical types such as Jimmy. 'Although we were Catholics and we went to Mass every Sunday, we weren't political people at all,' he says. 'But this didn't feel like a political issue. It was a civil rights movement, about jobs and housing, and almost everyone got involved one way or the other.'

On Sunday, 30 January 1972, Jimmy Doherty took the

bus from Strabane to Derry to join a crowd of thousands in the latest protest march, organised by the Northern Ireland Civil Rights Association and the Northern Resistance Movement. He was late getting there. 'The march had been re-routed, so I had to make a detour on foot,' he says. 'By the time I reached Free Derry Corner, there were riots starting on William Street. Bernadette Devlin [the 24-year-old civil rights activist who was the independent MP for Mid Ulster] was on the back of a lorry, shouting into a megaphone, saying it was meant to be a peaceful protest and asking people to leave the area. Then suddenly we heard gunshots in the distance and everyone fell to the ground. I froze. I was lying on my belly in the street. It was amazingly scary for a few minutes. And then things seemed to die down. I walked through the Bogside a few hours later, back to the bus station, and the place was in darkness. It was the evening, in winter, but all the street lights were off. I wandered back and caught the bus to Strabane. There had been rumours about people being shot, but it was only when I got home that I heard thirteen people had been killed. Because of the type of area it was, I knew some of them. Hugh Gilmour [a seventeen-year-old victim] had lived next door to me. Bloody Sunday. And things escalated from there.'

Strabane was still relatively untouched by the Troubles when Jimmy and Geraldine Doherty's first son, Gareth, was born on 13 May 1971, but the picture had changed dramatically by the time Geraldine fell pregnant again the following year. On 9 June 1973 she went into labour and was taken once more to Strabane hospital. Jimmy was concerned for his wife, whose father had died earlier that week, but he was advised to stay at home to look after the two-year-old Gareth. 'In those days the matrons didn't want you there at all,' he says. 'You kept your distance.'

Jimmy went to bed that night without receiving the expected bulletin from the hospital. The following morning, 10 June, he awoke at 6.30 a.m. and, after leaving Gareth with Geraldine's sister Marie, he set off for Mopack, the plastics factory where he worked. 'It was the nearest place I knew that had a phone,' he says. 'I had to climb over the gateway into the factory to use the phone there and ring the hospital. They told me our second son had been born at half past midnight, and he and Geraldine were doing well. And that was Adrian.'

Eleven days later David Smith, a 31-year-old dog handler for the Royal Welsh Fusiliers, was killed by an IRA booby trap while searching derelict houses on the Ballycolman estate. It was the fourteenth death caused by the Troubles in the Strabane area in less than two years.

Jimmy and Geraldine Doherty are an adorable couple. People in Strabane tell me, from my first visit, that they and their sons and daughter are 'the nicest folk you could wish to meet'. Over a succession of meetings, always revolving around coffee and cakes, they sit in their lounge, always next to each other on the two-seater sofa, and cast frequent glances towards the mantelpiece, where – among the various photographs of their children, Gareth, Ciara and Peter, and their ever-expanding collection of grandsons – a black-and-white photograph of a teenage Adrian takes pride of place.

What kind of boy was he? 'Energetic,' says Jimmy with a chuckle. 'Lively,' laughs Geraldine. 'Oh, definitely lively.'

'He was into everything,' Gareth, now in his forties, says. 'I think I was maybe a typical first child, and I would usually think things through before acting, but Adrian was head-first into everything – spontaneous, fearless, full of mischief.'

The first nine years of Adrian Doherty's life were spent on the Ballycolman estate. At number 209, Jimmy and Geraldine shared one bedroom and Gareth and Adrian shared the other. Geraldine's mother, known to the kids as Granny Barrett, lived on the estate with her daughter Christina, while another three Barrett girls – Nellie, Annette and Geraldine's twin sister, Marie – had also settled there with their families, respectively the Ferrys, the Sharkeys and the O'Dohertys. Granny Barrett's house was the hub of the family. 'It was always hiving there, always full of aunties, uncles and cousins,' Gareth says.

The cousins were constantly in and out of each other's houses, with Sean Ferry and the Doherty boys becoming so inseparable that neighbours assumed they were all brothers. 'It was that time when kids constantly played out on the streets,' Gareth says. 'A group of us would all have races down the hill – a couple of us on bikes, a couple in home-made go-karts and the odd other "improvised" vehicle. It was like *Wacky Races*. One time I remember Adrian coming off his bike on a tight bend, just round the corner from the house. The doctor was called and there was no serious damage, but he was told to stay off the bike for a few days. Then, typical Adrian, he kidnapped our wee sister's favourite toy, Snowy, a grey dog on wheels. That was brave because Ciara was the boss of the house from an early age. I was sceptical, but, as it turned out, Snowy was a flying machine, with Adrian's feet pounding the pavement, Fred Flintstone-style.'

The Doherty family had swelled to five when Ciara was born in January 1978, a sister for Gareth and Adrian. As much as her oldest brother might have considered her the boss of the family, Ciara insists she barely got a look in, particularly after a third brother, Peter, was born in July 1984. 'Everything in our house was always like a competition because the boys were sport-mad,' she says. 'Because I was a girl, I wasn't really included in all that, but I just loved being around my brothers. I know you might say we must have argued, but when I look back now, there are no bad memories. Only good ones. There were never any arguments.'

'Apart from playing sport,' Peter interjects.

'Oh yes, apart from sport,' Ciara says. 'Adrian was really *really* competitive.'

'He was an unbelievably bad loser,' Gareth says. 'That would probably surprise most people who knew him later as quiet and laid-back. Ninety-nine per cent of the time he was laid-back. But when he was playing sport . . .'

'He just hated losing,' their cousin Sean Ferry says. 'Football, snooker, anything, he had to win. And even though he was two years younger than us – and the stan-dard was always decent on the Ballycolman – he would hold his own. There was a wee green behind where we used to live and sometimes now, when I walk past it on my way into town, I can't believe how small it is.'

'Hannigans' Green,' Gareth says. 'It was just across from where a couple of mates of ours, the Hannigans, lived. Obviously they didn't own the land, but that's what we all used to call it. The matches sort of just happened. People would go home for dinner or be called in for homework and other lads would join in – coats for goalposts, a pitch full of bumps and what must have been a 75-degree slope. To us, it was like Wembley.'

By now, Jimmy Doherty, having hung up his football boots, was working for DuPont, the American chemicals company that had a factory nearby, initially as a machine operator, then in charge of the conveyor system before moving to the warehouse. 'We didn't have much in terms of luxuries, but my da worked hard to make sure we didn't go without anything,' his son Gareth says. 'He worked a lot of twelve-hour shifts, nights and weekends too, and we would often drag him out to play football after three or four hours' sleep. He could never resist a game of football. My ma worked in the other local factory, Adria, as a machinist, but gave it up in the end to look after us. She lived for the family. She used to put up with a lot in a house full of lads, constantly playing or watching sport on TV. If it wasn't sport, it was Bruce Lee or cowboy films or *Spiderman*, *Tarzan*, *The Six Million Dollar Man* or *Monkey*.'

Ah yes, *Monkey*, the weird Japanese TV drama which had Buddhist or Taoist philosophies as a background for the 'funkiest monkey that ever popped'. The young Adrian was obsessed with it, re-enacting the fight scenes with his friends, using his mother's yard brush for Monkey's magical wishing staff.

The Saturday-night routine in the Doherty household would involve bathtime, pyjamas and a couple of hours in front of the television as a treat – *Starsky & Hutch*, *The Generation Game*, *Kojak*, perhaps even *Match of the Day* if the boys could stay awake long enough, which Adrian, exhausted, rarely could. 'One Saturday night we were waiting for Adrian to come down in his pyjamas and we went up to check on him and he wasn't there,' his father, Jimmy, says. 'He must have slipped out the front door. We were panicking and then Louise Ferry, our niece, came over, panicking, and said Adrian had appeared on his bike and been hit by a motorcycle. Luckily he had only cut his knee, but anything could have happened. We said to him: "Adrian, you must never go out like that. What were you doing? Where were you going?" He told us he was going out to play snooker. He was only about eight or nine. He certainly kept you on your toes.'

Give or take the odd bike-related drama, it sounds like a fairly typical 1970s/1980s childhood. But it was not. The Troubles, like that faint hum of the turbines in Brian O'Nolan's day, always seemed to be there in the background – on the television news, on the radio, in the paper, in people's conversations. And when they were not in the background, they were in the foreground.

'The army would have armed foot patrols on the Ballycolman when we were running about,' Gareth Doherty recalls. 'When the police drove through, some lads would throw stones. You would see the odd riot. You would see on the news that people were getting killed in Belfast or Derry and occasionally Strabane, but we were kids, and it was the norm to us, so we didn't think about it all that much. I remember getting stopped by a couple of soldiers when I was about nine or ten. That was a bit scary. They made you take your shoes off and they checked your pockets, asked you questions. That was seen as a common occurrence back then, but it didn't affect you on a day-to-day basis.'

They learned to make light of the Troubles. When they looked out of the bedroom window one evening to see a car ablaze and petrol bombs being thrown, Gareth and Adrian, along with their cousins Karen and Louise Ferry, tried to convince a frightened Ciara it was 'Mickey Mouse's surprise birthday party and they're having a bonfire and fireworks for him'. They learned to recognise the warning signals, like if they were called inside early, which might suggest a riot was taking place, or if an area had been cordoned off. 'The odd time you would spot "masked men" running about,' Gareth says, 'and you knew there was something serious going on when you heard the helicopter out.'

John Tinney, who would play football alongside Adrian in school and district teams through their early teens, recalls the troubles in starker terms. 'I lived in a Nationalist area, the head of the town, and there were a lot of house raids,' he says. 'You didn't have to be an IRA suspect to have your house raided. Once they came into a Nationalist area, they just randomly raided, going into your house, through your personal stuff. I remember soldiers in uniforms coming in with Alsatians. They were looking for explosives, so there would be sniffer dogs tapping your bed. You could walk out in the morning and find a soldier lying at your front door. They had been lying in your front garden overnight and you wouldn't know. We didn't know any different, but you were trying to fit your day-to-day activities, your normal childhood, into what was basically a war zone.'

Kevin Doherty (no relation), who would become one of Adrian's best friends once they started at St Mary's Boys' Primary School, has a slightly different take on Troubles-era Strabane. 'John was brought up in a more traditionally Republican neighbourhood than Adrian or I grew up in,' he says. 'I would say Adrian's family environment shielded him from it to a large extent. We were all Catholics, but you still wouldn't necessarily venture into the tougher neighbourhoods if you didn't really need to. It did play on your mind when you were walking home at night. You were mindful of cars if they were travelling slowly. We were all aware of it – it was impossible not to be – but only as something that was in the background.'

Dee Devenney, who also grew up on the Ballycolman, agrees. 'To be honest, the Troubles went over my head until I got older,' he says. 'We didn't know it was any different to anywhere else. Nobody had much money, but, for us kids, it was a fantastic place to grow up.'

CHAPTER 2

At St Mary's Boys' Primary School, in Strabane, Bob Crilly took his position as coach of the football team seriously – a little too seriously, he claims, for the school principal's liking. Crilly ran two teams and took time to watch during lunch breaks to see if there was any new talent emerging in the playground. One day he witnessed something entirely unexpected – a seven-year-old darting between his classmates and older boys with a tennis ball at his feet, manoeuvring himself and the ball through gaps that seemed not to exist. It was nothing new to those lads who lived on the Ballycolman, but to Crilly and to some of the boys in the playground it was startling. As Adrian Doherty's friend Niall Dunphy puts it, 'There was this moment playing in the playground where you suddenly realised: "Jesus Christ, he's about twice the speed of the rest of us."'

Adrian was known as one of the brightest boys in his class at St Mary's, but not, until now, as a footballer. Crilly marked him down as a dead-cert for the school team, but was shocked when word came back that the latest star of the playground did not fancy it. Why? 'Because he was shy and he didn't want to put himself forward in public,' Crilly says with the same booming laugh that used to scare the bejesus out of Adrian and his classmates. 'It took a bit of work from his father and me to persuade him to play.'

As Jimmy Doherty recalls it, Adrian was worried by the thought of leaving his friends behind to play with the P6 and P7 boys, who were so much bigger. In the end, he was persuaded. He was a revelation in the school team, first of all in the second XI and, quickly, the first XI. 'He was far and away the star of the team,' Kevin Doherty says. 'It was a real surprise to people just how good he was when they had never seen him before.'

That much is confirmed by John Farrell, a local referee, who used to take charge of the school matches. 'Even aged eight and nine, he was just too good,' Farrell says. 'He would get the ball and –' he shakes his head – 'I can't even describe. He was just a wizard with the ball at his feet. He was like Johan Cruyff out there.'

It says something about Adrian Doherty's quiet demeanour that his sporting talent should have surprised so many. Football, after all, was in the Doherty family's genes. His father, Jimmy, had been a tricky left-winger – so tricky, in fact, that in August 1963, at the age of sixteen, he was invited to go on trial with Middlesbrough. Jimmy's excitement at being offered a two-year contract was lessened when he learned the same courtesy had been offered to dozens of others and so, rather than move to England, he concluded he would be better off staying at home, working at the Birmingham Sound Reproducers factory in Creggan, making record-player turntables, and signing for Derry City.

Jimmy Doherty was a popular figure during his three seasons as a first-team regular for Derry, gaining international recognition with the Northern Ireland amateur team, in matches against England, Scotland and Wales, and earning a professional contract. But the beginnings of the Troubles saw the club engulfed in sectarian tension – not least with the Belfast-based Irish Football Association. Security concerns surrounding the Brandywell would see Derry forced to play home matches thirty miles away in Coleraine and, ultimately, withdrawing from the Irish League in 1973 and spending twelve years in the wilderness before joining the League of Ireland, south of the border. Doherty did not stick around to watch things deteriorate. Before the end of the 1960s he moved on to Coleraine and then Finn Harps, spending a season with each, but he had reluctantly settled for a more stable career, as a machine worker at Mopack, near the new family home in Strabane, by the time he became a father for the second time in 1973.

It did not require any great paternal encouragement for Jimmy Doherty's sons to play football – 'they just started kicking a ball about, the same as every other boy in the area', he says – but he remembers thinking Gareth was a natural and Adrian even more so. 'Suddenly at the age of eight or nine Adrian looked outstanding,' Jimmy says. 'He scored goals in practically every match. He was incredibly skilful and, unlike his dad, he could use both feet. He really stood out, but we had seen a lot of young players in Strabane stand out over the years, so I wasn't going to get carried away at this stage.'

The Doherty boys had followed their father in nailing their colours firmly to the Manchester United mast. 'My da always talked to us about the Munich disaster and regaled us with stories about the players who were killed, like Duncan Edwards and Tommy Taylor, and how Harry Gregg had been a hero, trying to save the other lads,' Gareth says. 'He told us about the time he saw George Best play at Windsor Park. I watched football whenever it was on TV, but Adrian was more into playing. He wanted to be outside doing something all the time.'

Faced with a long summer holiday in which to try to find entertainment for his two hyper-energetic older boys, Jimmy Doherty, along with his friend Jim Devlin, decided to set up a junior team to play in local tournaments. They went by the suitably local-exotic hybrid name of Mourne Santos, reflecting Jimmy's love of Brazilian football. On his first eleven-a-side match for Santos, Adrian, the smallest player on the pitch, drew gasps from the small crowd of parents by dribbling around five or six players before being tripped in the penalty area. 'All of us in the team insisted he took the penalty,' his brother Gareth recalls. 'He took this huge run-up, but because he was so small, the ball barely reached the keeper. I can still see the look of disappointment on his face. But two minutes later he got the ball and off he went again.'

The Mourne Santos experience did not last but it gave the Doherty boys another taste of organised football. After that, they joined a more established Strabane junior side, which went by the mundane name of Melvin. Here, under the management of Liam Kennedy, the set-up was more structured and more serious. Adrian quickly made a strong impression as his goals helped Melvin win a couple of trophies. As in the primary school competitions, they were playing against teams not only from Strabane but from Derry and the surrounding areas. Once again the thought occurred to Jimmy Doherty, on the sidelines, that in his admittedly biased opinion Adrian might just be the best player in the district in his age group.

It was not just football that interested Adrian Doherty. He was into everything. His fascination with *Monkey* led him to ask to be enrolled in the local judo club, where his parents were amused to note that he enjoyed the spiritual aspect as much as the combative. Dee Devenney remembers him obsessively reading fantasy books and finishing off the *Lord of the Rings* trilogy by the age of nine. Then there was the inevitable *Star Wars* bug when *Return of the Jedi* hit the big screen – or, in the case of Strabane's cinema, the medium-sized screen – in the summer of 1983.

Music was another passion that was taking hold as Adrian developed a sudden liking for the Police (favourite song 'De Do Do Do, De Da Da Da'), Adam and the Ants and Michael Jackson. He would try to copy Jackson's dance moves and even pleaded with his parents to send away to America to get him a replica of the jacket from the *Thriller* video. 'Adrian got so into music that he actually stopped playing football for a few weeks,' Gareth says. 'He was about nine and he told Bean [Sean Ferry] and me he had decided to give up football and was going to start a band instead. I think he just wanted a break, because we had been playing from morning until night all summer. Eventually we were playing a grudge match against some other lads from another part of the Ballycolman and I needed him to play. He kept refusing until I finally, in desperation, offered him my week's pocket money, 20p, if he played one last game. He scored the winning goal and that was the start of his comeback. And he became obsessed with it. He would hit the ball against the wall in the back garden hundreds of times and then he would start to juggle the ball, keeping it up. Soon enough he could do that 100 times, 200, 300. Then he would move on to a tennis ball. Again, 100, 200, 300. Whatever he was into – football, music, reading, computer games, anything – he was obsessed with it.'

Adrian was a bright boy, bubblier than his natural shyness suggested. 'His intelligence was very natural,' his friend Gerard Mullan says. 'He was a good all-rounder, one of those boys who could turn his hand to anything. He would also get these mad laughing fits. He wasn't the class joker or anything like that, but something would make him laugh and he would totally go off on one.'

Memories of a hysterical Adrian tend to inspire similar reactions among his friends now. 'I don't just mean laughing. I mean laughing to the point where he would hyperventilate and he'd need a paper bag,' Niall Dunphy says. 'He would just laugh his head off. He was a ridiculously happy kid.'

He was at his happiest, it seemed, when running rings around opponents on the football pitch. He was a 'goal-scoring machine', according to Bob Crilly, as St Mary's made an unstoppable charge towards the Derry and District Primary Schools League title. It was a proud moment for the boys, captured on camera by the *Strabane Chronicle*. 'That's me there with a lot more hair than I have now,' Kevin Doherty says, as he hands over the picture of the title-winning team. 'I was captain, but only because it was a question of who could shout loudest. That's Dee Devenney there. And that's your man there. That's Adrian. And I've just remembered something bizarre. We got these dinky little medals in plastic bags and Adrian, for some reason, was going through a phase of chewing plastic. I remember asking him afterwards: "Where's your little bag to put your medal in?" And he had eaten it.'

Adrian Doherty and his team-mates were developing a taste for success. As if the Derry and District title were not enough, they were starting to dream that their goalscoring star, in his final year before moving to high school, might shoot them to glory in the Northern Ireland Primary Schools Cup. They made it through to the last eight, but were beaten 2–1 by the eventual winners, St Anthony's of Craigavon, in the quarter-final. Through the mists of time, there are even a few hazy memories that Adrian might have missed a great chance to equalise late on. He was not quite infallible as a footballer, but it had begun to seem that way.

Life was changing for Adrian Doherty. He now had a baby brother, Peter, and the family had left the Ballycolman behind for a slightly larger property on the new Carlton Drive estate. Ciara was delighted, with a bedroom of her own now, but her older brothers were dead against the move. 'It was only about a ten-minute walk from the Ballycolman, but to us it might as well have been ten miles, as we were leaving all our mates behind,' Gareth says. 'But we made a lot of new mates and Kevin Doherty was just up the street. What really sealed the deal was that we could walk out of our back gate, take twenty steps and open the gate to a perfectly flat green. It was our very own Old Trafford.'

That summer of 1984 was spent playing football, watching the Olympics, attempting to emulate Daley Thompson's track-and-field exploits, whether outdoors or on the ZX Spectrum, and trying to avoid the whiff of nappies. Then it was time to join the exodus from St Mary's to St Colman's High, where Adrian would be a smaller fish in a much bigger pond.

Adrian Doherty's school friends are a warm, engaging and impressive bunch. Kevin Doherty works in wealth management in Canada; Gerard Mullan is a secondary-school teacher in the West Midlands; Dee Devenney is a software engineer in Dublin; Niall Dunphy is chief financial officer for a global entertainment company based in London. Of those who have stayed in Northern Ireland, Brian McGillion owns a successful car dealership and Mick Winters, to his friends' considerable amusement, is a police inspector. All of them suggest Adrian Doherty was perhaps the brightest among them, his talents stretching far beyond the football pitch. 'He was, honestly, the most talented fella I have ever met,' McGillion says. 'Anything he turned his hand to, he would excel at it.'

The last part is not quite true. Doherty's friends have a list of things he was terrible at. Kevin Doherty proposes swimming ('one of the few people who could swim worse than me', 'the only swimming race we would win would be one to the bottom of the pool') and goalkeeping ('the worst goalkeeper I've ever seen in my life', 'for a lad who was so talented with his feet, he just couldn't use his hands').

That might account for his lack of proficiency with pen or pencil. 'Oh, his handwriting,' Dunphy says. 'It was appalling. Then there was his drawing. It was horrendous! His "Battle of Marathon" drawing was legendary. "Jesus Christ, Aidy, what is *that*?!" But the academic side of things came easily to him. To be honest, he found most things easy. He was that kind of boy.'

It is one of the most celebrated concerts ever to have taken place in Ireland: Bruce Springsteen at Slane Castle, County Meath, on 1 June 1985. Jimmy Doherty was adamant he and his older boys would be there. 'It was our first ever gig,' Gareth Doherty says. 'Springsteen live, outdoors, 80,000 people, the *Born in the U.S.A.* T-shirts, the denim jackets and the mullets. We looked the part.'

Music was already a big part of Adrian Doherty's life. 'We had Michael Jackson and the Police when he was younger and then we both got into Springsteen,' his older brother says. 'He started to pick up a guitar around this time as well, twelve or thirteen. Then my da's brainwashing really started to pay off because I remember coming home from school and all you could hear was Bob Dylan, which Adrian was playing at full volume.'

The summer of 1985 was an unforgettable one for Gareth and Adrian. In their school holidays they went abroad for the first time, flying to California with their cousin Sean Ferry to visit their uncle Paddy, aunt Joanne and cousins Kevin, Dennis and Alana at their home in Burlingame, just outside San Francisco. They went to various theme parks – Disneyland, Great America and Ponderosa Ranch, which were quite a step up from Barry's Amusements at Portrush – and to Lake Tahoe. They were the envy of their friends back home when they went to see *Back to the Future* (twice) before it was released in the UK. Adrian sent his parents a postcard from Disneyland, warning that Strabane would seem incredibly boring when they returned home. He told them he was having a 'class' holiday, the rides were 'killer' and that they had 'seen Mickey Mouse and all them dudes'. 'He was talking like that after about two days there,' Gareth says. 'Everything was "killer", "awesome" and "dude". That didn't last long once we got home.'

One of Ferry's overriding memories of that trip was another sign of his twelve-year-old cousin's sporting prowess. 'The first two days, Adrian was totally wiped out by jet lag,' he says. 'We were playing basketball and he was just lying in the shade on the side of the court, unable to join in. By the third day we thought we were getting quite good and then Adrian was on his feet and straight away, having never played basketball before in his life, he was almost as good as the local boys. It used to sicken me how good he was at sport. Whatever he did – football, golf, snooker, basketball – he was brilliant at it.'

It had not taken long for Adrian Doherty to make a name for himself at St Colman's. He would draw crowds with his keep-ups in the playground, which would go well into the hundreds – and that was just with a tennis ball. His exploits on the Gaelic football pitch did not always go down so well. John Tinney remembers him infuriating the teacher by running the length of the Gaelic pitch with the ball on his head, like a performing sea lion. Dee Devenney recalls him dribbling around everyone else on the pitch and then crossing for him to score with a header. 'To this day, Adrian is the only player I've seen get sent off by his own manager,' Brian McGillion says. 'He just refused to use his hands when we played Gaelic – simply because he was so good with his feet, he didn't need to – so the teacher sent him off and left his own team a man down.'

'We had no interest in Gaelic. We were all football-mad,' Devenney says. 'Adrian had always been good when we were at primary school. Playing youth football with him at Melvin, from eleven years of age, he was outstanding. Now he was getting even better.'

'He looked quiet and unassuming,' Tinney says. 'But once he went onto a football pitch, he was like Clark Kent turning into Superman. It was like he had super powers when he put his football kit on.'

'I always told Adrian he ruined my football career,' Gareth Doherty says. 'About halfway through my fourth year, the manager of our Under-15 team told me he was going to call up Adrian for a cup tie. This was unheard of. He was only twelve. He was named as a sub and I was on the right wing. Then he came on at right-wing and I was moved up front. I think he scored the equaliser with five minutes to go. As for me, I couldn't play up front at all, so Adrian was now the star of the Under-15 team at the age of twelve, and that's when you start to think: "You know what? My little brother is getting pretty good."'

CHAPTER 3

It had been a long time since Jimmy Doherty had seen a crowd like this at the Brandywell. It was packed an hour before kick-off, with football fans flocking from far and wide for a rare glimpse of glamour in the form of Nottingham Forest, whom Brian Clough had brought over for a friendly match against Derry City. The size of the crowd put an unexpectedly intense spotlight on the warm-up act, which was an Under-14 match between a Derry representative team and Home Farm, the all-conquering youth team from Dublin.

John Clifford, the Derry Under-14 coach, warned his players and their parents it could be a difficult experience – not just because of the crowd, but because of the opposition. Home Farm took many of the best players from Dublin and the surrounding areas. Their Under-14 team were reputed to have gone fifty games unbeaten, dating back to when they were Under-9s, winning tournaments in England as well as in the Republic. This would be a step up in class for the Derry boys and Clifford was anxious to see how they coped.

What happened on 5 May 1986 left Jimmy Doherty speechless. Like everyone at the Brandywell, including the delegation from Forest, he was blown away by the performance of his son Adrian, still not a teenager for another five weeks. Home Farm's proud unbeaten run came to an end with a 2–0 defeat, with Adrian scoring both goals. Highlights of the match briefly appeared on YouTube in late 2014. The goals were of a startling technical quality. It was not just the mesmerising dribbles but the sheer impudence of the finishes. The first of them, cutting in from the right wing, ended up with an improvised shot – something between a flick and a scoop – of a type now synonymous with Lionel Messi. It was precocious. It was utterly brilliant.

'He was, honestly, absolutely exceptional that day,' his team-mate Peter Hutton, who went on to serve Derry City with distinction as player and manager, says. 'Afterwards, people weren't talking about the senior team or Nottingham Forest. They were talking about this incredible prospect they'd seen in our game.'

It was a proud moment for Jimmy Doherty, his son excelling on the ground where he himself had played on the wing for Derry. Some of Jimmy's former team-mates, now involved with the club in other roles, suggested young Adrian was on course to follow in his father's footsteps. But there was another former Derry player who had something bigger in mind for the young prodigy he had seen that day. Liam O'Kane, who was Clough's assistant, got in contact with Jimmy soon afterwards and, following some small talk, reminiscing about old times playing together in the 1960s, he cut to the chase. O'Kane wanted Adrian to go on trial with Forest.

Is sporting talent innate? The question has divided opinion in recent decades. The Swedish psychologist Professor K.

Anders Ericsson proposed that 'many characteristics once believed to reflect innate talent are actually the result of intense practice extended for a minimum of ten years,' a theory based not only on studies of sportsmen but on the practice habits of, among other groups, violinists and typists. Ericsson's idea was taken on and popularised by the Canadian journalist Malcolm Gladwell, who proposed his 10,000-hour rule in *Outliers: The Story of Success*, citing the Beatles' experience in Hamburg in the early 1960s to support his belief that world-class expertise can be attained in many fields through sustained practice over a period of ten years.

More recently, the former *Sports Illustrated* writer David Epstein has led a pro-talent backlash of sorts, endorsing nature over nurture by placing renewed – though not total – emphasis on genetic influences. Epstein points out the genetic advantages seemingly held by certain groups, for example Jamaicans and Kenyans, in certain athletic disciplines. He cites the importance of ACTN3, a gene that allows for the production of the protein alpha-actinin-3 in muscle fibres. The mutant version of ACTN3 is generally associated with endurance, the non-mutant version with sprint performance. He does not claim to have found all the answers. He simply believes the importance of innate talent has been downplayed – with considerable commercial success, it must be said.

Jimmy Doherty felt from the first time he saw them kick a ball that his three sons, Gareth, Adrian and Peter, had inherited some kind of basic skill – technical, athletic, motor or whatever. All three were quick, agile and tricky on the ball, just as Jimmy had been when playing on the wing for Derry City in the 1960s. Adrian, though, had something else, whether it was his boundless energy, a competitive intensity or an instinctive game-intelligence. 'It was just all-round ability,' Dee Devenney says. 'He was, honestly, the best player on the pitch in every game I ever saw him play.'

In his primary-school days, Adrian's commitment to football started and finished on the field. If he was doing something else – on his bike, at the snooker table, in front of the television – he was quite capable of turning down a kickaround. That changed as his focus on football became more serious. It was no longer enough for him to play those chaotic, large-sided matches involving boys of varying ability. He wanted to improve – and improvement meant individual training, working on the physical and technical qualities he felt would take his game to a much higher level.

One of them was speed. This would shock anyone who encountered him in his prime as a footballer, but Adrian, whatever his ACTN3 status, was not extraordinarily fast during his primary-school days. 'He didn't win many races on sports day back then,' his father says. 'He was quick, but not lightning quick. It amazed me how quick he became. I always thought you were either fast or you weren't, but it didn't come as a gift for Adrian. He worked on it, doing sprints, working on his acceleration.'

Often he would train on his own. Other times his father, his older brother or a friend would join him. 'He would work on both feet, so that, although he was right-footed, he became very good on his left,' Devenney says. 'He used to get me pinging the ball at him so he had to practise his first touch – again with either foot. He didn't just want to practise controlling it. He wanted to work out how to control it to give himself the most time and space in different situations. He knew defenders would get tight to him because he was quick, so he figured he was going to adapt to different situations. He was very smart like that.'

The improvement did not go unnoticed among his team-mates in the Derry and District side. 'I remember him coming back one summer and, although he hadn't had a growth spurt or anything, gee, he was suddenly exceptional, unplayable,' Peter Hutton says. 'I think that's what we saw with that game against Home Farm at the Brandywell.'

It was not just his contemporaries who marvelled at the sight of Adrian training. 'I went up to the school fields one night to call him for his dinner and Adrian was having a kickabout with a few of the soldiers,' Gareth Doherty says. 'I couldn't believe it. If it had been anyone else, people would have been knocking on their door, asking questions about what they were doing. But that wouldn't even cross Adrian's mind. He just said they had been watching him and then they started playing two-on-two with him. They had actually put down their guns to play with him.'

The number of incidents and deaths had fallen since the Troubles were at their height in the early 1970s, but chilling reminders were never far away. On 23 February 1985 three IRA volunteers – Michael Devine, David Devine and Charles Breslin – were shot dead in an SAS ambush on the outskirts of Strabane. The three men were believed to have been returning arms to a dump following a planned ambush of their own which had not materialised. Breslin was given a paramilitary-style funeral, his coffin draped in the Irish tricolour as it was carried through the streets. Gerry Adams and Martin McGuinness, of the Republican political party Sinn Féin, were among the mourners. Afterwards, Adams made a brief address in which he described the SAS soldiers as 'strangers, people who are not from here, do not belong here and have no rights here'. He claimed the three IRA volunteers had been 'murdered in cold blood'. The riots and the bombings were far less frequent now, but these were still deeply confused, con-flicted, troubled times.

With a Nottingham Forest trial on the horizon, Adrian Doherty was no longer just the talk of the town. He was excelling in the Derry and District Under-14 team, whose coach Sean Davis was flabbergasted by the boy's talent. With Adrian their inspiration, Derry and District won the national cup, beating North Down in the final. 'I played him up front in the final and he scored twice,' Davis says. 'It was the first time we had won the trophy for twenty years.'

Adrian had outgrown his local youth team at Melvin, where Liam Kennedy had done so much coaching and coaxing to help unlock his potential. Now that people were beginning to discuss a professional football career as a genuine possibility, it was time to look for a more com-petitive environment, playing against teams from further afield. Along with a handful of other boys from St

Colman's High – Kevin Doherty, Dee Devenney, John Tinney – he signed up to play for Moorfield Boys' Club, based in Derry.

Moorfield was a serious club, run by Matt Bradley with assistance from Noel Kivlehan and Steven Nash. They sent teams to the Northern Ireland Milk Cup, an annual tournament in which Liverpool and Manchester United competed. But it was also, according to Kevin Doherty, 'a nicely run little club, with a tight-knit group, the type of environment in which all of us, particularly Adrian, felt comfortable'.

Bradley has worked in football for decades, coaching in Northern Ireland and scouting for Celtic and various English clubs. Never, before, had he witnessed a teenage talent like Adrian Doherty. 'The moment I saw him, I thought this kid is the best I've seen in the Northern Ireland area since the days of George Best,' Bradley says. 'He was incredible – off the cuff, no fear. He was multi-talented. He was, and I mean this, the nearest thing I have seen to another George Best.'

Adrian felt at home at Moorfield. He liked Bradley, Kivlehan and Nash and he had close friends around him on what might otherwise have been daunting journeys into Derry. It also suited him that he was not the only star of the team. His team-mates at Moorfield included Johnny McIvor, who was rumoured to be attracting interest from Arsenal.

It was McIvor whom John Dillon, Arsenal's Northern Ireland talent scout, travelled to Mallusk to watch play for Moorfield in a youth tournament. 'I went up there with Kevin Doherty's dad,' Jimmy Doherty says. 'We had heard

John Dillon was going to be there to watch the boy McIvor. Moorfield were playing against Linfield's youth team, I think it was, and I have to say Adrian absolutely blitzed them. John Dillon rang us that night and said he wanted Adrian to go to Arsenal for a trial.'

Liam O'Kane wandered over to where the schoolboy trials were taking place at Nottingham Forest's training ground. 'I always liked to watch the trials, especially when there were lads over from Northern Ireland,' the former Forest coach says. 'Adrian had his socks rolled down to his ankles and he stuck out like a sore thumb. I remember our coach Alan Hill said to him, "Have you no shinpads, son?" He said, "If you come from Strabane, you don't wear shinpads." That made me laugh because I knew what he meant. Adrian did very well. We let him and his father know we were very keen.'

In April 1987, in the Easter holidays in his third year at St Colman's, Adrian Doherty went to Arsenal. After the provincial charm of Forest, Arsenal was grander and more imposing, but, despite the odd feeling of homesickness, he enjoyed his time there. He played in three junior-team games, attended two first-team matches at Highbury, against Charlton Athletic and Newcastle United, and ate lunch in the company of the senior squad. The trialists were told this was a club with a renewed commitment to youth, as illustrated by the emergence of Tony Adams, David Rocastle, Niall Quinn and others. He returned to Strabane full of laughter about two things. One was how Arsenal had taken all the trialists around Highbury – marble halls and all – and then allowed them to be

photographed, one by one, in the centre-circle holding the
Littlewoods Cup, which George Graham's team had won
at Wembley a few weeks earlier. Adrian had lost his precious photo, which he found hilarious. The other story
came when his father asked him what feedback he had
been given by the Arsenal coaching staff. Apparently,
either Pat Rice or Theo Foley – he was not altogether sure
which – had described him, in full flight, as being 'like a
f***ing blur'.

Sunday evenings in the Doherty household came to
revolve around a certain routine. The family would
have their tea and then sit around watching television –
Bread or the like – waiting for the telephone to ring.
When it rang, they would all look over to Jimmy, who
would struggle to suppress a grin as he went to answer it.

'Hello?'

'Hello, Jimmy. This is Pat Rice.'

'Yes, Pat. How are you?'

'Great, thanks, Jimmy. How's Adrian? How did he get
on yesterday? Is he still looking forward to signing for
Arsenal?'

'Yes, he is, Pat.'

And he was. The whole of Strabane knew Adrian
Doherty was on course to sign for Arsenal, the club synonymous with some of the great names of Irish sport,
whether it was Terry Neill, Pat Jennings, Sammy Nelson
and indeed Rice himself from the north or Liam Brady,
David O'Leary, Frank Stapleton and Quinn from the
Republic. After some barren years, Arsenal had just won
the Littlewoods Cup and were beginning to re-establish a
reputation for developing their own young talent. The

promised contract offer had not arrived yet, but the Dohertys were told it was only a matter of time. The Sunday night telephone calls from Rice only added to Adrian's sense of affiliation to Arsenal. Nothing could be better than this. Well, almost nothing.

CHAPTER 4

Something was nagging at Matt Bradley. As manager of Moorfield, he was justifiably proud that one of his lads was about to sign for Arsenal, but he also felt miffed. He had long felt players in the outlying regions of Northern Ireland were too easily overlooked by the Belfast-based scouts employed by the English clubs. In one sense, Arsenal and Nottingham Forest had done well to find Adrian Doherty, but they could not claim to have unearthed this particular gem. He was simply a rough diamond who had been waved in front of their eyes. They could hardly miss such talent. The ones who were missing out were the clubs whose scouts had not ventured anywhere near Derry and Strabane.

Bradley expected the scouts to descend on Coleraine and Portrush for the Northern Ireland Milk Cup tournament at the end of July and was looking forward to seeing if some of the other Moorfield lads could catch their eye and earn a trial across the water. But Adrian might already have been snapped up by then; subject to certain assurances about his education, the plan was to sign associated schoolboy forms shortly after his fourteenth birthday on 10 June, with a view to starting an apprenticeship when he turned sixteen. Bradley could not help feeling that, as illustrious as Arsenal and Forest were, Adrian's talent was worthy of the ultimate recognition. And, as a Manchester United fanatic, he had only one club in mind.

Bradley took matters into his own hands. He wrote to Alex Ferguson, telling him a brilliant thirteen-year-old winger, the most exciting player he had seen in Northern Ireland since George Best, was about to sign for Arsenal. He urged Ferguson to send someone to watch Adrian as a matter of urgency. Within days Bradley got a call from Eddie Coulter, who had just been appointed as United's new scout in Northern Ireland in succession to Bob Bishop, the man who had discovered Best and Norman Whiteside.

'The sole reason I did it is that I'm a Manchester United supporter,' Bradley says. 'I would have been proud to see Adrian go to Arsenal, but I was desperate for United to sign him. He was the closest thing I had seen to another Best and I couldn't believe United hadn't been to see him. I said to Eddie Coulter: "This boy is going to Arsenal unless you act very quickly." He asked when Adrian's next match was. As it happens, he was playing for Derry and District in Cookstown a few days later. Eddie met me there. Within ten minutes he said: "We have got to get him over as soon as possible."'

No sooner had a delighted Jimmy Doherty heard the news from Bradley than he received a call from Coulter. 'We will get him over to Manchester in the school holidays,' Coulter told him. 'Do not sign for anyone else in the meantime. We want him at Manchester United.'

At the *Strabane Chronicle*, they were in no doubt. 'Adrian is set for stardom', read one headline in the summer of 1987, revealing that Adrian Doherty, having already been on trial with Nottingham Forest and Arsenal, 'is off again soon, this time to Old Trafford, home of the famous Manchester United'. He even agreed to share his thoughts ahead of the trial. 'I would find it hard to say which club would appeal to me more, but, as a Manchester United fan, I feel I have to wait to see what their set-up is like before I say or do anything else,' he is quoted as saying in his first newspaper interview.

His father, Jimmy – 'a modest man who will not rush his son into making any rash decisions,' the paper said – managed to contain his excitement. 'It really is all up to Adrian, but he agrees he will have to look after his studies first,' Jimmy said.

Adrian took it all in his stride. 'I was at his house when I heard United were after him,' his cousin Sean Ferry says. 'I was unbelievably excited but it was water off a duck's back to Adrian. "Aye I'm going over there. What's for pudding?"'

Sean Davis, his coach with the Derry and District Under-14 team, found that nonchalance delightful, if just occasionally exasperating. 'If anything, as a coach, you would think he was almost too nice,' Davis says. 'He was so laid-back, it was unbelievable. I never found him to be all that passionate about football. Boys would talk in the dressing room about this player or that player. The only times I heard Adrian talk, it was about music. You're thinking, "Sweet Lord . . . Do you realise the potential you have?" Sometimes you would have to tell him to gee up. But on the pitch he was incredible. Blinding pace, excellent on the ball, good control, two good feet, he was one of the best players I've seen in thirty years of coaching. As a coach, you're telling them to stick up for themselves, "Don't let yourself be knocked about." But then you look at it from the parents' point of view – "Have manners and be nice." Adrian was polite and shy and he was an incredible footballer. Not many find that happy medium.'

Davis's only concern was about whether Adrian's personality might prevent him rising to the occasion when the trial in Manchester came around. 'I had seen umpteen lads go across the water and freeze when they were there for a week or so on trial,' he says.

Jimmy and Geraldine Doherty were uneasy when the invitation arrived from Joe Brown, Manchester United's youth development officer. According to the letter, Adrian was required to report for duty at the club's training ground, at an address in Salford, at 10 a.m. on the morning of Monday, 10 August. There was also a mention of swimming. This was a worry because Adrian could not swim. To their relief, Brown proved more amenable when they called him. This was a standard letter, he told them. Yes, of course arrangements would be made to collect him from the airport. No, of course he did not expect their boy, who had barely ventured beyond Strabane, just to find his way to the training ground in Salford. Yes, of course he would be welcome to sit out the trip to the swimming baths.

Adrian and his parents were further reassured when they learned the Moorfield goalkeeper Michael Nash had also been summoned to Manchester, having caught Coulter's eye on the same afternoon in Cookstown. So too had a talented young midfielder from County Antrim, who made an impression while playing for Ballymena in the Milk Cup a couple of weeks earlier. His name was Brendan Rodgers.

On Sunday, 9 August, Rodgers, Nash and Doherty were waved away by their anxious families as they prepared to fly from Belfast to Manchester. There were a few nerves among the travelling trio too. Someone will be there to collect you, they had been told. How would that work? How would they recognise that someone? What if that someone wasn't there? What would they do then?

At the sight of three bedraggled teenage boys wandering across the arrivals hall, wide-eyed, sports bags slung over their shoulders, a man in his late sixties stepped forward. He introduced himself and led them outside. 'I don't know why this sticks in my head, but I think he was a relation of the actor [Ian] McShane,' Nash recalls. 'I think he might have played for Manchester United.'

Indeed, the driver was Harry McShane, a Scottish winger who had played under Matt Busby and alongside Roger Byrne and Johnny Carey in the team that won the league championship, United's first in forty-one years, in 1952. He had remained a part of the furniture at Old Trafford, not just scouting but even serving as the stadium announcer during the 1960s and 1970s. He had also served with the RAF in Italy and North Africa during World War Two. While he might have been proud to tell these three impressionable lads from Northern Ireland that his son was an actor whom they might have seen on their television screens, Harry McShane was rather more than just the father of *Lovejoy*.

To Doherty and particularly to Rodgers, from the harbour village of Carnlough, even Derry seemed like a big city. Belfast was like a metropolis. Manchester was something else again. Over the years that followed, Doherty would come to marvel at the architecture, particularly the neoclassical central library, but to the three youngsters in the back of McShane's car, as it chugged through the traffic towards Salford, Manchester was a concrete jungle, bustling with traffic, people and noise. Strabane it was not.

The three boys were taken to the halls of residence on Oakland Road. Each had a room to himself – always a relief. In the evenings they dined with their fellow long-distance trialists. Nobody ate much and they did not speak much either. The air was what the boys, for the first time in their lives, might have recognised as professional. The three lads from Northern Ireland were the quietest of all. According to Nash, they 'were seen as foreigners, for want of a better expression, so we just stuck together'.

Rodgers recalls that Alex Ferguson was there to meet the trialists on the first day. 'He had only been there a year or so at the time,' he says. 'But even then I remember being impressed by the interest he took in the young players. You would see him there every day, watching the youth team as well as the first team.'

Ferguson's presence on the touchline caused a buzz among the trialists, but in the first instance the man they had to impress was Brian Kidd, who had been invited back to work alongside Nobby Stiles in running the school of excellence. For the dozens of boys, summoned from across the British Isles, the objective was simple. Seize the moment and take the chance. Most, unlike Nash and Rodgers, had been on trial elsewhere and some, like Doherty, already had offers of traineeships. But this was

Manchester United. There were trialists from Wales, Scotland, Northern Ireland, the Republic of Ireland and all over England – all those young players of whom United's scouts had reported great things but who had been unable to get to Manchester to parade their talents until the school holidays. The trialists were said to include stars of the England and Scotland schoolboy teams. This was quite a step up from Moorfield.

Sean Davis had feared Doherty might 'freeze' in Manchester, but that morning at Ayrshire Road, just around the corner from the Cliff, the boy was red hot. 'He was head and shoulders above everyone else there, just like back home,' Nash recalls. 'We were up against England schoolboy internationals who had been coached by professional coaches since they were eleven. We hadn't had any of that, but Adrian was so much better than all of them. He stuck out a mile.'

'He was one of those who made you look up,' Kidd remembers of his first sight of Doherty. 'Very talented boy. Very, very talented boy. He had bits of everything. Good touch, but he could run past full-backs and beyond the back four. Very, very good turn of pace. Adrian could light it up. He was very, very quick over the first ten yards, which was unusual. Over those ten yards, bang. And he wasn't just quick. He was a good runner with the ball. He could unbalance a full-back, unbalance an opponent. And at that time, Manchester United were going for wingers in a big way.'

Ferguson, Kidd and the rest of the United coaches loved what they saw. 'I'm pretty sure that, even after that first training session, they had decided they wanted to sign Adrian,' Nash says.

After training, the trialists were taken to Old Trafford for a guided tour – the dressing rooms, the enormous communal bath, the boardroom, the trophy room, the executive boxes, the luscious green pitch and the sweeping terrace behind the goal at the Stretford End. Unlike Arsenal four months earlier, United were not in a position to take the boys to a first-team match, since the season had not yet started, so instead they were taken to Ewood Park to watch Blackburn Rovers play Wigan Athletic in the final of a pre-season tournament called the Lancashire Manx Cup. Blackburn prevailed in a penalty shoot-out, but the match passed Doherty by. So too, to a large extent, did the Old Trafford tour. As he saw it, he was there to play football and show how good he was. This stuff got in the way. Others were wide-eyed, but if the Ewood Park experience told Doherty anything it was that he needed to make sure he ended up with United. Playing at Blackburn, in the Football League's hinterland, held nothing like the same appeal.

That Thursday afternoon, the Doherty family got the news they had been hoping for. Ferguson took it upon himself to make the call. 'We've been looking at your son and we want to offer him a contract,' the United manager told Jimmy Doherty. 'When we look at young players, we assess them technically in different areas – speed, bravery, strength, technique, vision and so on. Adrian ticks every box, which is very rare. We know there are other clubs looking at him, but we feel he would be perfect for Manchester United. We think he would have an excellent chance here.'

If there were gleeful celebrations in the Doherty

household, Adrian took the news in his stride back in Manchester. He had expected it. He had sailed through every trial he had attended – with his school, with the Derry and District team, with Moorfield, with Nottingham Forest, with Arsenal. Why should Manchester United be any different?

For his two travelling companions, things were less certain as they entered the final day of the trial. Rodgers knew he had made a good impression but he was not sure which way it would go. Nash, on the other hand, was all but resigned to rejection. 'I would say I knew,' the goalkeeper says. 'After training we were taken to the boardroom at Old Trafford. Adrian had already been told he would be coming back. Alex Ferguson told the rest of us that we hadn't been successful.

'When we went outside, Brendan needed a bit of time to himself. He was very disappointed because he had really hoped and believed he would make it. I was disappointed too, but I had probably reconciled myself. I was there, training with England schoolboy internationals, Welsh and Scottish schoolboy internationals. I think I knew I wasn't at that level. They had different plans for Adrian.'

For Nash, that week in Manchester was as close as he would come to a career in professional football. For Rodgers, there would be further visits to Manchester to train with United in school holidays over the year ahead, but he never quite forced the club into a reappraisal. He would end up going on trial at Luton Town, then a top-flight club, before signing for Reading, where he was captain of the youth team. Injury would end his hopes of making it as a professional player, but he would re-emerge years later as a highly regarded youth coach before finding his vocation as manager of Reading, Watford, Swansea City and, most notably, Liverpool. He was not sure whether Ferguson would remember his days on trial at United – 'that skinny little rat', as he describes his teenage self – but he knew for certain the Scot would remember Adrian Doherty.

There was deep disappointment at Arsenal when Adrian Doherty's father called Pat Rice to let him know the boy would be joining Manchester United. So too at Nottingham Forest, where Liam O'Kane had hoped the Brian Clough factor, as well as the homely atmosphere, might tempt the kid from Strabane. 'We were disappointed, but we couldn't argue with it,' O'Kane says. 'They were such a big club. I said to Jimmy, "Let us know how you get on. If it doesn't work out, you know where we are."'

The more Jimmy and Geraldine Doherty thought about it, the more concerned they became about the idea of Adrian, just turned fourteen, starting an apprenticeship in Manchester two years later. They sought more clarity from Joe Brown about accommodation, care and practicalities – including the issue of continuing their son's education beyond the age of sixteen – and were more comforted by what they heard. Brown said all the apprentices were required to take further-education courses and, yes, this could include A-levels if they wished. Brown even travelled over to Strabane to meet them and to address the headmaster at St Colman's, who was reassured that any visits to Manchester would be restricted to the school holidays. It had been United's plan for any Northern Irish recruits to train at their new school of excellence in Belfast each week, but in Adrian's case, because of the travelling distance, these trips could be taken on an occasional basis so as to minimise interference with schoolwork. 'Joe Brown was a very nice man and he answered all our questions,' Jimmy Doherty says. 'We trusted him and we trusted United. We still had some concerns about whether Adrian would be ready to move to Manchester when he was sixteen, particularly Geraldine, but we felt and he felt it was an opportunity he could not possibly turn down.'

'*Old Trafford here I come!*' said the headline in the *Derry Journal*, accompanied by a picture of Adrian Doherty and his father holding a Manchester United scarf in their back garden. The reporter Keiron Tourish was happy to put his Chelsea allegiance to one side to declare that Adrian had 'fulfilled the ambition of every young footballer by signing for English First Division giants Manchester United'.

Tourish even managed to coax a few words out of the teenager. 'It's great to sign for United,' Adrian said. 'I was over on trial last week and I thought I did well and really enjoyed the experience. Mr Ferguson talked to each player and said he had rung home and had a chat with my father. He said he thought I was good enough to make it. I'm just over the moon.'

In October 1987, Alex Ferguson, approaching the end of a difficult first year as United's manager, spoke in the club's match programme about the 'quiet revolution in full swing at Old Trafford'. He talked about the steps taken to overhaul United's youth set-up, citing renewed efforts not only to find more of the best talent locally – much of which, to his horror, seemed to have been snapped up by Manchester City – but to tap into other rich hunting grounds, setting up new centres of excellence in Durham and Belfast. Ferguson also discussed the return of Brian Kidd and a renewed emphasis, in United's coaching at youth level, on playing 'with speed and at speed'. 'I feel these developments are very important for United and hopefully we will be able to produce some exciting youngsters who can progress through our youth ranks and maybe into the first team one day,' the manager said.

One of the new recruits merited a special mention. Adrian Doherty, Ferguson said, 'is like greased lightning. He plays wide on the right and he's a very exciting discovery.'

CHAPTER 5

Adrian Doherty did not grow up dreaming of playing for his country. When the Northern Ireland national team enjoyed its finest hour, defeating the hosts, Spain, at the 1982 World Cup, he was a fairly underwhelmed nine-year-old. That was the summer when he and his mates well and truly caught the football bug, but, while much of the country went mad for Billy Bingham's team, it was a different story for Doherty and his friends, growing up in the far-flung Republican stronghold of Strabane. Rather than Norman Whiteside, Billy Hamilton and Gerry Armstrong, they were seduced by Sócrates, Falcão, Éder, Zico and the rest of that wonderful, if ultimately flawed, Brazil team.

The first few days of the World Cup had passed the Doherty boys by, but one Monday evening they were summoned into the lounge by their father, Jimmy, and asked to sit and pay attention. 'He told us, "You have to watch this",' Gareth Doherty recalls. 'It was Brazil against the USSR. Sócrates and Éder scored great goals. From then on, we were buzzing about Brazil. In the past we'd be playing out and we'd be Frank Stapleton, Steve Coppell or Norman Whiteside, but now it was all Zico, Falcão, Éder. That was when we really got into it, the game against

Scotland and the Éder chip. We were all trying to do that chip and we'd all be falling over.'

When people in Strabane remember the young Adrian Doherty, they remember him wearing his treasured Brazil shirt. Nobody seems quite sure whether it was just one jersey he never grew out of, or a succession of them, but he did not like to play football without it. Never had he been more impressionable as a young football fan than he was during the 1982 World Cup. Nor had the Northern Ireland football team held stronger appeal than that summer. But Billy Bingham's boys did not capture his imagination as Brazil did. And by the end of his first season with the Northern Ireland schoolboy team six years later, his sense of affinity had not grown.

If you grew up in a Catholic household in Strabane during the Troubles of the 1970s and 1980s, then in most cases the concept of Northern Ireland was not an appealing one. Even now, even in a family as apolitical as the Dohertys, that label does not quite stick. Over the course of dozens of interviews with Adrian Doherty's friends and family, Northern Ireland is barely referenced except in a sporting context. They talk freely of 'the north', 'the north-west' or 'north-west Ireland', as a region, and refer to the wider 'Ireland', certainly, but 'Northern Ireland' rarely crops up. It is not taboo by any means, but it does not roll off the tongue easily.

This is the context in which the Northern Irish football scene of the 1980s has to be seen. There might have been an influential minority of Catholics in the senior national team – Pat Jennings, Mal Donaghy, Martin O'Neill and

Gerry Armstrong among them – but, up in Strabane and Derry, there was a deep-rooted suspicion that the day-to-day workings of the Irish Football Association (IFA), along with other sections of the Belfast-based establishment, were shaped by religious, political or even just regional agendas. 'If you were from this side of the Glenshane Pass, it seemed they didn't want to know you at that time,' Matt Bradley says. 'Not unless you were absolutely exceptional.'

Adrian Doherty was indeed exceptional. He sailed through the two rounds of trials for the Northern Ireland schoolboy team. 'He was head and shoulders above any-one in our team, anyone in the city and ultimately anyone in the country,' says Michael Nash, his Moorfield team-mate and fellow trialist with both Manchester United and the Northern Ireland schoolboy team. 'He was light years ahead. I played against lads who were good players who went on to play for the Northern Ireland senior team, but they didn't hold a candle to Adrian Doherty.'

To a combination of astonishment and derision in the north-west, though, Doherty was one of only two players selected from what was felt to be the best Derry and District team in years. Peter Hutton and Johnny McIvor were initially rejected. The only other member of Derry and District's cup-winning team to make the Northern Ire-land schoolboys squad was the left-back Kyle Quigley. That Quigley happened to go to a predominantly Protes-tant school, Clondermot, in the Waterside area of Derry, did nothing to dispel the conspiracy theories.

'It has totally changed now, thankfully, but that year was ridiculous,' Bradley says. 'Of course they picked Adrian – it would have been impossible not to – but how they left out Peter Hutton, in particular, I'll never know. They picked a big guy, Norman McCloy, from County Down, ahead of Hutton. I said to one of the coaches: "In ten years, Hutton will be a player and McCloy will be standing outside a nightclub in a dickie bow." I don't think I was far wrong.'

Mention of Norman McCloy – the guy 'standing outside a nightclub in a dickie bow,' according to Matt Bradley – brings an affectionate laugh from Peter Smyth. A gifted midfielder, Smyth was one of those selected for the Northern Ireland schoolboys team in 1988. He had also, like Adrian Doherty, been offered an apprenticeship with Manchester United. 'Big Norm is one of my best mates,' Smyth says. 'We grew up in the same village in County Down. He went to Glentoran, but he drifted out of the game. He was a man when he was eleven – hairy legs, shaving already, massive centre-half. He looked after quite a few of the lads on the pitch in terms of his physique.'

Smyth was grateful to have McCloy for company. 'I don't know what it's like now, but anybody who went into the Northern Ireland schools set-up back then, if you weren't from the Belfast area, you felt you were kind of frowned upon,' Smyth says. 'You were like the country bumpkin. That's how I found it, coming from a rural village, Killyleagh. It was intimidating. A lot of the Belfast lads would be cocky and loud. I think our year was one of the first when more of the kids were from outside of Belfast, but it was still hard for those of us that weren't.'

Smyth suspects the Catholics had an additional hurdle to overcome, even if it was mostly in their own minds. 'I don't remember anything happening or being said, but it was a grey area all the time,' he says. 'I was Protestant, British side, and it wasn't an issue at all for me, but at that time everyone had the religious thing at the back of their mind because it was something you grew up with. It's just something that was in your head – probably more so from the Catholic side. I can't honestly say there was something going on. It wasn't in your face. But I just think there was . . . something.'

Liam Coyle can think of few higher compliments for Adrian Doherty than the fact he was a Catholic from County Tyrone who walked into the Northern Ireland schoolboy team in the 1980s. 'I don't mean to politicise it, but there was a lot of political stuff around it,' Coyle, who went on to win a senior cap as a flamboyant and much-loved forward with Derry City, says. 'Very few Catholics played for Northern Ireland schools at that time. I never got picked. Adrian came about five years after me and, yes, he played, but, well, they could hardly have ignored him. That would have been ridiculous. He was too good for anyone to ignore.

'I got to the last twenty-two. I was on Nottingham Forest's books at the time and usually if you were with an English club, you were picked automatically. But I wasn't. It's totally different now, but that was the way it was then and you just had to accept it. The north-west in general was just dismissed. With the people who ran it, it was very much Belfast, County Antrim, County Down.'

The only surviving member of the coaching staff from the Northern Ireland schoolboy set-up at the time is Bob

Nesbitt, who managed the team and is now involved in coach education for the IFA. He vehemently rejects the inference of any kind of bias – regional, religious or political – either now or then. 'I can say categorically there was never any sectarianism,' Nesbitt says. 'I can say that to you hand on heart. It wouldn't have come into the psyche. I could give you a long list of players we picked from Derry and an even longer list of Catholic players we picked. We were only interested in picking the best players. If you look at the IFA now, our team manager is Michael O'Neill and our elite performance director is Jim Magilton. Both are Catholics. Both came through our schoolboy set-up before the Adrian Doherty period and they would stand by what I'm saying.

'Northern Ireland was a very different country back then, but football was one thing that brought it together. I'm surprised if anyone would say otherwise. Whether players were Protestant, Catholic or Hindu, they were looked after and treated the same way. Total – and I emphasise total – impartiality was the foundation on which squads were selected in all my time. I wouldn't have stood for anything less and I hope this puts the record straight.'

Adrian Doherty was not the only Catholic to make it through the Northern Ireland schoolboy trials held on the outskirts of Belfast in early 1988. There was also Moorfield's new midfield recruit Brendan Rodgers – 'an exceptional player at youth level,' according to John Tinney. Rodgers had only started playing organised football at the age of thirteen, having attended a school where Gaelic sports and basketball took precedence, but he had quickly shown a flair for the game, even earning a trial at Manchester United, and now needed to look further afield in search of a suitable stage. The move to Moorfield meant a three-hour round trip to Derry every week from his home in Carnlough, County Antrim. Such were the sacrifices Rodgers and his father, Malachy, made as they tried to make up for lost time in the pursuit of a career in professional football.

'It was only after I went to school in Ballymena that a friend introduced me to the local team there,' Rodgers says. 'Then after that I played for Matt Bradley at Moorfield. A great man, Matt. That's where I came across Adrian. He was someone I got to know well for a year or two. He was such a talent – so fast and brave as a lion. He was just a natural. He was quiet, shy, such a nice guy, but there was a big personality underneath that. He was an individual, quirky in his own way, funny, too. And on the pitch, great balance, two feet, could score a goal. A massive talent.'

Already, selection for the Northern Ireland schoolboy team was beginning to feel like a mixed blessing for Adrian Doherty. He did not like the long journeys to Belfast or what he saw, heard and sensed of the city through the window – the size of the place, the noise, the concrete jungle, the sectarian graffiti, the omnipresent smell of conflict. He didn't enjoy the training sessions, which were far more regimented than anything he had known before. He felt uncomfortable among the Belfast kids, who were tough, streetwise and spoke in a harsh accent. He was different and he knew it. He also knew that they knew it. 'He didn't like it,' Doherty's school friend Dee Devenney says. 'He was doing quite a lot of travelling up and down to Belfast and he didn't like the set-up or the training. He felt it wasn't friendly.'

When Peter Hutton was finally called into the Under-16 squad later that year, he too disliked the atmosphere he and Doherty encountered. 'It was very much a Belfast clique,' Hutton says. 'It was very tough. All the coaches were from Belfast. They would have been on first-name terms with all the Belfast players, so even to get into that team from the north-west you really had to stand out. It wasn't a very nice environment at that time, to be honest.'

Does Hutton recall that Doherty disliked the Northern Ireland youth set-up? 'No, but I can understand where he was coming from,' Hutton says. 'I would have concurred. It could be intimidating. Adrian was from Strabane. He wouldn't have been streetwise like a lot of the lads from Belfast were. It was hard to go into that, with big charac-ters from Belfast who dominated the changing room. The religious thing was very rife at the time. Myself and Adrian and a few others experienced that.'

What are we talking about? Bullying? 'I wasn't aware of any bullying,' Hutton says, 'but there was a religious thing in the air.'

It was an inauspicious start to Adrian Doherty's inter-national career. His debut for the Northern Ireland schoolboy team, on 27 February 1988, ended in a 3–0 defeat by the Republic of Ireland at New Grosvenor Field, Ballyskeagh. If anything was 'schoolboy', it was his team's defending. Their youth was certainly not going to spare them criti-cism in the *Belfast Telegraph*, where John Laverty laid the blame for the Republic's first goal on the shoulders of

Alan McReavie, the Belfast-born full-back who, like Doherty and Peter Smyth, was bound for Manchester United. At least, according to Laverty, the Northern Ireland coaching staff could draw some consolation from the performances of Philip Macauley and Doherty on the wings. Both were deemed to have made excellent contributions, even though Doherty was playing on the left-hand side rather than his preferred right flank.

There was a happier outcome the following week at Vetch Field, Swansea, where Northern Ireland beat Wales 4–3, with Brendan Rodgers scoring the winning goal, and there was talk of a carnival atmosphere around their next match, a friendly against the mighty Brazil at Windsor Park. For Doherty, brought up on the brilliance of Sócrates, Falcão, Éder and Zico, it was a red-letter day. Likewise for Rodgers, whose father, Malachy, organised a bus to bring friends and family down to Belfast from Carnlough. Malachy Rodgers got there to find out that his son, the match-winner in Swansea twelve days earlier, had been left out of the starting line-up for this showpiece game. Rodgers Sr was furious.

In the end, both the occasion and Brazil – no future household names in their line-up – left the 8,000-plus spectators disappointed. '*Samba time turns out to be a big yawn*', as the *Belfast Telegraph* headline said. Their venerable football correspondent Malcolm Brodie mentioned in passing that he was impressed by Doherty, but he called it 'a lacklustre, undistinguished game', in which the visitors from Brazil fell a long way short of expectations. The spirit of *joga bonito* was certainly not evident as Alexandre Damasio was sent off for a headbutt in the closing stages.

*

Adrian Doherty did not enjoy his away days with North-ern Ireland at schoolboy and Under-16 level. 'If you were on a team bus going somewhere, you would have most of the lads sat around in twos and threes and Adrian would be on his own with his earphones on,' Bob Nesbitt says. 'He was happier listening to his music and they would leave him to it. It wasn't like he was ostracised or anything like that. The other players recognised his talent. "Let the Doc do what the Doc does."'

In May 1988, Adrian was part of the Northern Ireland schoolboy team that travelled to Geneva to play a game against Switzerland. 'I couldn't get him to eat anything,' Nesbitt says. 'It was before the days of teams having nutri-tionists and dieticians, but we knew we had to get the lads to eat carbs and proteins. But Adrian was living off diges-tive biscuits and cups of tea because he wouldn't eat the salads and continental breads.'

So what happened? 'I sat him down and said: "Adrian, you're going to have to eat. It's your fuel. If you don't put fuel in a car, it doesn't go. If you don't eat, you can't play,"' Nesbitt says. 'He did eat something in the end. I was con-cerned about him more than anything. If he was away with the team and wasn't going to eat, I was concerned about his general health, never mind how he would expect to perform.'

Whether because of some deeper underlying issue, or simply the frustration of being asked to play to a more defensive game plan in a struggling team, Adrian Doherty was already feeling deeply disaffected with the whole Northern Ireland set-up when he was called up to the

Under-16 squad for three matches in the space of ten days in October 1988: two away games against Denmark followed by a home fixture against the Republic of Ireland. This time he had Peter Hutton for company, as well as Brendan Rodgers, but the experience was more dispiriting than ever. Northern Ireland were beaten 5–1 by Denmark in Vejle and 2–0 in Aabenraa, a game in which Doherty limped off midway through the first half and Rodgers was sent off on the hour. On returning to home soil, they played the Republic at Mourneview Park, Lurgan, and were beaten 2–0. For Doherty, this was the last straw.

'After the game, I was waiting in the car and Adrian came out and said he had to go back to speak to Roy Millar, the coach,' Jimmy Doherty says. 'Ten minutes later he came back. He didn't say anything about it on the way home. He just sat there calmly. The next day Roy Millar called up and said Adrian didn't want to play for the team any more. He said he would rather not play football if it was just going to be about running around trying to stop someone playing. He wanted to enjoy it and let someone else worry about trying to stop him. Roy Millar said that was a bad attitude. I can see why it's not the attitude a coach wants from a young player, but it tells you two things about Adrian: 1) he needed to enjoy what he was doing and 2) he was incredibly strong-minded and wasn't afraid to say how he felt. He didn't play for them again and it didn't bother him.'

Even now, the idea of a young footballer switching his allegiance, from Northern Ireland to the Republic, is a highly controversial one. The former Northern Ireland Under-21 international James McClean, a Catholic from Derry, attracted death threats when he did so as a 22-year-old. That was in 2012, fourteen years after the Good Friday Agreement. Adrian Doherty, remarkably, pondered doing so in the late 1980s, when even the beginning of the peace process was a long way off.

It is not entirely clear whether Doherty would have been eligible to swap allegiance and commit to the Republic, even under the famously lax dual-nationality rules of the time, but what is certain is that he talked about the possibility. 'He and I used to room together when we travelled away with the Northern Ireland schoolboy team,' Brendan Rodgers says. 'He opted out of playing for Northern Ireland after that. He turned down the Under-17s and we thought he was going to play for the Republic.'

Doherty also brought up this apparent crisis of national identity in conversation with Bob Crilly, his former football coach at St Mary's Boys' Primary School. A Manchester United fan, Crilly met up with his former pupil during the second year of Doherty's apprenticeship at Old Trafford. 'I remember Adrian said he would have liked to play for the Republic of Ireland,' Crilly says. 'He knew what the political repercussions would have been. He indicated that. I think he realised he couldn't have done it, though. It would have been a big step.'

Jimmy Doherty says this was never much more than a flight of fancy. There had been rumours of interest south of the border from Jack Charlton and the Football Association of Ireland should such a move be found to be permissible on ancestry grounds, but it never crystallised into a firm approach. The point was not really that Adrian Doherty wanted to play for the Republic, but that he had so disliked his experience of playing for the country of his birth.

'Did Adrian really want to play for his country?' asks Peter Smyth, who was to join him in going from the Northern Ireland schoolboy team to Manchester United. 'Even before he gets there, that long drive to Belfast, maybe he was thinking, "I'm a Catholic lad from Strabane. They probably don't want me to play for them." Not because he had been told that or experienced that, but because he might have thought that's just how it was.'

Rodgers wonders whether Doherty's frustrations were more tactical than anything else. 'Adrian knew what was going to get the best out of him,' Rodgers says. 'In the right set-up, he would be a superstar. At that time with Northern Ireland we were always 4-4-2 and he was always playing in a deeper role – often on the left – when he probably wanted to be higher up the pitch, giving the opposition something to worry about. Adrian felt that as a young player he was possibly not being used in the best way. He did work hard for the team; he wasn't one of those wingers who only run forward. It's just that he knew what was best for him – and he felt that would also be the best for the team. And the one thing all these stories will tell you is that he knew what he wanted.'

Rodgers lost touch with Doherty after that. 'He was about to move to Manchester and there were no mobile phones or any of that, so we lost contact and your life moves on,' he says. 'But I always wondered how he was getting on at Manchester United. Three or four years later, when I was at Reading, we took Jim Leighton on loan. I knew four or five players at Man United at the time, Northern Irish players. I asked Jim: "Do you know Peter Smyth? Do you know Alan McReavie?" He knew them vaguely. Then I asked him if he knew Adrian Doherty. Jim's eyes lit up and he said to me, "The Doc is a legend."'

CHAPTER 6

At times over the previous few years, Jimmy Doherty had wondered, like others, whether his son – so laid-back, so easy-going, so diverse in his interests – was totally committed to grasping the opportunity to be a top-class footballer. Those paternal concerns evaporated as the move to Manchester came closer and his son's aspirations and focus intensified.

'He had never been an obsessive watcher of football on TV, but he became obsessed with Diego Maradona,' Jimmy Doherty says. 'One day when he was fifteen he said to me: "Maradona is the best in the world. In five or six years' time, someone else will be the best in the world. Why shouldn't it be me?"'

Adrian's dedication to self-improvement increased. 'Most evenings he would go up to the field on his own with a couple of balls and a stopwatch and six Coke cans and he would dribble in and out of the cans – in and out, in and out, in and out, against the stopwatch – and you could see him getting quicker and quicker, better and better,' his father says. 'He taught himself to get quicker. He taught himself to be two-footed. And I don't know about best in the world, but there can't have been many better fifteen-year-olds in Britain at that time. It was inspirational, really.'

*

Football was by no means Adrian Doherty's only obsession at this stage. Father Michael Doherty (no relation) remembers sitting in the Parochial House and watching Adrian train on the playing fields night after night. Then, an hour or two later, the doors of Melmount Parish Church would swing open and the same boy would pitch up for evening Mass. 'He was very devout,' his mother, Geraldine, says. 'At first we thought he must be out visiting somebody, because it was too dark for him to be playing football, but then friends would tell us Adrian had been at chapel. Every night. We actually started to wonder if he might want to become a priest.'

Then there was music and, increasingly, reading. 'For most of us, reading at that time, at fifteen or so, was specifically around the reading we had to do for school,' Kevin Doherty (again, no relation) says. 'Adrian was far more interested in reading whatever he wanted to learn about than whatever he was meant to be reading for school.'

Between his playing commitments with St Colman's, Moorfield, the Derry district XI and the Northern Ireland schoolboy team – not to mention visits to Manchester United in the school holidays and the occasional trip to Belfast to train at the club's centre of excellence – Adrian Doherty was finding his free time squeezed. In the face of pleas from his parents to focus on his schoolwork, he still insisted on going out to train on his own almost every night. Evening Mass took up another half-hour and was not, he said, up for negotiation. Something was clearly going to have to give. His schoolwork suffered – not drastically by any means, but to the point where his classmates and his parents felt he could and should have got more than the clutch of Bs and Cs he got in his GCSEs in the summer of 1989. 'If Aidy had taken his schoolwork really seriously, he might have been one of those who got straight As in everything,' Niall Dunphy says. 'Just as long as he didn't take art. Oh, or chemistry . . .'

None of his friends is quite certain how the situation came about, but at one stage at St Colman's, Adrian Doherty felt an overwhelming need to flunk an end-of-year chemistry exam, perhaps in order to dispel the growing pressure to push him down the science route when it came to his choice of GCSE subjects.

'We were all seated alphabetically, so Aidy was sat just to the side of me,' Kevin Doherty says, 'and I saw him get up, walk to the front of the class and stand in front of the periodic table, which was hanging on the wall. There was a question in the exam, "What is the periodic table?" or something like that, and I thought: "OK, Aidy must be taking a different view on this one." And boy, did he take a different view. Let me give you an example of some of the answers. The periodic table? His opening gambit on that was, "The periodic table was created by the Fisher Company" – or whoever it was that made the poster – "in 1972 . . ." And it went on like that.'

Dee Devenney is laughing. 'There was a long list of them,' he says. ' "What is a compound?" "A compound is a place where enemy prisoners are kept." "Give an example of a solvent." "An example of a solvent is Sherlock Holmes." The chemistry teacher went nuts when he marked the papers, but, as Adrian saw it, it was a means to an end. He just didn't want to do chemistry.'

Niall Dunphy remembers another exam – GCSE physical education, he suspects – in which Adrian misread the rubric and answered questions at length on twenty different sports, including synchronised swimming and ballroom dancing, rather than on the two or three specialist subjects they were meant to choose from a long list. 'Aidy had that sort of attitude: "No need to read what it says. Synchronised swimming, you say? OK, here I go . . ."' he says.

Gerard Mullan, like the rest of them, laughs at the reminders of Adrian's unusual exam technique. 'Being a teacher now, I would say you would probably be a bit frustrated because Adrian was one of those who was so intelligent that you'd think about what he could do, academically, if he had applied himself more,' Mullan says. 'People, not least his parents, said to him: "Make sure you get your GSCEs. You still need to make sure you do well" – even though he had already been signed by then and knew what was on the horizon. The world was his oyster, but he was totally committed to making it as a footballer.'

'That expression "happy-go-lucky" is used far too often,' Dunphy says, 'but that's exactly what Aidy was like. Whatever would make his friends happy, he would want to do it. Maybe Jimmy and Geraldine wouldn't always see the funny side at the time, but his outlook on life, even from eleven or twelve, I would just describe as hedonistic – but without any of the negative connotations. It wasn't selfish. It wasn't "Let's go and get drunk or take a load of drugs." It was just "Whatever is a laugh, let's do it."'

That spirit was certainly in evidence when Adrian and his friends went on holiday together after their GCSEs, camping in Downings, in County Donegal. 'We were out one night and people were saying to us, "I think your friend has had a bit too much to drink,"' Dunphy recalls. 'And we would say, "Actually he's the one who's not drinking." He would be on the dance floor and you'd look at him and think, "Jesus Christ, Aidy . . ." Another day, for some reason, he wrapped himself up as a mummy. He was covered in toilet roll, walking around this campsite in hysterics. He was a really funny guy. Intelligent, interesting, kind, caring and, yes, really really funny.'

Peter Doherty was a few days short of his fifth birthday when his older brother left for Manchester. His memories before that are limited. 'One of the earliest things I remember of Adrian is that I always thought he was magic,' he says. 'The most prominent image I have of him is that – obviously – he used to have a stash of 10p mixes in his bedroom, but he used to pretend he could make them appear and he would give them to me.'

Another of Peter's early memories involves a family trip to Manchester in March 1989 as the Dohertys were invited to Old Trafford to meet Alex Ferguson and his staff and to learn a little more about Adrian's apprenticeship, which was to start in July. 'We were picked up at the airport and taken to a hotel and we were all impressed because, for Peter and me, it was the first time we had been on a plane or stayed in a hotel,' Ciara, who by then was eleven, says.

The Dohertys were given the VIP treatment, taken on a tour of Old Trafford and seated in the directors' box – just behind Brian Clough, who was serving a touchline ban – for a match against Nottingham Forest. More importantly, Jimmy and Geraldine received reassurances from Ferguson and United's youth development officer Joe Brown about the supervision Adrian would receive when he began his apprenticeship four months later. They were not taken to see the digs, but the phrase they both remember is 'a home from home'. They travelled back to Strabane feeling much more positive about what was looming on the horizon.

Adrian paid three other visits to Manchester in school holidays over the course of that season. He made two appearances for United's B team (fourth XI) the previous August and then in the February half-term he was elevated to the A team (third XI), where, as a fifteen-year-old playing among professionals, such as Mark Robins, he scored the only goal of the game away to Burnley reserves. Then, in the final weeks of the season, there were outings against Bury and Blackpool, for the A and B teams respectively. Those trips to Manchester were always testing for schoolboys, staying in digs with rowdy apprentices and young professionals, but the message Jimmy and Geraldine Doherty received from United all along was that Adrian would be given the best possible care and supervision. It was in the club's interest, after all, to do everything possible to help their young players feel at home as they strove to fulfil their potential. In the case of Adrian Doherty, that potential was felt to be sky-high.

Nobody talked of bucket lists in those days, but one of Adrian's dreams was to see Bob Dylan perform. That dream came true on 3 and 4 June 1989, when he and his father travelled to Dublin to watch the latest leg of the great man's Never Ending Tour. These were Dylan's first performances in Dublin since May 1966, when he was the 24-year-old voice of a generation, performing at the Adelphi Theatre in front of a crowd that included a young Jimmy Doherty. Twenty-three years on, Jimmy was at RDS Simmonscourt with his son Adrian, the pair of them entranced by a Dylan show which began with 'Subterranean Homesick Blues' and culminated with 'All Along the Watchtower'. They were there for the second night too, when Dylan was joined on stage by U2's Bono for an encore of 'Knockin' on Heaven's Door' and 'Maggie's Farm'.

On the journey home to Strabane, Adrian was still exhilarated by the experience – not just by Dylan but by the whole atmosphere, with amateur musicians sitting outside in the sun beforehand, busking away. 'He just loved it,' his father says. 'Absolutely loved it.'

CHAPTER 7

A hush descended over the apprentices' dressing room at the Cliff as Alex Ferguson, his initials emblazoned on his tracksuit top, walked in. No knighthood back then, of course, but even in the summer of 1989 the Manchester United manager commanded a combination of respect, fear and awe, particularly among the younger players. The new apprentices steeled themselves in anticipation of a powerful address about how honoured they were to be at United, with the chance to follow in the footsteps of greatness, and how they must do everything possible to seize the opportunity they had been given. Ferguson cleared his throat. 'Right, lads,' he told them. 'Get yourselves changed. There's a minibus outside.'

The apprentices did as they were told, changing into the training kit that had been laid out for them and, all the while, looked around, sizing each other up. There were a handful from the immediate area – Mark Gordon, John Sharples, Jimmy Shields and Les Potts – and those from a little further afield in the north of England, which included Ian Wilkinson (Warrington), Jonathan Stanger (Blackburn) and Marcus Brameld (Sheffield). Then there was Colin McKee (Glasgow) and the Northern Irish trio of Alan McReavie (Belfast), Peter Smyth (Killyleagh) and

Adrian Doherty (Strabane). Gordon and Shields had played together for Salford Boys and knew Sharples and Potts through having trained with United at Littleton Road as schoolboys. There was far less familiarity among the out-of-towners, but, already holed up in digs around the corner from the Cliff, some of them had begun to strike a rapport. 'You could tell from the outset that people were starting to form their own little cliques,' Potts says.

Some of them had encountered Doherty before, in the school holidays, but Stanger remembers raising an eyebrow upon spotting his new team-mate for the first time. 'His kit was miles too big for him,' the goalkeeper recalls. 'You were just looking at him and thinking, "Really? What's all this about?"'

'You wouldn't have looked at him as a footballer,' Shields says. 'He was scrawny compared to a lot of us. He was like the lad in *Kes*. He was quiet, just getting changed in the corner, not saying a word.'

Within five minutes, Doherty and the rest of the new apprentices had joined Brian Kidd and Eric Harrison on the minibus that was chugging out of the gates at the Cliff. Eventually they pulled up next to a park – Heaton Park, the signs said. There were no goalposts, no pitch markings and no footballs in sight. 'Right, lads. Out you get.'

Barely had the apprentices climbed out of the minibus than they were off in pursuit of Kidd, running around the park. 'It was early in the morning and there was no one else there,' Smyth recalls. 'All we did was run around, doing circuits. One group went this way around, one group went the other and it was all very regimented, almost like

Marine training. Round and round and round. That's all we did that first day. Some of the lads were being sick.'

For Doherty, after all those hours performing shuttle runs against his own stopwatch back in Strabane, this was second nature. 'None of us could get near him in the sprints,' Potts says. 'He was like a greyhound. What I remember most is the brutality of it all. "Sprint over there, then sprint back here, then sprint back over there, then sprint back here." In hindsight, it was probably very wrong in a way, but as a kid, when you've just joined Manchester United, you don't question any of it.'

And the next day? 'The same,' Smyth says. 'And the day after that. Get your miles in first, build up your fitness. I think it was two weeks before we kicked a ball. If not, then that's what it felt like. It was very physically demanding, very tough. You would go back to digs exhausted. You were sore and you were too tired even to talk about it. You would just collapse onto your bed.'

The digs were on Lower Broughton Road, 200 yards from the Cliff, a large house belonging to a Salford couple named Mike and Eve Cody. They also had a couple of large dogs, which immediately put Adrian Doherty on edge. He was one of six Manchester United youngsters living in the house. The senior figures were Wayne Bullimore, a second-year pro from Nottinghamshire, and John Shotton, an eighteen-year-old forward from the north-east. The hierarchy within the house would be challenged by Mark Bosnich, a seventeen-year-old Australian goalkeeper whose laid-back yet boisterous demeanour made him popular with the players, if not always the coaching staff. Then there were the three new apprentices from Northern Ireland: Alan McReavie, Peter Smyth and, last but not least, the shy one who had already been christened 'Doc' – 'a milky, pasty lad who came over with a grown-out crew cut,' as Shotton recalls.

It was quite a mix of characters and indeed accents. 'It was a democracy,' Shotton says. 'Or maybe more of a commonwealth, actually, what with Bozzy, the Irish guys and me, because being from the north-east I don't think I qualified as English. It was friendly banter, but it was competitive too. Who would be first to the dinner table? Who could eat the most toast at breakfast? It was ridiculous things like that, competitiveness in everything we were doing.'

The initial inclination among the others was to regard the Northern Irish lads as a trio, but it quickly became clear this was not the case. From an early stage, there were McReavie and Smyth and then there was Doherty. Bosnich recalls it as being two Protestants and one Catholic, 'two guys from the Shankill Road in Belfast and Doc from wherever he was from'. In fact, Smyth was from the rural village of Killyleagh and had always felt like a 'country bumpkin' on his trips to Belfast with the Northern Ireland youth teams, but he felt he had a little more in common – far beyond religious background – with McReavie than with Doherty.

The new apprentices were told there was one large bedroom, which two of them would have to share, and a smaller single room. No lads want to share a bedroom when they are sixteen going on seventeen, but if they really had to do so, then McReavie and Smyth were the obvious two. That suited Doherty just fine. They saw little of him in those first few days except for training and when the six of them congregated in the common areas – the TV room and dining room, where breakfast and dinner were served. The food, Bullimore says politely, was not a highlight. 'Yes, Eve did the odd fry-up, but that was in the days before dieticians,' Smyth says. 'None of us knew any different.'

These days there are training grounds where a form of apartheid exists, with different staircases and different canteens so that apprentices, reserves and first-team players barely cross paths, never mind exchange words. It was not like that at the Cliff. There were three separate dressing rooms, but there was an unmistakable sense of community, albeit one with a clear hierarchy. At the bottom of the stairs was a corridor containing five doors: the boot room, the apprentices' dressing room, the reserves' dressing room, the first-team dressing room and the sauna. As Gary Neville says, 'It was incredibly close-knit, a real family atmosphere, a wonderful place for team spirit. Everyone knew each other inside out.'

Even as an apprentice, at the bottom of the food chain, you could not avoid rubbing shoulders with Bryan Robson, Mark Hughes and Brian McClair. Norman Whiteside was on his way out, controversially sold to Everton within days of the apprentices' arrival, as Ferguson stepped up his crackdown on the drinking culture in the squad, but Smyth recalls the new intake from Northern Ireland being given a pointedly Protestant welcome by his fellow Ulsterman. 'He welcomed the three of us – myself, Adrian and

Alan McReavie – and I can remember him whistling "The Sash",' Smyth says. 'He did it to wind up Paul McGrath, who is a Catholic and was coming down the stairs at the time.

'You go there thinking it's going to be like Hollywood. It wasn't like that at all. It was down to earth, so close-knit. Everyone knew everyone. Every morning Alex Ferguson would come into our changing room, have some banter, take the mickey out of someone and then he would go to the young pros' room and do the same. He was brilliant with us. So was Archie Knox.'

The one who terrified the first-year apprentices was Eric Harrison, whose craggy features, brusque manner and booming voice made even Ferguson seem gentle by comparison. If Brian Kidd, Nobby Stiles and Jim McGregor, the physio, were all seen as good cops, Harrison would frequently be cast as the bad cop, taking what Alan Tonge, an apprentice in the year above Adrian, calls a 'sergeant-major approach'. The first thing Harrison told every group of apprentices was that wearing the Manchester United crest did not mean you were talented enough to be able to get away with less than 100 per cent effort. On the contrary, it meant you always had to work harder than every opponent. 'It's not about the badge. It's about what's underneath it,' he told them. 'If you're wearing that badge and you're not competing harder than your opponent, then I'll drag you off and you'll never wear it again.'

'Eric was great,' Jimmy Shields says. 'We were all scared to death of him. He knew when to put his arm around your shoulder, but he knew when to give you a rollocking too.'

*

There were other ways in which that first week at Manchester United proved a rude awakening for the new apprentices. They had dreamed they would be spending their days pinging balls around lush training pitches with some of the best players in the country. They had imagined it as a finishing school, a place to hone their technique in preparation for their destiny as first-team players. They had been told there would be other duties, but they had not realised that these would take up quite so much of their time.

'It could be anything,' Alan Tonge says. 'You could be working in the development office or the ticket office at Old Trafford, doing maintenance on the ground, cleaning the trophies, helping the groundsman do the pitch, or you could be back at the Cliff, pumping balls up, cleaning the gym, cleaning the showers, cleaning boots, cleaning the stands, sweeping the dressing room.'

'It was tough, very tough,' Peter Smyth says. 'You had to be there before everyone else in the morning and then leave after them in the afternoon – cleaning, scrubbing the showers out, scrubbing the sauna out, getting all the kit and the balls ready. It was knackering.'

Another piece of housekeeping in those first few days involved finding further-education courses for the apprentices. They would train Monday to Wednesday, doing their jobs in the afternoon, training again on Friday before playing on Saturday, but Thursdays were set aside for college. Joe Brown made it clear to the youngsters that, while a two-year apprenticeship at Manchester United was something to be treasured, it came without guarantees, so they must continue their education in order to give themselves the best chance of a career after football – whenever that might be. The majority, based on their predicted GCSE grades, were expected to register for an NVQ at North Trafford College, not far from Old Trafford. The dubious reward for the higher achievers would be a weekly two-hour round trip to Accrington and Rossendale College, in Lancashire, for their day-release course on a BTEC national diploma in sports and leisure management.

Adrian Doherty scrutinised the list of BTEC courses on offer. None held the slightest appeal. If he was to be sent on a course, he would prefer to do something he was interested in. He asked about A-levels, about whether it might be possible to study English, music or history, something like that. Brown said he would make some enquiries and get back to him.

It was time for the new apprentices to be introduced to another Manchester United tradition. Some of the second-year apprentices had been waiting twelve months for this, the chance to impose their new-found seniority on the unsuspecting first-years. With all the apprentices sitting on benches in the dressing room, one first-year after another would be told it was their turn to get up and perform. 'It could be anything,' Jimmy Shields says. 'You might have to dance or sing in front of the group. There were hundreds of things.'

One of the traditions involved chatting up a mop in front of their peers and being required to show an appropriate level of self-confidence. So far, so harmless. Another was called 'Shag the Bed,' where the apprentice was required to climb onto the treatment table and, in front of the group, simulate sex, sound effects and all. A later twist was 'Shag Sunbed', where, rather than thrust up and down on the treatment table, they would have to perform the same actions on a life-size picture of Clayton Blackmore, the first-team full-back, who, by virtue of his miraculous year-round tan, was known as 'Sunbed'. If the technique was considered up to scratch by these all-knowing second-years, then there would be the cheers that signified approval and acceptance. If not, there would be shrieks and howls of derision because it would be time for a forfeit. One of the most common was known as 'The Lap'. 'They used to lie you on the treatment bed with your head down, looking through the hole, and they would kick the ball through at you, in your face,' Peter Smyth says.

'Or someone would be put in a tumble dryer,' Shields says. 'I can remember Mark Gordon being put in the tumble dryer for a spin. Another one was where someone would be gagged and put in a kitbag and taken to Old Trafford on the bus. They would fall out when the cleaners opened the bags.'

This stuff had been going on for years, the forfeits varying between the nonsensical, the brutally inane and the sinister. One player, years earlier, had been dressed up in several layers of tracksuits and barricaded into the sauna until, Houdini-style, he managed to get them off and escape. Then there was what was known as 'The Bong' – a series of bashes on the head with a pumped-up football wrapped in a towel. Keith Gillespie, in his autobiography, says another punishment involved being 'lined up for a flurry of punches that would leave you with a dead arm'. Gary Neville, in his autobiography, *Red*, recalls apprentices 'being stripped naked and having the United kit – the shorts, the shirt, even the number on your back – rubbed on to you in dubbin with a wire brush. After that it would be two minutes in an ice-cold bath and then into a tumble dryer.'

These anarchic ceremonies required the services of a lookout to give warning when Alex Ferguson, Archie Knox, Eric Harrison or another member of the coaching staff appeared at the top of the staircase. They have become part of the modern Manchester United legend, the 'toughening-up process' that made men of Ryan Giggs, David Beckham, Paul Scholes, the Neville brothers and the rest. All have referred to them in their autobiographies and, at some length, in *The Class of '92*, the documentary film about their remarkable success story. They wince and shake their heads as they cast their minds back, but there is a little laughter there too.

Paul Scholes, like Adrian Doherty, was a painfully shy teenager. He did not find the 'initiation' culture funny when he began his apprenticeship at Manchester United in 1991 and he does not find it funny now. 'It happened, didn't it?' the former England midfielder said with a shrug when we met in November 2013 for an interview to promote *The Class of '92*. 'There was . . . Some of the stuff, you just wouldn't be able to speak about these days. It would never happen. I suppose the whole point of the initiations was to make you mentally tougher and mentally stronger and it did that.'

All of this forced exhibitionism must have been

anathema to someone like Scholes, though. 'Oh, I hated it, yeah,' he said. 'It got stopped around our year, actually, all the stuff you had to do. I think one of the players' parents complained and that was it.'

How bad can unspeakable be? 'I can't tell you,' he said. 'You would be in trouble for it these days, some of the stuff that went on. Seriously.'

The word 'initiations' offered some kind of reassurance that this stuff was a one-off, merely part of a getting-to-know-you process, but it was not. Much of it continued through the year as ad hoc punishments for, say, a poor performance in training or shoddy workmanship when it came to the menial jobs. Jimmy Shields remembers being stripped down to his underwear and made to run around in the snow, his team-mates laughing at him from the warmth of the corridor. Similarly, Gary Neville made the remarkable claim in his autobiography that 'the coaches would see an apprentice running around the pitch in the freezing cold in nothing but his boots, yet turn a blind eye'. Les Potts says: 'I wouldn't say I was bullied, but I would try to avoid the dressing room. For the first year, they probably made my life hell.'

'It was ridiculous, some of the stuff that went on,' Jonathan Stanger says. 'It was a tough school. At Manchester United at that time, you just had to show the mental attitude and aptitude to get through it. I don't think I was mentally strong enough to survive in that environment. That was professional football at the time. In fairness, I can't remember Doc being picked on all that much. He had the strength of character and was the type of deep thinker who would make his own decisions. There were plenty of others who were picked out and picked on and made to do different things.'

'As an apprentice at that time, you didn't know what you were going into,' Marcus Brameld says. 'It was a tough upbringing, dog eat dog, everyone vying for places, all trying to get up the ladder. You had to deal with the older ones. You had to become a man overnight. Some of us, like me and Doc, had to deal with being away from home too. If you look at some of the lads in our age group, some of them crumbled a little bit. That was just what happened back then.'

The first week of their apprenticeship had been a combination of 'brutal' Marine-type training, college-course admin, hours of errands and now humiliation and intimidation at the hands of the second-years. Welcome to Manchester United. The only times they had come in contact with a football was when pumping them up for the professionals or being whacked over the head by the second-years. It was not quite what Adrian Doherty and the rest of them had in mind when they signed their contracts in front of their beaming parents, or indeed when they were waved off a week earlier.

For the local lads, it was a case of going home every evening and, while emphasising how exhausting it was, keeping quiet about the things their parents would not want to hear. At least they had their home comforts. For those in digs, there was no such refuge. There was a payphone in the hall, but it was in near-constant use, particularly in those first weeks. Family and friends wanted to hear all about it. As Potts says, 'You found yourself trying to hype it up to be everything it probably wasn't at the time.'

For the sake of their peace of mind, Doherty spared his parents many of the details when he spoke to them on the telephone. Then he called some of his friends. 'At the start Aidy was, like, "This isn't quite what I thought it was going to be,"' Niall Dunphy says. 'It wasn't so much the training. It was just that, from a very early stage, with the jobs, the dress code and everything else, on top of the training, it was spelt out to the players that this was their job now and it wasn't going to be fun. And Aidy, because he was such a free spirit, so laid-back, so hedonistic in the sense that he liked everything to be fun and had always played football to enjoy it, found that a bit of a shock.'

CHAPTER 8

It was uniform day for the new recruits at Manchester United. The first-year apprentices were being measured up for their new club blazer, with crisply ironed white shirt, grey trousers and shiny black shoes compulsory. Some of them, not a hair out of place, felt like Joseph putting on his Technicolor dreamcoat. By contrast, Adrian Doherty felt like a scarecrow, his blazer hanging off him, his shirt cuffs flapping around his knuckles. He knew he looked daft, so he held his arms out to accentuate the point. Better to be laughed with than laughed at.

The blazer was intended to heighten the apprentices' sense of what it means to represent Manchester United. But to Doherty, it was just a glorified school uniform. Moreover, he was worried by something they had just been told about the need to stock up on white shirts.

He had, on his parents' instruction, travelled to Manchester with a couple of white shirts and a pair of black shoes, but the advice to the apprentices from Joe Brown was that it would be worth investing in more unless they were to spend their weeks fretting about laundry cycles and ironing. Any player who needed another white shirt or two was advised to take the bus into Manchester city centre and stock up at Marks & Spencer or the like.

The city centre. The bus. Shopping. Spending money. All of these ideas filled Doherty with trepidation, but he knew he would have to do it. This was the first test of his new-found independence. He would get the bus in, buy a shirt and then get the bus back to his digs on Lower Broughton Road. How hard could it be, really?

Francie McCauley, a schoolteacher from Strabane, heard the telephone ring at his home in Salford. 'It was Jimmy, Adrian's father,' Francie recalls. 'He told me Adrian was stuck in the centre of Manchester with no money. He was outside Marks & Spencer in a phone box and didn't know what to do. I told Jimmy to try to let Adrian know I would come to pick him up.'

The Doherty family had asked McCauley to keep an eye on Adrian, to have him around for dinner occasionally and to be a point of contact in case of emergency. McCauley was happy to do so and had planned to make contact after the hurly-burly of the first week or so. He had not expected the first SOS call to come quite so soon.

'The thing you have to understand,' McCauley says, 'is that, for a young lad coming over from Strabane, Manchester was a totally different environment. For one thing, you could walk everywhere in Strabane. You could walk from one end of town to the other in ten minutes. And if you wanted to buy some clothes, you would go into a local draper's shop and if it came to £23, they might tell you it was £20 for cash.

'Adrian had gone to Marks & Spencer to buy a new shirt. He went to the checkout and they told him it was £15 or whatever and he thought he could do the same as you would back in Strabane, offer them less for cash. Well of course they said no. As it was, he had just enough money to cover the shirt, but it meant he only had something like 20p left, which wouldn't cover his bus fare back to Salford. So he rang his dad and told him he was stuck in Manchester with no money and didn't know what to do. I set off as soon as I could, but when I got there, he was nowhere to be seen. I found a payphone and rang Jimmy. It transpired that Adrian had set off walking and had got all the way back to his digs, a couple of miles away. That was typical Adrian. It was a big undertaking for a lad from a rural town in Ireland to be away from home in Manchester, but he dealt with it in his own way. He had an inner confidence. He had that by the bagful.'

Above all, Adrian Doherty had confidence on the football pitch. He longed for the opportunity to show it. During that gruelling and unsettling first fortnight at Manchester United, he and his fellow apprentices drew solace from the fact that every day – every hour spent running around the training pitches, every hour spent sweeping floors or enduring humiliation by the second-years, every hour wiled away in the boredom of the digs – took them closer to the moment when they would start playing matches. That Marine-style pre-season training regime, as Peter Smyth describes it, was a means to an end, the first steps on the long journey which they hoped would lead to United's first team. The next steps, they knew, would come on the pitch. Their first big test would be in the Milk Cup, back in Northern Ireland in the last week of July. Accordingly, the training regime was adjusted and the emphasis switched from fitness drills to ball work. It is the way every footballer likes it, particularly those as talented as Adrian Doherty. 'He stuck out a mile,' Jonathan Stanger says. 'He had absolutely unbelievable skill.'

Doherty loved training – or rather he loved what he considered training, which was what he had done every night back in Strabane, dribbling in and out of Coke cans or traffic cones at quite astonishing speed, against the stopwatch, and then looking to shoot past an imaginary goalkeeper or cross to an imaginary team-mate. At the Cliff, it was a different kind of training, far more structured, far more punishing. Eric Harrison was determined to drill good habits into the apprentices, to the point where best practice would start to come instinctively. Much of the emphasis now was on conditioning them to think like United players, both in forging the right attitudes on the pitch, in terms of workrate and diligence, and in making them aware of what was expected of them with and without the ball. Harrison would accept losing the odd match – or so he claimed, at any rate – but he told the apprentices quite forcefully he would never tolerate a lack of application.

'The first thing Eric would say to us was that thing about the Manchester United badge and how, underneath it, we had to work harder than everybody else,' Peter Smyth says. 'The other thing he used to say to us, particularly the midfield, was "Check there and there –" a quick glance over each shoulder – "before you get the ball. Don't rely on other people to tell you." Eric would say: "If I don't see you checking there and there, I'm taking you off." That's why the likes of Paul Scholes were so good. It was drummed into you – "there and there" all the time.'

One of the drills was called man-to-man marking. As a right-winger, Doherty would be expected to run at and torment the left-back – Les Potts in the first-years, Sean McAuley in the second-years, both of them dreading these assignments – but that was just one part of it. When the opposition had the ball, Doherty's job was to double up and provide defensive cover for the right-back Alan McReavie. Whatever United's fascination with flamboyant wingers, they were expected to do far more than just dribble, cross and shoot. Under Alex Ferguson's management, under Harrison's tuition, a winger was expected to work his flank relentlessly – terrorising the opposition when United had the ball, protecting his full-back with equal ferocity when they did not. In terms of intensity and the demand to put work before talent, it was far closer to the joylessness of the Northern Ireland schoolboys set-up than Doherty had ever imagined. Maybe this was just the reality of professional football. Either way, it wasn't great fun.

Home, sweet home. Adrian Doherty was back in Strabane. With the Milk Cup taking place on the northern coast of Northern Ireland, in Coleraine, Portrush and other towns nearby, he, Alan McReavie and Peter Smyth had been granted permission to see their respective families before joining up with the rest of the squad, who flew over from Manchester a couple of days later. For now, however briefly, Doherty was back among his family and his home comforts. Everything felt right again.

The Manchester United squad were staying in the coastal resort of Portrush, just across the road from Bertie's Amusements. Les Potts remembers the United players getting 'a lot of attention' from the local girls on their trips to the fairground. Under the management of Brian Kidd and Nobby Stiles, though, it was a serious business, with a tough schedule of seventy-minute matches starting on the Monday morning and taking place every day – sometimes two games a day – building up to the final on the Friday. United got through their first-round group, beating Coleraine 1–0, Heart of Midlothian 2–1 and Star of the Sea 3–0. Doherty started the first game, sat out the second and came on as a substitute in the third, in which Colin Telford, a fifteen-year-old from Belfast, scored a hat-trick to underline the potential that had already secured him an apprenticeship to begin a year later.

Jimmy Doherty recalls that his son suffered with back trouble both before and during the Milk Cup, but by the Thursday he was able to manage two games in a day. In the morning he played in the quarter-final victory over Dundalk Schoolboys League. In the afternoon, with United trailing 1–0 to Clydebank in the semi-final, he equalised in the closing stages before Mark Gordon scored the winner in extra time. That set up a final against Newcastle United, whose squad included five future Premier League players in Lee Clark, Alan Thompson, Robbie Elliott, Alan Neilson and Lee Makel. Clark, in particular, had a big reputation. Potts recalls that the Newcastle captain was being hyped as a future £1 million player and that, rather than play it down, he would shout out whenever he had done something to add another £100,000 to his valuation. This did not endear him to the United contingent. 'I remember in the final Jimmy Shields took him out,' Potts says. 'He got a bit more than the ball.'

Clark had the last laugh as Newcastle claimed the trophy with a 2–1 win, but the Milk Cup was a productive experience for United's youngsters. Telford was one of the main beneficiaries, scoring four goals in as many starts, but he was more impressed by a team-mate who was still feeling the effects of a back problem. 'That was the first time I had played with Doc and I thought he was out of this world,' Telford says. 'He was just unbeatable at that level.'

A new season was looming, but the excitement felt by most at the Cliff was not coming so easily to Adrian Doherty. Homesickness was one concern. Frustration with the daily grind, even on the training pitch, was another. Both were compounded by his persistent back problem, which meant making regular visits to the treatment room. He was encouraged to continue his stretching exercises, but then he was advised to rest, which meant sitting out training, the next round of pre-season matches and, less dishearteningly, some of the apprentices' day-to-day duties.

The life of an injured footballer is a lonely one at the best of times, never mind when the player has just begun an apprenticeship in a strange city and does not have the luxury of being able to pop home to see his friends and family. Doherty was not settling in well. He was not enjoying the training, the day-to-day routine, the machismo and the so-called banter, whether in the dressing room at the Cliff or back at the digs. He missed his friends and family, but he craved solitude and quiet, closing his bedroom door behind him while his housemates gathered together to watch television, some of them wearing football boots to help break them in. 'It's hard trying to fill the time after training,' Peter Smyth says. 'After training, you're supposed to rest, but there's only so much resting you can do. It's hard to fill the boredom.'

Doherty was not the only new apprentice who was finding it tough. Jonathan Stanger says: 'You would go back to the digs and there was the homesickness element to deal with as well. My personal opinion is that the local lads had it easier because they didn't have to go through living in digs, on your own, away from home, away from your parents, with a group of lads who had nothing to do. That is a lot harder than people realise.'

In his autobiography, *My Idea of Fun*, Lee Sharpe recounts a story of how, at another digs, on Priory Avenue, they would play a game called 'Darkness'. Essentially this involved turning off the lights in the living room and closing the curtains, so it was pitch black, at which point you were free to throw things around the room – ornaments, shoes, cutlery, anything at all – but you were not allowed to make a noise if you were struck by a missile. If you did, the others would have carte blanche to give you a dead arm or a dead leg. 'No, you don't need me to run that past you again,' Sharpe says. 'That was it, just one of the ways in which the gilded youth at the world's most glamorous football club used to pass the time in the evenings of their apprenticeship.'

There was much worse, Sharpe claims, for some of the schoolboys arriving for trials in the holidays. 'During the day they would train with their heroes, then in the evening they would be lined up in the living room of these digs, a porno film would be put on and these poor unfortunate young lads would be made to watch it,' he says. 'If one of them got a hard-on, he would get a dig off all the lads.'

Initially, some of the local lads might have envied their team-mates who were staying in digs, with their crazy games and their independence, away from their parents. Quickly, though, they came to pity the out-of-towners. Kieran Toal, a local lad who was a second-year apprentice at the time, recalls going to the digs on Priory Avenue – known to every United player of that generation as 'Brenda's', with reference to Brenda Gosling, the long-suffering landlady – and witnessing a game where the lodgers would stand in the lounge and take turns to throw a cushion at the wall. The twist was that the cushion had to land in the six-inch gap between the clock and a picture hanging on the wall. If it hit either, then there was a forfeit. As for the forfeits, a typical example would be having to call Brenda through to ask her an embarrassing question while a pornographic film played in the background. Poor Brenda.

You are left with the impression that life in digs was entirely at odds with the professionalism demanded by Alex Ferguson, Eric Harrison and the coaching staff at the Cliff on a daily basis. 'It was just an inane existence,' Toal says. 'Look at that from the perspective of someone like Doc, who also not only a lot more intelligent than the typical apprentice but also on a totally different wavelength. What must he have been thinking?'

It was made worse for Doherty by his back problem, which denied him even the regular cycle of training and matches to break the monotony. He missed a couple more friendly matches as well as a five-day north-west youth tournament, which United won, allowing first-year apprentices to pick up the first trophy of their Old Trafford careers along with a fifteen-year-old schoolboy named

Ryan Wilson, who would go on to be known as Ryan Giggs. With more rest required and with the coaching staff recognising that he might be better off among friends and family at home, Doherty was allowed to spend a few days back in Strabane. Again it was a relief to get away from Salford, away from the Cliff, away from the digs, away from the conflicting forces of mundanity and anarchy that summed up the life of an apprentice at Manchester United in the late 1980s.

By the time Adrian Doherty was fit to play, the season had started. This was a strange, turbulent period in Manchester United's history. The club was the subject of interest from Michael Knighton, a flamboyant property developer who followed up his public £20 million takeover bid with a bizarre ball-juggling, kiss-blowing appearance on the Old Trafford pitch before the opening first-team fixture of the season against Arsenal. Swept along by a feel-good factor – and a couple of expensive new signings, in Neil Webb and Mike Phelan – United won 4–1, raising hopes that this could be the season when they finally awoke from their slumber. More high-profile additions followed, in Gary Pallister, Paul Ince and Danny Wallace, as United continued what was at the time the biggest spending spree in English football history, but within weeks the Knighton takeover collapsed in embarrassing fashion and this star-studded team was dragged into a grim battle to avoid relegation as Alex Ferguson's popularity plummeted among a disillusioned fanbase.

So distant did the first team feel from the apprentices – perhaps even more so after the early-season influx of expensive new talent – that such concerns passed them by. For the younger players, it was all about getting onto that ladder. In Doherty's case, that meant making up for lost time after five weeks on the sidelines. He returned to action to inspire United's B team to a 3–0 win over Liverpool, scoring the opening goal. That was more like it. Victories over the Merseyside club, at any level, were always treasured by everyone at United.

Doherty's performance against Liverpool came in time to secure his call-up for the next day's departure for the Grossi Morera tournament in Italy. It was a ten-day trip for a seventeen-man squad. The majority were second-year apprentices, but six first-years (Ian Wilkinson, Alan McReavie, John Sharples, Jimmy Shields, Peter Smyth and Doherty) made the squad too. More surprisingly, so did Ryan Wilson, six months Doherty's junior, who was required to take a week off school to play in the tournament.

It was a step up for Wilson, playing in an Under-18 tournament at the age of fifteen, but he started five of United's six matches. Doherty, by contrast, started just one, the 4–0 win over the Viterbese select XI, coming on as a substitute against AC Milan, Atalanta and Torino and in the final against Auxerre, which United won 4–1 to secure another trophy.

Tony Park, an obsessive follower and peerless chronicler of United's youth teams, recalls that Doherty was 'outstanding' at times during the tournament, while Alan Tonge remembers there being 'one game where he got absolutely unbelievable praise afterwards'. But Doherty was never at his happiest on those trips. The enforced ritual of the pre-match walkabout was not to his liking.

Neither were the long journeys – the flight to Rome via Heathrow, the one-hour bus trip from Rome to their base in Bagnoregio and the daily trips on winding roads to the outlying towns, Viterbo, Gallese and Civita Castellana, for the matches. Where possible, Doherty listened to his music on his personal stereo. He was no keener on foreign food than he had been in Switzerland as a fourteen-year-old. 'Off the pitch, the only thing I remember of Doc on that trip is at the guesthouse, sort of floating about a bit,' Tonge says. 'We would be having dinner around a table, with tracksuits on, and he would wander down in a vest – an old granddad-type vest – grab a piece of bread and wander off again.'

Kieran Toal has to double-check a photograph of the winning squad, about to fly back to Manchester the morning after the final, in order to be certain that Doherty was involved. 'I can remember Giggsy on that trip, but not Doc, which is unusual because he was such a good player,' Toal says.

At last, seemingly free of back trouble and with no more foreign jaunts on the horizon, Adrian Doherty got into a rhythm with his training, building up to his Saturday run-outs in the A or B team. The problem was that, even with the errands and jobs and the daily routine taken into account, that rhythm involved so many empty afternoons and evenings. Mark Bosnich, his housemate, had settled into a pattern of going for a couple of pints in the after-noon and sleeping it off. Better than staring at the walls, the Australian reasoned. Doherty looked for alternative means of stimulation. He found a couple of Catholic churches nearby, St Boniface's and St Sebastian's, but he was disappointed to learn there was no daily service. His college courses would not start until late September.

Homesickness was a problem for many of the lads holed up in those boarding houses in Salford, including Giuliano Maiorana, a talented winger who had joined United from Histon, of the Eastern Counties League. 'You're thinking, "Why have they put us right in the middle of one of the roughest parts of Salford?"' he says. 'I remember the first day I went back for pre-season one year – I think it was that year, 1989 – a few of us went up the road to a shop and we got chased back to our digs by two or three lads who got out of a car with a crowbar. You're thinking, "What's all this about?"

'Before I went there, I had a full-time job. Up at United, I used to start training at half-ten, finish at midday and I had nothing to do in the afternoon. You would get bored and homesick. Everyone thinks, "You're at Man United. What have you got to moan about?" But the main thing was boredom and being away from your family. I used to drive around on my own, getting lost, thinking, "Who can I go and see?" And I was nineteen, with a car. It was a three-hour drive back to Cambridge, but I could do it if I wanted. Doc was sixteen and his family were a flight away, so he didn't have that option.'

Doherty was spending his afternoons and evenings in his room, listening to music, and he found that his weekly £29.50 pay packet was beginning to build into quite a stash. He decided it was time to do something he had been thinking about for a while. One afternoon he went into Manchester, found a music shop and bought a guitar and some books to teach himself how to play it. The shopkeeper took a shine to him, even giving him a free record player to go with the guitar. He and that guitar would quickly become inseparable.

Teenage boys do not tend to bare their soul in telephone conversations, but Jimmy and Geraldine Doherty were worried that Adrian was homesick in Manchester. They asked Francie McCauley to get in touch again and, if possible, to try to take him out one evening. 'I only lived about ten minutes away so I would go and pick him up and we would go for a bite to eat,' McCauley says. 'We would chat about Strabane, about football, watch some TV. He was a lovely, well-mannered, quietly spoken young man, but he didn't seem to fit in with the general atmosphere around the other lads. They were watching football videos all the time, going out for a drink, going out to see what the local talent was. Adrian went and bought himself a guitar and taught himself how to play it.

'Adrian was also a religious lad. I taught in a Catholic school and I knew the local priests. One of them, Father Houlihan, told me one night he had a knock on the door at St Sebastian's and found this young lad asking if there was an evening Mass like he had gone to every night at home. There wasn't, but he got to know Father Houlihan well. He was a big Manchester United fan as well, so he would have been excited to get to know Adrian. But Adrian missed evening Mass. I think he felt that would have given him something else to focus on.'

In late September, back in Strabane, Dee Devenney found an envelope waiting on his doormat. The almost-indecipherable handwriting, along with the Manchester postmark, left him in no doubt who the letter was from. Devenney opened it quickly, anticipating exciting tales about life inside the Old Trafford dream factory. His heart sank. He did not have to read for long to realise his good friend Adrian Doherty was finding life at Manchester United far less pleasurable than anyone had imagined.

'The apprenticeship isn't very good,' Doherty announced early in the correspondence. 'In fact the daily routine is cat and boring.'

'Cat', as Devenney explains, was a slang word they used, meaning something approximate to 'terrible'. 'You get fed up playing football when you play the way the people over here play it,' Doherty went on, 'but you have to put up with it. The training isn't really hard but you still can't wait for it to finish. Today for example we did jogging and then something that was really stupid. Then all the second-year apprentices played the first-years and beat us 5–0 or something like that. This is normal and all the second-years will be eighteen soon and will have to make their own dinner. I don't care at all, but I'm just saying it anyway. I went to an adult-education class by accident last night. Then I missed the bus and didn't get home for nearly two hours.'

On it goes, at one point enthusing about a 'class picture house' in Bury, 'which looks like a spaceship', and at another lamenting the fact that 'nearly all the apprentices are U2 fans and none of them are hip so I can't go to the same places as them on Saturday nights or anything'. He also refers to his YTS income being 'a good lot', and says 'I don't really know what to spend it on', before adding that he has bought a guitar. He tells his friend: 'I hope you enjoy yourself on Saturday night and sing about elephants and envelopes' – 'He used to come out with these mad, nonsensical lines,' Devenney explains – and finishes by saying he hopes to see him soon, 'about next weekend or the weekend after'. Oh, yes, and he suggests he has had trouble remembering to clean his teeth on a regular basis. He signs off 'Adrian Doherty'.

In that letter, Doherty does not exactly sound like a kid who was living the dream. 'I knew he was homesick as soon as I got it,' Devenney says. 'We were real country boys, very naive sixteen-year-olds from a small community where everyone knew everyone. He had gone to a big city. You could see a bit of the novelty being there, but, reading between the lines, you can see he was a bit lost. He's not mentioning games or the joy of playing. It's just about the training and the grind. I think, looking at it, even in those first weeks, maybe he was falling out of love with it a wee bit.'

'It is really difficult,' Wayne Bullimore, one of Doherty's housemates at the digs on Lower Broughton Road, says. 'I'm quite shy and I was from Mansfield, which was a back-water, so it was hard for me, but it was much harder for Doc. Coming to a big city like Manchester, a big club, a lot of expectation from your family and friends back home, living with a group of strangers night and day, it really is tough. You come over at sixteen and you're in a group, com-peting with each other. The dressing room, with all that banter, can be cruel, very competitive. To me, he seemed painfully shy. I would try to have conversations with him, but it would be minimal. "What did you do last night?" "Ah, I just played some music." I would ask what kind of music and he would say something that was a bit obscure for me.'

Mark Bosnich says he too found it hard to engage with his young housemate. 'Doc was different,' he says. 'If I can put it this way, a football club is a very conformist society. If you don't conform, people think you're not normal. He knew he was different and I always thought he was some-one who was extremely comfortable in his own skin. He wouldn't change just to fit in. Fair play to him. When we went to play snooker, he stayed in and read. I must have asked him a million times if he was OK. He always gave the impression he was. He would have made a great card player because you never knew what he was thinking.'

Peter Smyth says it was only afterwards that he realised his housemate was struggling. 'He was never left out of anything, but he wouldn't get involved either,' Smyth says. 'If we were going into Manchester, going around the shops on the odd afternoon when we were bored, we would ask if he fancied coming. He would prefer to do things on his own, reading, playing his guitar. I thought he was happy doing his own thing. He didn't mention being homesick. He didn't say he was thinking of going home. I just remem-ber coming back from training one day and he was gone.'

CHAPTER 9

Adrian Doherty woke up to gloriously familiar surroundings: in his own bed, in his own room, in his own house, in his own town. He was away from Salford, away from the raging testosterone of his fellow apprentices with their flashy clothes, hair gel, banter, mainstream music and stupid games. He was home. Nothing had changed apart from Peter growing another couple of inches and following him around like a shadow. Ah, it was good to be back.

He had told Manchester United's youth development officer Joe Brown he was homesick, was not enjoying the apprenticeship and felt like giving up. Brown offered the standard line of reassurance, telling him that another Northern Irish winger, called George Best, once cut short a trial with United on account of homesickness and was back in Belfast within twenty-four hours – but ended up returning and being rewarded for his perseverance. Doherty meant it, though. He did not like the training, the digs or being away from home. Brown discussed Doherty's situation with Eric Harrison, Brian Kidd, Nobby Stiles and the rest of the coaching staff, all the way up to Alex Ferguson. This was serious. Ferguson asked him to explain how he felt. Doherty told him he wanted to go home and did not want to continue with the apprenticeship. The manager was concerned. Doherty was a real talent and had to be handled with extra care. The decision was taken to allow him to return home and take as long as he needed, but to leave him in no doubt that they held him in the highest regard and that he had an extremely bright future at United. They wanted him to take time out and then return with his enthusiasm renewed, ready to adapt to the demands of his apprenticeship, both on and off the pitch. In the meantime, they would look into ways to make his life more comfortable when – or, as he saw it, if – he returned to Manchester.

It was a Thursday. Most of his mates would be in college. He was looking forward to seeing them, looking forward to the *craic* but dreading the inevitable questions about what the hell he was doing back home, back in bloody Strabane. Still, off he went for a walk, out past the golf club and up through the Ballycolman estate, all the way to Melvin Park, where he had been coached by Liam Kennedy years earlier.

John Tinney is sitting in the lounge at the Dohertys' house in Strabane. He is in his forties now, a father of four. He is lean and athletic and likes to keep busy. He is bright, enthusiastic, good-natured. At the time we meet, he is unemployed. 'Strabane is still an unemployment black spot,' he says. 'It actually seems worse now than it was when Adrian and I left school. You just have to get on with it.'

Tinney is one of those guys who recalls his youth in the sharpest detail. He will not just remember an incident, he will pinpoint a date. He certainly remembers the day in November 1989 when he was shocked to see Adrian

Doherty, his former classmate and team-mate, traipsing across Melvin Park when he should have been serving his apprenticeship at Manchester United.

'It was a Thursday afternoon and the reason I know that is because I was doing a welding course and we got a recreation period on a Thursday afternoon, when we used to go and play football, usually at Melvin Park,' Tinney says. 'I remember on that particular day I was down there with the YTP [youth training programme]. We got talking and he said it was too fast over there, too busy, too many bright lights – coming from here, from a town like Strabane, to a big city like Manchester. I would find that myself if I was stuck over there, to be honest. I don't think it was so much to do with the football side of it.'

Doherty's difficulty in adjusting to the training regime at United did come across, though. 'I remember him telling me they were being taught how to kick a ball,' Tinney says. 'I thought he was joking. He said, "I'm serious. They actually show you how to kick a ball." He was, like, "Well, I can definitely kick a ball. If I couldn't, they wouldn't have signed me in the first place." He was joking about it, but I think he found it ridiculous.'

Tinney asked if Doherty fancied joining the kickaround: 'You could show us all how to kick a ball.' Doherty politely declined. A kickaround on Melvin Park was a million miles from the intensity of life back in Manchester, but he had come back to Strabane to get away from football. 'Maybe next time,' he said.

Adrian Doherty's friends wanted to know why he was home, but he kept turning the conversation on its head, asking what they were up to at college. They were left to read between the lines. 'I think he was a bit confused by it all,' Gerard Mullan says. 'He didn't like all the stress. He was so relaxed and everyone there was so uptight. He liked – no, loved – playing football, but he didn't like all the pressure and that feeling of "We're paying you X amount. We expect you to be like this."'

Niall Dunphy felt the demands of the apprenticeship were taking a toll on his friend. 'It quickly became his job, rather than what it had been before,' Dunphy says. 'He was being told where he had to go, what time he had to be there and – a big thing, this – what he had to wear, how he had to look. That irritated him, being told he had to wear a shirt and tie and blazer and had to comb his hair. I remember him saying he got grief for not combing his hair. That went completely against the grain for Aidy. His view was "I'm going to turn up, play well, work for the team, score two goals and set up another goal. Why does it matter what my hair is like?" He wasn't a big fan of the training either. We reminded him he used to go and train by himself for three or four hours at a time and he didn't mind that, but I think a lot of the enjoyment was being taken out of it for him.'

It would be hard, too, for those back in Strabane to understand the problems he was encountering in Manchester. Whatever his grievances, they would sound like a price worth paying many times over for a career at Manchester United. How could he possibly explain, as someone living the supposed dream, that all of these difficulties were building up to one big nightmare?

'I think he was reluctant to say things explicitly because

he didn't want to let anyone down,' Dee Devenney says. 'Everyone had that expectation for him. I don't just mean his family or his mates. I mean the whole town.'

'I had severe doubts about whether he was going to go back,' John Tinney says. 'Everyone was just thinking, "Jesus, he's going to be stuck here in Strabane in the employment centre like the rest of us." To the rest of us, it looked like he had a stark choice between staying here, with nothing to strive for, and going over to England and making a go of it. And I suppose, with it being a small town, everyone was asking him, "Adrian, what's happening? Why are you back here with all this carry-on and these shootings and everything else?"'

Kevin Doherty views it slightly differently. 'I think many people in Strabane wouldn't have found it that unusual that Aidy missed home,' he says. 'A lot of folks in Strabane thought it was the centre of the universe, so it would have seemed daunting to be away from home. Plus the support framework he had grown up with just wasn't there in Manchester. He was a young sixteen anyway. In terms of life experience and outlook on life, he would have felt even younger over there.'

Dunphy feels Doherty was also craving the intellectual stimulation that was not available to a Manchester United apprentice. He had started his A-level courses in Manchester, but even that was a bind, involving bus journeys into and out of the city for night classes. 'Aidy really wanted to re-engage his brain,' Dunphy says. 'He had always been a big reader, but, perhaps because he had so much free time, he decided to start reading anything and everything. My father has a load of old books in the house that he never reads – old Russian authors, old Russian music. I would get back from college and my father would say, "Adrian was around this afternoon. He wanted to borrow some books" or "He was asking me about Shostakovich."

'Now when I say some of these things, you might think, "Well this guy sounds pretentious," but Aidy absolutely wasn't. If something interested him, he would think, "I want to know more about it." So he started reading Dostoyevsky or Tolstoy or whoever. He was also teaching himself the guitar. Looking back, you can see he wanted to engage and expand his mind.'

He was not above a cheap joke at his own expense, though. 'I remember one morning when he was back, Aidy and I went to watch a match his brother was playing in down the bottom of the Ballycolman,' Dunphy says. 'We were standing there and some guy standing beside us, typical eejit, points at Gareth and says, "See that Doherty boy? He's useless." Aidy latches on to this: "Oh, I know. He's useless." This guy says, "And you know that brother of his at Manchester United? He's no better." And Aidy's going, "I know him. He's rubbish. And he thinks he's good. He's an eejit." I was in hysterics. I can imagine a lot of footballers taking offence at that, but Aidy loved it. "Adrian Doherty? Oh he's a complete tube, that boy."'

Back at the Cliff and the digs nearby, it was business as usual – professionalism with a liberal sprinkling of anarchy when authority turned its back. The first-year apprentices were still copping a lot of flak from the second-years. Les Potts remembers Adrian Doherty 'disappearing for a while' and being told it was due to homesickness, but says nobody knew any more than that. Peter Smyth says he frequently asked Joe Brown whether Doherty was coming back, but 'they didn't give too much away'. Derek Brazil says Alex Ferguson's usual approach was to give homesick players, particularly from Ireland, as much time off as they needed, but four weeks seemed extreme. 'I remember thinking he wasn't going to come back,' Wayne Bullimore says.

The first sign that Adrian Doherty might be coming around was when he agreed to go and train with Derry City to work on his fitness. This arrangement was the result of a conversation between his father and Tony O'Doherty, who had played alongside Jimmy in the Northern Ireland amateur XI in the 1960s and was now on the club's coaching staff. It was designed as a stepping stone back to Manchester United, but there was a growing feeling that, at sixteen, he might end up deciding his long-term ambitions would be better served by cutting short his apprenticeship in order to sign for Derry.

'He was talking about not going back,' Gareth Doherty says. 'And for him to have been talking in those terms, having been so totally focused and totally obsessed with becoming a professional footballer, makes me wonder what had triggered it.'

'He didn't explain it,' Dee Devenney says. 'When you're sixteen, there aren't many heart-to-hearts. I just know he didn't like it, particularly the digs and that set-up. I think if he had had to go back to the digs, he wouldn't have gone back at all.'

Jimmy and Geraldine Doherty always asked Adrian what the real issue was and what, if anything, might persuade him to resume the apprenticeship. They would never have forced him to go back – they had been concerned enough about him leaving home at sixteen in the first place – but they were understandably worried about him sacrificing such a bright future for the sake of something as potentially fleeting as homesickness. They reassured him that, if his brother Gareth got the A-level results he was hoping for, he would be moving to Manchester or Salford to study the following year. In the meantime, maybe there was something they could do to make the transition easier for him. Again, Adrian told them he did not want to go back to digs.

Between them, Jimmy and Geraldine came up with an idea. It began with a plan to ask Manchester United whether they might find a family who would offer Adrian the kind of calm environment that seemed impossible in the accommodation the club provided. They had a eureka moment. What about Dee Devenney's aunt Geraldine, a Strabane girl who had settled in Manchester with her husband, Frank? They dreamed up a scenario whereby Adrian would lodge with Frank and Geraldine. It would be peaceful there, a refuge from the intensity and the lairiness of the day job, and, in the care of the aunt of one of his best friends, it might feel like an oasis amid the hurly-burly of Manchester. They put their idea to Adrian. Would he return to Manchester and give it another go if they could arrange something like that? Maybe, he said. The club would probably go for it too, if it helped get him back on the pitch, doing what he did best. Now it was a question of persuading Frank and Geraldine to open their house and their arms to a sixteen-year-old Manchester United footballer they had never met. Jimmy and Geraldine wondered how best to broach the idea. They tentatively proposed it to Dee's parents, who felt it might appeal to Frank and Geraldine. Adrian and his parents sat and waited, aware that his hopes of a professional football career might hinge on the outcome of this conversation.

Geraldine Manning recalls the telephone call from her brother, ringing on behalf of the Dohertys. 'They thought maybe he would settle more if it was someone from his hometown, a home from home, like a second family,' she says. 'Well, we just said yes.'

Jimmy Doherty informed Manchester United there had been a breakthrough but that, if Adrian was to return, it would only be on the condition that he was allowed to live with these family friends in Levenshulme. The arrangement was not entirely to the club's liking, because it was on the other side of the city, six miles from the Cliff, but they agreed for now in the hope that it would help an outstanding young player to settle. In the final week of November 1989, Adrian Doherty left Strabane for Manchester once more. Four and a half months into his apprenticeship, it was time to give it a real shot before it was too late.

CHAPTER 10

In the sitting room of their semi-detached house in Levenshulme, Frank and Geraldine Manning are casting their minds back to the day Adrian Doherty walked into their home and their lives in November 1989. What were they expecting from the Manchester United apprentice? Swagger, testosterone and hair gel?

Frank: 'We didn't know what to think.'

Geraldine: 'I knew he wouldn't be like that.'

Frank: 'Not with his mum and dad.'

Geraldine: 'And not from Strabane.'

Frank: 'It was fun thinking "Great, a footballer," "Wow, a United player," but he wasn't like that at all. He was just a lovely kid.'

Geraldine: 'He was so young when he came here.'

Frank: 'He was going to pack it in, wasn't he? He didn't feel at home.'

Geraldine: 'He had no family around him where he was before.'

Frank: 'If he had been kept in that atmosphere in the digs, I think he would have packed it in and gone home. I don't think he could have taken it much longer. But from the moment he came through the door here, he felt at home.'

Geraldine: 'It gave him a sense of being at home.'

Frank: 'It's hard for them lads in them homes. They were lacking a bit of home life. But then he came here and it was like a second Strabane to him. It gave him a bit of peace and quiet.'

There were no races to the dinner table at Milford Drive, no toast-eating contests, no football videos on loop (and certainly no pornography) and nobody raising an eyebrow if you chose to stay in your bedroom playing the guitar rather than sitting in the lounge watching TV, wearing football boots. Neither was there an abundance of testosterone or inane machismo in the air. It was quiet. It was like being back in Strabane. True, it was not ideal, since the Cliff was now two bus journeys away, but getting up an hour earlier every morning was a price worth paying for this new-found sense of sanctuary.

Adrian Doherty was given a warm welcome on the morning he returned to the Cliff. Most of the out-of-town lads could sympathise on the homesickness front. The coaching staff understood it too, recognising that this was one of those times when they needed to go out of their way in order to make a young player feel at home. Eric Harrison's sergeant-major approach gave way to something softer where Doherty was concerned. 'Eric treated everyone as an individual,' Brian Kidd says. 'If someone had a special talent that needed nurturing, we would do whatever we possibly could to get it out. I wouldn't call it special treatment. It was just a case of knowing how different players need to be handled.'

Kidd's point is a pertinent one. Doherty was a completely different character to, say, John Sharples or Alan McReavie. The natural inclination among coaches, when presented with a new group of apprentices, is to treat them even-handedly, as equals, but perhaps only for the first few weeks until different personalities and different challenges come to the fore. Doherty was one who needed the arm-around-the-shoulder treatment, at least in the short term, as the coaching staff strived to persuade him this was a far warmer environment than he had felt previously. 'It takes all kinds to make a team,' Kidd says. 'You don't have to be a Jack the lad, a tough lad, with muscles in your spit. Adrian was a quiet, well-mannered boy, never a minute's trouble. He wasn't head in the clouds. He was quiet, but what a talented boy.'

Where Kidd's interpretation is debatable is in the suggestion that even Harrison's renowned man-management skills extended to a mastery of the lad that the coaching staff knew as Doc. 'Eric could relate to Salford lads like Ryan Giggs, Mark Gordon and Jimmy Shields and he could relate to lads like Nicky Butt, Paul Scholes and the Nevilles, but I don't think he ever really had the measure of Doc at all,' Kieran Toal says.

'In sports psychology, you look at two types of motivation,' Sean McAuley, now a coach for the Portland Timbers in Major League Soccer, says. 'You're either an ego-oriented individual or a task-oriented individual. Most elite footballers, in any age group, tend to be more on the side of ego-oriented individuals. But Adrian had no ego whatsoever. That is incredibly rare, particularly for someone so talented. He had no ego-motivation whatsoever and that made him an unusual character for the coaching staff to deal with.'

'In my opinion, Aidy played football because he enjoyed it and because it came naturally to him,' Toal says. 'He probably couldn't be dictated to. What motivated him? It's hard to say. If you look at all the ones who made it from the Class of '92 – David Beckham, Nicky Butt, Paul Scholes, Gary Neville and so on – they were all very different personalities, but Eric was able to identify what motivated them. It's very rarely fame or money at that age. In the case of those lads, I would say it was a fear of failure. But with Doc, you never got that sense. You always got the feeling that, if football didn't work out for him, he could happily go off and find something else that gave him pleasure. Even someone like Eric Harrison, who was an expert in pressing people's buttons, couldn't really identify what the correct button was.'

Harrison seems to agree. 'Vague is the word I would use,' the former United coach says. 'He was a fantastic lad, a really really lovely boy, but you could never get into his head. I think he was listening – he did what he was told – but you were never sure. He was very withdrawn. He was a good team-mate but he found it very difficult to mix. But he was very very good. And so brave. I've never seen a player so brave.'

Sir Alex Ferguson always treasured players who had what he called physical courage. That was one of the characteristics he admired most in Cristiano Ronaldo. Such bravery was cited by Ryan Giggs, Brendan Rodgers and others as the quality that, for a time, appeared to elevate Doherty from a possible to a dead-cert in the eyes of the United coaching staff. Some initially wondered whether he lacked application, such was his tendency to daydream in the dressing room, but Doherty was an entirely different beast on the pitch. 'He would get kicked, but he would just carry on, taking people on,' Giggs says. 'He was such a brave player.' Alan Tonge says Doherty 'used to get booted about' but would still demand the ball time after time, eager for another chance to outwit his aggressors. Harrison agrees. 'He used to go into tackles like you wouldn't believe,' the coach says.

Harrison might not have felt able to 'get into his head', but he was increasingly certain about Doherty's importance to whichever team he played for. 'I can hear Eric now: "Give it Doc. Give it Doc,"' Peter Smyth says. Wayne Bullimore remembers the same, saying that whenever either Doherty or Giggs stepped up from the B team, the A team would be required to adapt and to play to the strengths of the young wingers. Marcus Brameld says that, in some training sessions, the rest of the squad felt like they were 'there as guinea pigs to improve those two – not that they ever needed improving'. Smyth adds: 'It knocked the stuffing out of some of the other lads in a way, because we had decent skill ourselves, but Eric used to say to me, "Win it, pass it. Give it Doc." And when you saw what he did when you gave him the ball, you couldn't argue with it.'

Doherty returned to action on 2 December, appearing as a substitute in the A team's 7–0 victory over Accrington Stanley's reserves. The following week he scored the only goal of the game as the B team beat Chester City A. 'I think that was the day I really noticed what a talent he was,' Ian Brunton, another avid watcher of United's reserve and youth teams, says. 'Some of his mazy runs were absolutely mesmerising. I can remember he went on one brilliant run that took out several defenders and he then played a wonderful pass inside the centre-half. Once he was playing regularly, he began to stick out and look a certainty to become a first-team player.'

Frank and Geraldine Manning had immediately taken a shine to their lodger, even if he was not terribly communicative. 'He was always rushing in the mornings,' Geraldine says. 'He wouldn't sit down for breakfast. He would just have a cup of tea and maybe a slice of toast on his way out. He would finish up at something like two o'clock and then he would often go into Manchester for a wander around. Sometimes he would look at the cathedral, museums or the library – he would go to the library for hours – but mostly he would just come back and read or play the guitar. I would do dinner in the evening, after we had finished work, and he would say, "Don't worry about anything for me. I get fed at the club." Again he would maybe just have a slice of toast. He was very polite, but he didn't stay down here with us too much. He liked his own room, his own space, listening to his music, playing his music.

'He would worry you as well. He would go out for these long walks in the evening and he would go wandering through Moss Side at night. I would say, "Adrian, you can't do that!" "Why?" "Because you'll get killed!" He said there were gangs around, but nobody ever bothered him. I remember him coming down one morning and there was a lad asleep on the floor. "Who's this, Adrian?" "Oh, I was talking to him at Piccadilly. He's an American lad and he had nowhere to stay, so I just brought him back." Again, "Adrian, you can't do that!" But he never saw bad in anybody. He trusted everyone. He was just so . . . different. He gave you the sense he was from a different world.'

Did he go to church? 'Not when he was here, no,' Geraldine says. 'When he first came to Manchester, he would go to Mass all the time. And then I think I'm right in saying one of the priests told someone at United, "We've had one of your lads coming to church here." This is just an impression, but I think maybe he had been teased about it. I don't think he ever went back. He never came with us on a Sunday anyway.'

'He was very private, Aidy,' Frank says. 'He was laidback, but you could upset him if you went too far.'

Doherty could take a hint, though. 'He couldn't sing, you know,' Geraldine says with a laugh. 'When he first came here, he used to go upstairs with his guitar and it would sound like a strangled cat. I would say to him, "Adrian, are you all right in there? It sounds like someone's killing you." "Why?" "Because you can't sing, Adrian." "Oh. Can I not?" "No, dear. You haven't got a note in your head." So he went out and found someone who could teach him to sing. Because he could write music, you know. He was teaching himself to do that and to play the guitar. He was clever – very, very clever. That might not have been obvious to everyone because he was so laid-back. He was just so different. Oh, he was a lovely lad. He was nothing you would expect from a young footballer. Sometimes in the evening he would just saunter out and go for a walk. Other times he would go out into the street, playing football with the young lads who lived here. There were no airs and graces with him at all.'

One of the young lads in question was David Furey. He was fourteen when he was told, to his amazement, that a young Manchester United footballer had moved in with the Mannings. 'We were always trying to get Adrian out to play football with us,' Furey says. 'He was very good-natured. He would stop in to have a brew. He was very easy to talk to and get along with, but he didn't really chat about football much. He enjoyed playing the guitar and listening to Bob Dylan and the Monkees. We were at that funny age of fourteen/fifteen/sixteen, when you have time on your hands but can't do adult things like go to pubs. I would go round to his and listen to him play music or he would come round to ours and we would play computer games.'

That Doherty bonded more easily with his fourteen-year-old neighbour than with most of his fellow apprentices at Manchester United was not altogether surprising. He was, as the first-team goalkeeper Jim Leighton puts it, 'as green as they come' when he first arrived. At the Cliff he was sharing a dressing room with second-year apprentices who had already turned eighteen and, whether from Manchester, Sheffield, Glasgow or Belfast, they tended to be streetwise – or were eager to give the impression of being so – in a way that he was not. Intellectually, he was maturing at a considerable rate, as his literary tastes developed, but there were still times when he was happier to play computer games with his young neighbour. 'In some ways he was very mature, but in other ways he was a very young sixteen,' Geraldine Manning says. 'There was an innocence about him.'

Frank Manning had grown disenchanted with football over the years, but one Saturday morning he asked his young lodger whether he could come to watch him play for Manchester United's A team at Littleton Road. Of course, Adrian Doherty said. 'I had no idea how good he would be because he hadn't told us anything and, well, he didn't really look like a footballer,' Manning says. 'But blimey, when he got the ball, it was like watching a jackrabbit. He dribbled down the wing like George Best or Willie Morgan. I remember one goal he scored where he beat three players and then turned and let rip and it flew into the back of the net. Even the referee was applauding.'

Doherty's performances, in training and in matches, were getting better and better. 'Every time he played, he was amazing,' Marcus Brameld, another first-year who was beginning to force his way into the A team, says. 'He would run past people for fun. Yes, he had pace, but also, all these tricks you see on TV now, he was doing them back then. He was mesmerising at times.'

'He absolutely stood out in his year group,' Mike Pollitt, a second-year apprentice who would go on to become Wigan Athletic's goalkeeper in the Premier League, says. 'He was so lightning quick. It was something you don't normally see. Looking at him, you thought he was only going one way – to the first team.'

Word of Doherty's surge in form reached the first-team dressing room. 'Everyone was talking about the talent this kid had,' says Gary Pallister, who at the time had just joined United in a record-breaking £2.3 million transfer, says. 'And when you hear stuff like that, you stop after training to go and watch him, to see if what they're all saying is true. That's what I remember, watching him at the Cliff and thinking, "This kid is really really talented. This kid can do things that your mere mortals can't."'

Away from the pitch, Doherty remained a mystery. Everyone recognised and revered his talent, but no one could quite understand his character. 'It was like night and day,' Wayne Bullimore, his former housemate on Lower Broughton Road, says. 'On the pitch, he wanted the ball, he wanted to express himself and he knew what he was about. He was brave too, as tough as old boots. Off the pitch he was completely different. The word that comes to mind is "enigma". He would love this, but, to me, he was just like Bob Dylan. It was like having Bob Dylan in a No. 7 shirt.'

One of the great traditions at Manchester United, even to this day, is the apprentices' Christmas cabaret, performed in front of the first-team squad and all the coaching staff. Paul Scholes recalls being cast as one of the seven dwarfs in *Snow White* – probably Bashful, unless the casting director missed a trick. A couple of years earlier, in December 1989, the first-year apprentices decided on a nativity play. Nobody seems terribly sure on the details, but there is a feeling that perhaps Les Potts played the part of Mary while Alan McReavie was a mustachioed Baby Jesus. 'I might be wrong about that,' Potts says. 'I think I've tried to wipe it from my mind.'

Someone suggested Adrian Doherty should play something on the guitar. After all, he was taking it to training practically every day, attracting some strange looks as he strummed away to himself in the canteen. Why not perform for an audience? To their surprise, he went along with the idea. Yes, he would perform for them. No problem.

The big day arrived. Alex Ferguson and his coaching staff were there. All the first-team players were there – Bryan Robson, Mark Hughes, Brian McClair, Paul Ince, Gary Pallister, Steve Bruce and the rest. So were all the reserve-team players and second-year apprentices. The nativity play came and went, attracting the usual groans and jeers, and then it was Doherty's turn. As he stepped forward with his guitar, wearing the usual baggy sweater, faded jeans and scruffy trainers, there were eyebrows raised in the audience. This was going to be interesting.

'He looked terrified at the start, but it was like *X Factor* in that, as soon as he got into it, he was just buzzing,' Peter Smyth says. 'He did really well. It was a Bob Dylan song.'

'It was "The Times They Are a-Changin",' Alan Tonge says. 'He went through the whole song, all of it fantastic. It must have been daunting because all the first-team lads were there and he was only a young, wide-eyed apprentice, but it went down really well. Usually you would get booed off, but Doc got a standing ovation for that.'

'I think he loved it,' Jim Leighton, the first-team goalkeeper, says. 'For him, the guitar was a way of opening up a bit in front of the rest of the lads.'

'To meet him one on one, you would never have thought he could do that,' Wayne Bullimore says. 'That seemed to be at odds with everything he was about, but he brought the house down and I think he began to come out of his shell a bit after that.'

The times really were a-changin'.

CHAPTER 11

Manchester was in the grip of a reawakening. Economic-
ally it had still to emerge from the post-industrial doldrums,
but deprivation had sparked rather than stifled the city.
'Music repopulated a lot of the derelict spaces,' Dave
Haslam, the former Haçienda DJ and author of *Manchester,
England*, wrote. 'Warehouses turned into clubs and
rehearsal rooms. Youth culture doesn't really worry about
how tidy space is. It's just about how cheap it is. Music created an energy in the city.'

'Madchester', as it came to be enthusiastically billed on
the front page of *NME*, had not come about overnight.
Whether it was characterised by the Happy Mondays, the
Stone Roses or the Ecstasy-popping hordes at the Haçienda,
the energy described by Haslam had built up over time
before exploding into the realisation that something special was happening. Manchester music aficionados point
out this was already the case when Joy Division (and later
New Order), the Smiths and the Fall were dominating
the local scene, even if much of the country was stuck in
the musical nightmare of Stock, Aitken and Waterman,
and when the hedonistic atmosphere of the Haçienda was
another of the city's best-kept secrets. The T-shirts pro-
claimed that 'On the sixth day God created Manchester',

but those behind this apparent cultural revolution – not least the Factory Records producer Tony Wilson – took the view that it was the result of years of unseen perspiration and creative inspiration.

Sir Alex Ferguson might say something similar of the glory that would return to Manchester United over the course of the next two decades, particularly the contribution made by a core of home-grown youngsters. The energy and cavalier spirit that came to define the Ferguson years were built up through the grim late 1980s – not least at underground level, in terms of invigorating the club's youth set-up. The problem for United's supporters was that, as the 1990s dawned, the prospect of Ferguson taking them into a new golden era seemed barely more feasible than a Manchester music revival being led by Timmy Mallett.

Three Irishmen walked into a bar. They were told to get out and come back when they were eighteen. They tried another bar. This time they did not even get through the front door. A third bar. 'What can I get you, lads?' They scanned the bar in search of something familiar, something that would make them sound like seasoned, sophisticated boozers. 'A crème de menthe please,' one of them said. 'Make that three,' said another.

'So we sat there, three sixteen-year-olds from Strabane, drinking crème de menthe all night,' Niall Dunphy says. Dee Devenney adds: 'I think that was pretty much the extent of our wild night out in Manchester, drinking crème de menthe in the Continental. Classy, eh?'

The New Continental was a Manchester institution of

sorts. Affectionately known to Mancunians of a certain generation as 'Conti's', it was a dingy, smoky bar with a sticky floor and – mercifully for Adrian Doherty and the other two boys from Strabane – no dress code. The music was decent, or at least varied, and it was one of those places whose popularity was enhanced by its reputation for attracting large numbers of nurses. Even better, late-night food was served from a hatch in the wall. Service without a smile, burgers of questionable provenance, chips with everything. What a place.

Doherty, Dunphy and Devenney – you could not find a better name for an Irish solicitors' firm – were together for New Year. The other two had cooked up the trip when Doherty was briefly home for Christmas and they had sold it to their parents as a charitable visit to a homesick friend in need – and, in Devenney's case, a chance to see Uncle Frank and Auntie Geraldine. In truth, they were even more excited than he was. After all, they did not get out of Strabane much.

By the time the other two woke up – Devenney in a terrible state, due not to excessive amounts of the green stuff but to an untimely dose of flu – Doherty had left for training. He returned in the afternoon. It was New Year's Eve, the final day of the 1980s, and, with United's youth teams not back in action until 3 January, they wondered if they should hit the town again. After all, that crème de menthe was not going to drink itself. Devenney was feeling so groggy that he could not face it, so Doherty and Dunphy left him to it and boldly took the bus into Manchester once more.

'We were walking down Piccadilly, New Year's Eve, and Aidy was dressed in a way that meant very few pubs would let us in,' Dunphy says. 'I can't remember what it was, but I think his shoes were falling apart. I probably wasn't much better, but I had at least tried to make an effort. Halfway down Piccadilly, Aidy shouts, "All right, boys?" and goes over to all these young lads, about our age, very dapper, suits and everything, about eight of them. I'm thinking, "Why is he trying to tag along with these lads?" And then he said, "These are all the lads I play with at United. This is so-and-so, this is so-and-so . . .' And I'm looking at them and thinking, "This lot look so bloody serious. They're not just out for a laugh." That's what Aidy was out for – a laugh. He would be happiest in a dirty old pub, chatting to unusual people. He loved meeting different people. I was thinking, "You lot are so different to my mate."'

The next evening, New Year's Day, they went to the cinema. Dunphy and Devenney do not recall whether it was the 'spaceship' one in Bury, as described in that letter a couple of months earlier, but one thing they do remember is the journey back. 'We were stopped at some traffic lights in the middle of nowhere and Aidy suddenly jumped out and said, "I'm going to walk the rest of the way. See you later,"' Dunphy says. 'We were, like, "What??? Where did he go? We can't leave him here." But the lights went green and we had to drive on. Frank was saying, "He'll be back." So we sat up and then a couple of hours later, sure enough, Aidy gets back and says, "I just fancied a walk." If I heard that kind of story about someone I didn't know, I might think this guy was just trying to get attention, but Aidy was the exact opposite. He was just impulsive. He would get something into his head and he would just do it.'

*

On the Wednesday night Adrian Doherty was back in action for Manchester United in an FA Youth Cup second-round tie away to Burnley. Niall Dunphy and Dee Devenney had tried to gain some insight into life at the Cliff, but he had told them little apart from the fact the training was boring. Asked whether his team-mates were any good, he told them Ryan Wilson (later Giggs), who played on the left wing, was a very talented player. When they suggested they might come to watch him play at Burnley, he had discouraged them. They might even have begun to wonder whether their friend was making all of this up had it not been for the sudden arrival in the Mannings' living room that afternoon of Nobby Stiles, the former England World Cup winner, to pick him up before the journey to Burnley.

Devenney took a photograph of Doherty in his United blazer, about to set off for the game. He looks fairly smart. There is even a suspicion of hair gel. Minutes earlier, he had been in the midst of one of his frequent wardrobe malfunctions. 'He couldn't find his blazer, but he was saying, "Oh, it'll be all right. I'll go without,"' Dunphy says. 'I remember him saying he had got in trouble for that sort of stuff, turning up without a blazer or without a tie or wearing trainers instead of shoes or – the classic one – turning up for matches with his boots in a Sainsbury's bag. Even when we were staying with him, he was saying, "Yeah, they gave me a bag. I don't know where I've left it." He found his blazer in the end. He wasn't rebellious or anti-establishment. He was just extremely laid-back. He would forget bits of clothes and he wouldn't think it was a big deal.'

Doherty's guests had wondered why he did not want

them to go to Burnley to watch the match. 'I was thinking, "Well maybe he's struggling at this standard. Manchester United – a big step up. Fair enough,"' Dunphy says. 'But Dee's uncle took us up anyway. Ryan Wilson, as he was called then, was very good, but so was Aidy. Skill-wise, there wasn't much between them, if anything. Speed-wise, Aidy was much quicker. And we were thinking, "He's at United now and he's still at the top of this."'

By the time they were jeered off after a o–o draw at home to Queens Park Rangers on 1 January 1990, Manchester United had gone eight games without a win. Those eight games had yielded just three points and three goals, a desperate run that saw United, after that extravagant outlay in the transfer market, languishing just two points above the relegation zone at the halfway stage. These were desperate times for Alex Ferguson, who would confess years later to having felt 'subdued and withdrawn', racked not by self-doubt but certainly by the additional pressure of self-examination. The sense of despondency among many fans was summed up by the banner unfurled after a grim home defeat by Crystal Palace a few weeks earlier: '3 YEARS OF EXCUSES AND IT'S STILL CRAP . . . TA RA FERGIE'. In a *Daily Express* article under the headline 'Fergie the Flop!', Steve Curry, referencing 'the worst record of any United manager of modern times', wrote that, once the Old Trafford crowd expresses such disenchantment, 'as they are doing now, then the wind of change blows in over Stretford'.

In fact, the wind of change was blowing over Salford, at the Cliff, where Ferguson felt his staff's labours on the youth-development side over the previous three years were promising to bear fruit. His coaching staff felt it, as did an expanded scouting team. The standard of the young players they were bringing to the Cliff seemed higher than before, whether it was Ryan Wilson, Nicky Butt, Ben Thornley and Paul Scholes from the Greater Manchester area or Adrian Doherty, Colin McKee, Raphael Burke, John O'Kane, David Beckham and Keith Gillespie from further afield. With that higher calibre of player came a similar type of creative energy – albeit not chemically enhanced – to the one Dave Haslam identified in the Manchester music scene. From that creative energy came increased competition and spirit. That was the spirit that would drive Manchester United forward. Ferguson's big problem was that this spirit and energy were so absent at first-team level.

It has gone down in history – correctly or otherwise, we will never know for certain – that Ferguson would have lost his job had a relegation-threatened United lost at Nottingham Forest in an FA Cup third-round tie on 7 January 1990. Both Ferguson and Martin Edwards, the club's chairman at the time, maintain the situation was not as reported because the board recognised the bigger picture. 'I had actually approached him that week and told him that whether we won or lost at Forest in the cup, he wasn't losing his job on that one result,' Edwards said in 2013. 'We knew how hard he was working behind the scenes, how hard he was working on the youth set-up. We had to give that time.'

A winning goal from Mark Robins, on a muddy pitch at the City Ground, brought Ferguson some desperately needed breathing space. That goal is cited as the one that saved the manager's career because it laid the foundation for the FA Cup success that in turn brought the momentum for everything that followed. But it is worth asking another question: would Edwards and the board have been quite so resolute as they claim, in the lead-up to that match in Nottingham, had United been eliminated from the FA Youth Cup by Burnley in midweek? They had been knocked out by Brentford the previous season and, given that faith in the Ferguson regime had by this stage become so inextricably linked to his hopes for the next generation of players, perhaps that 4–1 victory in the Youth Cup second round, achieved with Doherty on one wing and Wilson on the other, was almost as significant for Ferguson's survival prospects as the famous one that followed in the East Midlands four days later. Either way, Ferguson was desperate for United's next generation to get their hands on the FA Youth Cup by the end of the 1989/90 season. As desperate as he was for FA Cup success? Certainly not, but desperate nonetheless. With victory at Burnley, Adrian Doherty and his team-mates were up and running. Manchester United, like the city they represented, were finally in the grip of a reawakening.

CHAPTER 12

Gary Neville had been going to Old Trafford from the age of six, but these days it was different. Now fourteen, he had signed schoolboy forms with his beloved Manchester United. He was no longer just another wide-eyed young fan. He was a part of the club now. Only a small part, true, but when he left school in a couple of years he would be joining full-time as an apprentice. Rather than line up to squeeze through the turnstiles he had used in the past, he was now ushered in with a respectful nod as he went along on a Thursday night in February 1990 to watch the latest crop of United youngsters in an FA Youth Cup tie against Sheffield Wednesday.

Neville knew, like all the best young footballers in Greater Manchester did, about Ryan Wilson, the Salford lad who was the captain and star of the England schoolboy team and who was already, at sixteen, an integral member of United's Youth Cup XI. But Wilson was not the only one who was turning heads and turning defenders inside out. Lately Neville and his fellow schoolboys had begun to hear excited talk about the first-year apprentice on the opposite wing, a young slip of a lad from Northern Ireland.

'At a club like Manchester United, because of its history in bringing through young players, people are always

asking and talking about the next one to break through,'
Neville says. 'At that time, the chat on the street was all
about Ryan Giggs – Ryan Wilson as he was then – and
Adrian Doherty. They were always the first two names out
of people's mouths. They were very highly thought of.'

Settling into his seat, Neville looked down the team-
sheet. John Sharples, a fellow Bury lad, was wearing No. 4.
Wilson was at No. 11. Doherty at No. 7. Neville was keen
to see what the standard was like, as a young midfielder-
cum-defender who was hoping to carve out a future on
the stage that had captivated him for almost as long as he
could remember.

Elsewhere in the Main Stand that evening was Paul
Vaughan, a student at Manchester University. He was a
Manchester United fan, a regular at first-team matches,
but he would not ordinarily have concerned himself with
a Youth Cup tie on a cold night in February. He was there
to watch Adrian Doherty, whom he had heard all about
back in their home town of Strabane.

'I went along with a friend and he was telling me beforehand that all the talk was about this Welsh lad on the left
wing, who was going to be a superstar, so he wanted to go
along and watch him,' Vaughan says. 'I thought I would go
along to see how Adrian Doherty was getting on. For the
first ten minutes he didn't touch the ball and I'm sitting
there thinking, "Well, this is Manchester United. It's a big
step up for Adrian. It must be difficult."

'Then suddenly, after ten or fifteen minutes, he got the
ball and he danced around two or three of them, chipped
the goalkeeper, hit the crossbar and the whole place

erupted. For the rest of the game, he absolutely dominated. They won 3–1. He scored one and set up the other two and after the game all the talk was, "Who's this lad on the right wing? Who's this Doc?" He was head and shoulders above everybody – Giggs, all of them.'

Sitting in his office at Cardinal Newman College in Preston, where he is now deputy principal, Vaughan keeps emphasising that his recollections of that evening in 1990 are not clouded by a rose-tinted view of the boy from Strabane. He need not worry. His version of events is backed up elsewhere. In *Sons of United*, an encyclopedic chronicle of the club's youth teams, Steve Hobin and Tony Park describe Doherty 'waltzing around three defenders to lob a shot onto the bar in the ninth minute'. 'The main feature of the match,' they add, 'was the inspired display of Doherty, who continually lit up the ground with a bedazzling array of skills, which the visitors were bemused and befuddled by.' Lee Costa put United ahead and, after Wednesday equalised late in the first half, Doherty 'delivered a cracking cross from the right' to set up Colin McKee for the second goal. 'Nine minutes later,' the book says, 'Doherty turned goalscorer . . . , pouncing on a mix-up in the Wednesday defence to execute a crisp drive and give the Reds a two-goal cushion.'

Park's eyes mist over whenever he talks about the boundless potential of the young Adrian Doherty. 'He was a hell of a player,' Park says. 'If you can imagine this, he was like a bit of Ryan Giggs, a bit of Andrei Kanchelskis and a bit of Cristiano Ronaldo, all rolled into one. He was unstoppable when he got going. I remember one of the coaches telling me that, of all the kids at the club at that particular time, the only ones who were nailed on to make it as footballers were Ryan Giggs, Paul Scholes and Adrian Doherty. This coach said to me, "Giggs has a left foot and great pace. Scholes has two great feet. Doherty has two feet and great pace." If you watched the youth team at that time, you didn't watch or remember Giggs more than Doherty. One didn't stand out above the other. They were both as outstanding as the other.'

It is an interesting debating point. Who was better at that age? Peter Smyth, a member of that youth team, says Giggs and Doherty were 'definitely on a par'. Another, Lee Costa, puts Giggs slightly ahead, but Sean McAuley says Doherty was the better of the two at this age, adding, 'You were potentially looking at two world-class players.' Derek Brazil, who was a regular in the reserve team, says, 'There's no doubt in my mind that Doc was better than Giggs at that time.'

The young Gary Neville was not just impressed by Adrian Doherty, he was daunted. 'That night I watched him for the first time, he was frightening,' the former England defender says. 'He stood out in that youth team like you wouldn't believe. As a young player, I was looking at the standard of the players at the club, the standard I've got to get to. He would have been sixteen. As a fourteen-year-old, looking to make a career at Manchester United, looking at players like him and Ryan Wilson, you were just really scared by how good they were.'

Neville is not one for hot air or misplaced hype. He is not one to overplay the potential of those, among United's youth-team players of that era, who did not make it. He is certainly not one to discuss a player in the same breath as Ryan Giggs, in terms of talent and potential, without thinking about it.

'Adrian Doherty was a fantastic talent, he really was,' Neville says. 'Watching him dribble a ball and beat players, he had really wonderful ability. I had never seen anything like it. You have to be careful when you're making comparisons, but he had that Messi-like ability to have the ball at his feet, with a low centre of gravity, and then just accelerate away with the speed of his feet and a change of direction. He had the quickest feet. You know like Messi has that tight control? It's that style of play. Doc would have been like Messi or David Silva with that low centre of gravity and an ability to beat players. He was out of this world, he really was.

'He was ideal for Manchester United. When you think of Manchester United playing with two wingers and you looked out there at Adrian Doherty and Ryan Wilson in that youth team, they just looked absolutely sensational together. Those two – Doherty and Wilson – were the two that came off everyone's tongue, not just because they were so good but also because Manchester United has a love affair, a total fascination, with wingers. Adrian Doherty and Manchester United ticked every single box.'

Up in the press box, David Meek, the *Manchester Evening News* correspondent, agreed. 'Manchester United's depressed fans should get themselves down to watch the youth team,' Meek wrote. 'Not only would they see a winning team but one which has turned back the clock to play two clever, jet-propelled wingers. It's like a breath of fresh air to see Ryan Wilson streaking down the left and the smaller, but equally fast, Adrian Doherty running at defenders down the right.

Both are still only sixteen, with great skills as well as pace, and they bring a refreshing dimension to the game. While it may be difficult to appreciate Alex Ferguson's work at first-team level at the moment, his impact is looking good at junior level.'

Paul Vaughan could not wait to tell his friend Sean Ferry, Adrian Doherty's cousin, what he had just witnessed. It was music to Ferry's ears. A diehard Manchester United fan, Ferry dreamed of seeing his cousin play for the first team. He passed the message on to the rest of the Doherty family, who would otherwise only have heard from Adrian himself that the match had gone 'OK'. Ferry and Vaughan talked about how, seemingly, the only real obstacle to Doherty's progress was the homesickness that had almost caused him to abandon his dreams at United. Ferry was hoping to arrive in Manchester the following September to go to university, as was Adrian's brother Gareth. That would help cure the homesickness. In the meantime, maybe Vaughan – 'Gonzo' to his friends back in Strabane – would fancy meeting up with the young prodigy, offering a familiar accent, if not necessarily a familiar face.

'We met up and he was totally different to what I had expected,' Vaughan says. 'He actually looked scruffier than your average student, which is saying something. We went out for a couple of pints. He wasn't a drinker at all, but he wanted to go to the student places rather than the places you would expect a young footballer to be. We went to the Student Union bar and we hung around in Fallowfield – the Queen of Hearts, a student pub. I'm a big Man U fan and I would ask him questions. I remember him telling me a story about Bryan Robson giving him a pair of boots, about Viv Anderson being a very funny man, but he wasn't really interested in talking about football. He was into his music, Bob Dylan, and his poetry. He would rather talk about that or about Strabane and normal things. I got the impression he enjoyed the student world because he was probably more comfortable with that scene than the typical footballer places. And also I was probably the only other person in Manchester at that time who could understand the Strabane accent.'

Doherty paid another visit to Fallowfield a few weeks later and ended up dossing on the floor at Oak House, Vaughan's hall of residence. 'He literally stayed on the floor,' Vaughan says with a laugh. 'I'm sharing with a few other fellas. They come in and I say to them, "This is Adrian. He's from back home in Strabane," and I'm thinking, "If they knew who this was . . ." At that stage I'm thinking he's definitely going to make it, 100 per cent convinced, and there he is, lying in the corner in a sleeping bag, looking like the furthest thing from a footballer you could imagine. Not in a million years would you think this boy has a good chance of being a superstar at Manchester United. I said to him, "Adrian, sleep on the sofa," but, no, he's on the floor in a sleeping bag. "Ah, see you in the morning, Gonzo. Good man."'

By the time Vaughan got up in the morning, Doherty was long gone – back to the Mannings' house in Levenshulme, then the bus in and out of Manchester to Salford, back to the Cliff, back to training, back to the daily grind, the student life left far behind.

*

For Adrian Doherty, the second half of the 1989/90 season felt like a turning point. He had begun to feel more settled in Manchester, at last, and his performances reflected not just a sense of contentment but a feeling – encouraged by Eric Harrison and the rest of the coaching staff – that he was developing into the player they all wanted him to be. He was becoming a regular in the A team. Then there was the FA Youth Cup, which had given all the younger players at the club a sense of purpose and helped provide some of the first-year apprentices, such as John Sharples, Colin McKee and Doherty – and even a schoolboy, in Ryan Wilson – with the opportunity to test and establish themselves alongside Darren Ferguson, Alan Tonge, Lee Costa, Sean McAuley and the rest at Under-18 level.

Doherty was still only sixteen, but he was not merely a first-year apprentice any more. When most of his peers were playing in the B team on a Saturday morning, he and Wilson tended to be in the A team. Then came another call-up for the reserves as substitute for a match against Liverpool. Wilson had made a few reserve-team appearances earlier in the season, which was extraordinary for a schoolboy, but by March 1990 it was Doherty getting the fast-track treatment.

His promotion to the A team and the Youth Cup team had initially come about because Steven Carter, a right-winger in the year above, had broken his leg. Carter was approaching a return to fitness and, in the final months of his apprenticeship, was desperate for an opportunity to prove he merited a professional contract, but, in his injury-enforced absence, he had been overtaken by Doherty, a year younger. For Carter, the writing was on the wall.

'That must have been difficult for Steve, seeing Doc getting fast-tracked,' Costa says. 'Anyone who goes to Manchester United goes there with big hopes, big ambitions, and when younger players are fast-tracked ahead of you, it's soul-destroying. I can remember Doc playing very well in the A team and the reserves, and Steve congratulating him, but in truth you're devastated because you want it to be you. What more could he say, though? The fact is that Doc was being fast-tracked because he was worth it.'

Around this time, with such deep disillusionment in the air, plenty of Manchester United supporters would try to find ways to get out of their Saturday afternoon trips to Old Trafford. Adrian Doherty was one of them. In his case, it was less a reflection on the quality of the performances and more the feeling that, having done his business in the A team that morning, he was finished with football for the week. 'They would get complimentary tickets and quite often Adrian wouldn't go,' his father, Jimmy Doherty, says. 'He would just give his tickets away. Then he would get the bus into Manchester with his guitar and he would busk, playing Bob Dylan or even songs he had written himself. It wasn't for the money; I doubt he would have got much anyway. It was just what he wanted to do.'

'He definitely went busking,' Wayne Bullimore says. 'He would think nothing of it, but to us it was so out of the ordinary to see a young player who would think not "I'll go into town and buy some trainers" but "I'll go into town and do some busking."'

Brian McGillion, his friend from Strabane, who came to study in Manchester, says the busker's performances left something to be desired. 'I used to tell him he was awful,' McGillion says with a laugh. 'It was improvised versions of Bob Dylan, that kind of thing, and he wasn't a great singer. He just wasn't. But as far as he was concerned, he was as good at writing songs and performing as he was at playing football. And he had the confidence and charisma to carry it off.'

What did his team-mates make of having a busker in their midst? 'Well, that's the only Adrian we knew,' Peter Smyth says. 'You can't change people from what they are, can you?'

Adrian Doherty's face dropped when he learned he had been called up to Manchester United's reserve team again. It was an away game against Everton at Goodison Park on a Saturday afternoon – and that played havoc with his plans to get the train from Manchester to London with his father that evening to watch Bob Dylan's opening night at the Hammersmith Apollo on the latest leg of the Never Ending Tour.

Jimmy and Adrian Doherty had to change their plans, getting the train down from Liverpool Lime Street as soon as possible after the final whistle at Goodison. Jimmy was excited by the prospect of seeing his son play in United's reserves, on one of English football's great stages, but, as it transpired, Adrian was an unused substitute. He was – unusually – first out of the dressing room afterwards as the pair of them went straight to Lime Street. A few hours later they were rocking up outside the Apollo. That evening they met the late John Hume, a Northern Irish photographer who travelled around the world taking pictures of Dylan. As ever, Adrian was captivated by Dylan, but he was also full of uncharacteristic excitement at how things were progressing football-wise. 'He told me the coaches were saying very positive things about him and Ryan Wilson,' Jimmy says. 'At that time, Adrian was very confident he was going to get into the first team.'

One morning, as he was getting changed in the apprentices' dressing room at the Cliff, humming away to himself as always, Adrian Doherty was told he would be training with the first-team squad. He continued humming as his team-mates expressed a sense of awe. It was one thing to step up to the reserves, leapfrogging second-year apprentices and first-year professionals, but to be drafted into a first-team training session was something else entirely. 'We were chuffed for him,' Marcus Brameld says. 'No one was jealous. If it had been someone else, it might have been, "Why's he going with the first team?" But when it was Doc, you were OK with it because he was that good.'

Doherty traipsed out of the pavilion in the same casual style as ever – shirt and shorts hanging off him, socks around his ankles, boots still spattered with the previous day's mud. Jim Leighton, the first-team's Scotland international goalkeeper, recalls him looking 'like a wee waif, as if Manchester United had got him off the street'.

Leighton and the senior players, though, had learned not to judge Doherty by appearances. By now they were, like everyone at the club, well aware of his potential. 'People all around the Cliff were talking about this next kid coming up and being a superstar, if you like,' the former

United and England defender Gary Pallister says. 'There were big expectations if they could harness that talent. As a lad, he was a little bit different to everybody else, you would say, but he was a prodigious talent.'

Now he was going to have to do it in a first-team training session. Bryan Robson was injured at the time, but Mark Hughes, Brian McClair, Steve Bruce, Paul Ince and Pallister were all there. Archie Knox was running the session. Alex Ferguson was on the touchline, eager to see how the youngster coped with the step up. Some richly talented young players freeze in elevated company. Doherty did nothing of the sort. He had never been dazzled by them or their reputations. He trained as he always did, concentrating on himself. He did not say a word to the players, nor barely look them in the eye, but, rather than nerves, that was just his usual shyness. 'I don't think he was any more shy in front of the senior players than he was with the younger ones,' Leighton says. 'The management liked him. Fergie and Archie Knox loved him.'

'Adrian would train with the first team and he would never flinch a thing,' Knox says. 'He must have been about five stone wet through, but there was not a bit of fear in him. Hard as nails. He would never shirk a tackle or anything like that. Alec was saying, "I think we've unearthed a diamond here."'

CHAPTER 13

The headline in the *Manchester Evening News* screamed with excitement: 'Boy wonder standing by!' 'Manchester United', David Meek wrote, 'are considering a sensational first-team debut for 16-year-old unknown winger Adrian Doherty.' The story went on to say Alex Ferguson was 'being urged by his backroom staff to play the boy from Belfast at senior level' and that 'behind the scenes at Old Trafford, Doherty is tipped to make the kind of impact not seen since George Best was given his chance'.

Except for the Belfast reference, it was all true; the previous day, Doherty had travelled with the first-team squad to Southampton and had been told he would be named as one of the two substitutes if, in keeping with United's chronic injury problems at the time, either Neil Webb or Danny Wallace failed a fitness test. Had Doherty appeared at the Dell, he would, at sixteen years and 287 days, have become the club's youngest outfield debutant since the late great Duncan Edwards in 1953.

That was not, ideally, Ferguson's intention, for two reasons, which were reflected both in the *Evening News* article and in a conversation between the United manager and Doherty's father more than two decades later. The first was that Ferguson was hesitant to pick such a young player in a match which was, according to the newspaper, 'a bitter dogfight for first-division survival'. The second was that Doherty would be needed for a Lancashire FA Youth Cup semi-final against Manchester City two days later – a game Ferguson and his staff were desperate for United to win in order to prove the tide really was turning on the youth-development front. Despite those factors, both of them signs of United's fragilities rather than Doherty's, Ferguson felt the apprentice would be up to the rigours of first-team football if required. As Meek says in the article, which he recalls would have been sourced from either Ferguson or Archie Knox, 'If United had been safe, I think Ferguson would be ready to release his infant prodigy at senior level.'

This much is confirmed by Knox. 'I would be able to back that up,' Knox says when asked whether Ferguson would genuinely have been willing to pick Doherty against Southampton at the age of sixteen had the need arisen. 'He wouldn't have been there just so we could put a young lad on the bench, not to be used. Alec was always one to give the youngsters a chance and Adrian seemed to have the right temperament. That's an indication of how highly he was thought of. That was in his first year at the club – a lad who had just come as a schoolboy and all of sudden was travelling with the first team. I don't think David Beckham or Paul Scholes ever had that profile at sixteen or even seventeen.'

Niall Dunphy and Dee Devenney had always planned that when – not if – Adrian Doherty made his Manchester United debut, they would be there to see it. They had worked out this would probably happen during the 1991/2 season, by which time he would be eighteen and they would be over in England, having started university, ideally at Manchester, Liverpool or Leeds.

'And then suddenly,' Dunphy says, 'Aidy called up and said he was going away with the first team with a chance of getting on the bench. Dee and I were, like, "Shit. How can we get there?" Well we couldn't. There was no way we could get from Strabane to Southampton at a day's notice. We couldn't just bunk off college. It was impossible. We were kicking ourselves. Aidy said not to worry. He called up again from the hotel the night before to say he didn't think he was going to play but there was still a slight chance he would be on the bench – it was going to come down to whether someone passed a fitness test – and to look out for him on TV that evening, just in case.'

This was the first time anyone back in Strabane could remember Doherty calling up to instigate a conversation about football and his own prospects. 'He was absolutely buzzing,' his brother Gareth says. 'He rang up and he was saying, "I've travelled with the first team and I'm in this fancy hotel and there's a chance I might be on the bench." He was so excited and so were we. We thought that even if he didn't play at Southampton, it was only a matter of time. And he was only sixteen.'

On the Friday evening before an away game, United's players and coaching staff would eat together in the hotel dining room. This could be an unnerving experience for any young player, let alone a first-year apprentice who, the Bob Dylan act notwithstanding, was felt to be painfully shy. Doherty was used to eating in the same canteen as the first-team squad at the Cliff, but now he was going to have to sit at the same table as Gary Pallister, Neil Webb, Paul Ince, Brian McClair, Mark Hughes – household names. He was not star-stuck, but, in a social sense, he was just not comfortable around such big names and big personalities.

'I can distinctly remember him coming downstairs to eat with us,' the former United physiotherapist Jim McGregor says. 'How do I remember that? Because when he came down to dinner with the rest of the players, he was wearing slippers. We all remember that. Footballers generally came down in their tracksuit and trainers. Adrian was wearing his slippers.'

How would Alex Ferguson and his players react to that? Would they think the new kid on the block was a few cards short of a deck? Or even that he was playing the joker to ingratiate himself? 'Not at all,' McGregor says. 'The manager and the rest of the staff, we all knew Adrian. Everyone accepted it was normal for him. For him to do that, that wasn't ridiculous. He probably wore his slippers every night at the digs. When he was in his bedroom at the hotel, he probably just wanted to feel at home. I can visualise him now. That was Adrian. He was a lovely lad, very well liked.

'The fact he was included at all to go on that trip shows that obviously the manager must have thought, "Let's get the boy introduced to sitting with the players on the coach, in the hotel, at the meal on a Friday night, sharing a room." He was definitely in the manager's thoughts.'

By the Saturday morning, Doherty's chances of making the match-day squad had faded. Webb and Danny Wallace were passed fit and, in the days when only two substitutes were named, there was no need to put even such an exceptionally gifted sixteen-year-old on the bench just yet. But Doherty was still on a high. 'I could tell he was delighted because, for a start, he would never normally have phoned me on the day of a game and he wouldn't be talking about football – because football wasn't usually what he talked about when he rang up,' Devenney says. 'He probably got free calls from the hotel. Around the same time, I remember him saying he had played particularly well in a couple of Youth Cup games. Adrian would never usually tell you he had played well, so for him to tell you that, he must have been fantastic.'

United's league position was desperate. Between 25 November 1989 and 21 March 1990, they had played seventeen league matches, losing nine, drawing six and winning just two. Back-to-back defeats by Liverpool and Sheffield Wednesday left them in sixteenth position, just two points and two places above the relegation zone, with eight games remaining. At the Dell, to Ferguson's immense relief, they won 2–0. That was the first of four consecutive league wins, which, along with a promising FA Cup run, served to ease some of the pressure on Ferguson. It was a happy coach journey back to Manchester that evening. 'I remember Adrian telling me afterwards that, even though he didn't play, he was given a win bonus,' Doherty's friend Paul Vaughan says. 'I'm sure he said something like £200. That might not be right, but, whatever it was, it was substantial to Adrian.'

What would Doherty have done with £200? 'He would probably have bought records or a new guitar or something,' Vaughan says. 'He wasn't interested in flash cars or flash suits.'

His landlady Geraldine Manning can reveal exactly what Doherty used his first-team win bonus to buy. 'He bought a typewriter,' she says. 'One of those old-fashioned ones.'

'Aye, I can believe that,' Vaughan says. 'That's the sort of character he was.'

The sun was beating very ferociously down upon the playground fair. It was only just another normal day, with the clouds and azur overhead blocking out that which lay beyond the sky.

'Man, I sure am thirsty,' remarked Humphrey to nobody in particular.

Both he and his friend Bodegard were following the goings-on of the fair with a rather languid interest, keeping an eye on the seagulls above to ease their humdrum. Bodegard was also thirsty but his thirst was uncommonly much more perpetual and profound than that of his comrade. It was a thirst which could have only been quenched either by revelation or enlightenment. You see, Bodegard searches. He searches for some kind of meaning, which would tie everything up with each other. Life is a vast indefinable trail for him, though as of yet, he was yet to find or discover any new remarkable insights into the secret workings and causes of phenomena. Anyway, he was going to keep on trying and had presently immersed himself in following the philosophical, pseudo-religious, anti-social technique of development; he hoped that this would lead him onto the ultimate goal and much-dreamed-of achievement of absolute fulfilment.

(from *The Adventures of Humphrey and Bodegard* by Adrian Doherty, Prelude, page 1)

*

'He was a bit eccentric,' Steve Bruce says. 'He was certainly off the wall.' And this is without any knowledge of *The Adventures of Humphrey and Bodegard*, the absurdist and – regrettably – unfinished tale that Adrian Doherty spent months writing and painstakingly typing out over the course of his first couple of years at Manchester United.

It was a tale Doherty described, in an interview with *The Shankill Skinhead* in early 1991, as 'just an adventure story'. If the idea of an apprentice footballer writing an adventure story at sixteen or seventeen is an unexpected one, the content is even more so. Within the first page, Bodegard has been identified as a would-be philosopher, seemingly on a quest to discover the meaning of life. By page three Bodegard is 'locked in a kind of trance', telling himself, 'You must abandon all principles and morals. You must first empty yourself before experiencing fullness. You must vanquish all illusion and inconstancy from your mind and strive to control your thoughts in a boundless style.' Some might be reassured by the more adolescent content later on page one, in which Humphrey tries and fails to sweet-talk a snackbar attendant whom he recognises as a pornographic actress. Later, Bodegard hitches a ride to the North Pole and Humphrey declares himself the son of God.

Then there is the bulging folder of poems and songs Doherty wrote and typed out in Manchester between 1990 and 1992, as well as those he wrote in the years that followed. Some of them are dark, such as 'Invitation to a Voyage' ('Come, come, abandon all your care, Come with me to the valley of despair'), 'In Search of Purpose' and 'The Lost Soul'. Others are extremely light. Many of the most compelling are tongue-in-cheek, such as his song 'An Oblivious History', in which Doherty, in turn, skewers the reputations of Socrates (the Greek philosopher, not the Brazilian footballer), John the Baptist, Macbeth, King Arthur, Arthur Rimbaud, Friedrich Nietzsche, Muhammad Ali and even Bob Dylan, saying 'none of them really mattered'.

'It's true, he was off the wall,' Dee Devenney says of his mate. 'He was a quirky character, full of great invention. He would have crazy ideas. He just had a great imagination. Whenever he wasn't playing football as a kid, he was always reading. Later he got into French existentialism and stuff like that.'

'He was always a reader,' Gerard Mullan says, 'but more so after he went away to Manchester. He had a lot of spare time for it and maybe it was also the feeling that it was a safe, sensible thing to be doing rather than going out to pubs or into the Manchester scene. He was a deep thinker.

'The amount of stuff he used to read was unreal. I remember him going to the Corn Exchange, which had all these bookshops and music shops, and Adrian would spend hours looking at old records and old books, things like that. He would buy loads and loads of books from these shops. He loved Edgar Allan Poe. He would quote you things from books all the time and you would think, "Where the hell did he get that from?" But it was what he used to read. He had the weirdest concoction of books. Poetry yes, but philosophy, things about history, things about theology, things about politics, things about witchcraft, things about—'

Witchcraft? 'Yes, exactly,' Mullan says. 'I remember him saying in Manchester that he had met this white witch. If someone said something, he would want to know more about it, so he would buy a book and read up on it.'

This was not just a teenage pseudo-intellectual accumulating books to put on his shelves in order to impress people. Like Bodegard, Doherty wanted to learn. Away from the superficial world he inhabited as a footballer, he wanted to find depth. He was intrigued by all kinds of philosophy. He was intrigued, too, by theology, as he came to terms with an erosion of the Catholic faith that had underpinned him back in Strabane. One of the bookshops in the Corn Exchange specialised in books relating to esoteric thought. This stuff fascinated Doherty, even if he found some of it hilarious.

'It was so diverse,' Leo Cussons, a friend who encountered Doherty on the Manchester music scene, says. 'He knew about – or was trying to find out about – anything and everything. He had read the Koran. Not just the Koran, but Edgar Allan Poe, Dostoyevsky, Dante and all these amazing writers. Pretty much anyone who had made a major contribution to literature, he had read them all by the time he was seventeen, which makes it all the more incredible. I found him an enormously talented guy who had, through reading, learned an awful lot about a whole lot of things by a very young age. Whatever he did, whether it was writing a story or writing songs, he would do it brilliantly. And likewise football, presumably. I never saw him play football.'

Everybody knew Manchester United were approaching a quarter of a century since they were last crowned champions of England, in 1967. By the time Adrian Doherty arrived at Old Trafford in the summer of 1989, the club had already passed the twenty-five-year milestone in the FA Youth Cup. George Best was a seventeen-year-old, still feeling pangs of homesickness, when he helped United win the trophy in 1964. Perhaps the emergence of another prodigiously talented young winger from Northern Ireland – along with a home-grown 'new Best' candidate, Ryan Wilson, on the opposite flank – would help to land the trophy that would assure supporters the future was rosier under Ferguson than a wretched season at first-team level suggested.

After the Doherty wonder show against Sheffield Wednesday in the fourth round, United beat Leicester City to set up a two-legged encounter with Tottenham Hotspur in the semi-final. For the first leg at White Hart Lane on 4 April, Eric Harrison picked an experienced United line-up, including Mark Bosnich, Jason Lydiate, Sean McAuley, Darren Ferguson and Lee Costa. Doherty, Wilson and Mark Gordon, all sixteen, were the babies of the team. But Doherty also had an important part to play on the coach on the way down to London. 'I don't know how it started, but we used to have him singing and playing the guitar on the coach on the way to away games,' Jimmy Shields, an unused squad member against Tottenham, says. 'Away to Spurs in the Youth Cup, I remember him playing "American Pie". He knew all the words and he knew how to play everything. He was quite good.'

United's players were confident. 'The previous year we had lost away to Brentford in the quarter-final, conceding two very late goals, and I remember Alex Ferguson coming in afterwards and ripping us to pieces, each one of us,'

Costa says. 'The next year, with Doc and Giggsy, I remember feeling we had a golden opportunity to win it. But so many of us had a poor night at Tottenham. We got absolutely battered and we were lucky we only lost 2–0.'

Five days later many of the first-team squad were in attendance on a wet night at Old Trafford as United looked to overturn their first-leg deficit and reach the final. An early goal from Doherty, racing onto Colin McKee's through ball to beat the future England goalkeeper Ian Walker, was just what they needed. 'Nothing would faze Adrian,' Costa says. 'The average person, 2–0 down to Tottenham, second leg at Old Trafford, the whole club watching, you would be nervous. We were all on pins. Doc was the opposite. He was excellent that night, he really was. From what I remember, he outshone Giggsy. He was a real outlet for us. Unfortunately we missed a couple of opportunities to equalise and they scored again late on, which killed us.'

It would be another two years before United finally ended their wait to win the Youth Cup. Giggs would be the elder statesman of that team, leading a fresh batch of apprentices, who would become known as the Class of '92. But 1989/90 was a successful season at youth level, with Doherty getting his hands on a Lancashire League first-division winner's medal for his part in the A team's title success. True to form, he gave his medal away – offering it to Frank and Geraldine Manning to thank them for helping him to feel at home in Manchester. They said no, but he insisted. 'Stuff like medals wouldn't interest him,' Frank says.

*

The sight of Wembley Stadium's famous twin towers left Gareth Doherty and Sean Ferry awe-struck. So did the size of the crowd milling around outside. Kick-off in the FA Cup final, between Manchester United and Crystal Palace, was only half an hour away and Ferry was starting to worry that they had made a fatal error with their vague arrangement to collect their tickets from his cousin Adrian Doherty.

'Adrian just said he would meet us with the tickets near Gate G, or whatever,' Ferry says. 'We got there and there must have been 10,000 people outside. We were thinking, "How the hell are we going to find him?" But even in this huge crowd, he stuck out like a sore thumb – United suit on, but tie off, scruffy. He handed over the tickets and even then, there were fans spotting him and shouting, "That's Doc," "That's Adrian Doherty from the youth team." He was well known among some of the fans.'

It was a ding-dong of an FA Cup final, with the lead changing hands three times as United were indebted to Mark Hughes for his two goals, including an extra-time equaliser to force a 3–3 draw. That meant heading back to Wembley again for the replay five days later and, with his brother and cousin returning to Strabane, Paul Vaughan was the lucky recipient of one of Doherty's complimentary tickets as United beat Palace 1–0 and – although nobody knew this at the time – paved the way for Ferguson to lead the club into the most successful period in its history.

'I called over to his digs in Levenshulme a couple of days before,' Vaughan says. 'Adrian came downstairs playing Bob Dylan on the guitar and then he gave me the ticket. Anyway, I went down to Wembley and, ten minutes into the game, there's still a spare seat beside me. I'm thinking, "That's strange. The place is packed. You can't get tickets for love nor money." Five minutes later, Adrian appears next to me in his scruffs. "All right, Gonzo? Thought I'd come and watch the game with you." He tells me he was meant to be coming with the rest of the youth team but he missed the train or coach to the ground. I'm thinking, "This doesn't make sense. He must have realised this because he hadn't sold the other ticket." Looking back, it's possible somebody else was meant to pick the ticket up. I honestly don't know.

'Anyway, it gets to half-time and we're standing up, stretching our legs, and we're just in front of the section where the United officials and the youth team were sitting, all in their suits. That's where he's meant to be. They spot him. Some start waving and laughing. Others are shaking their heads. He's waving back. The people around us are wondering, "Who the hell is this?" They wouldn't have believed it. He looked as far from a footballer as you could imagine.'

There are countless stories of Adrian Doherty incurring the wrath of Manchester United's coaching staff – usually Eric Harrison – by turning up for matches in a less than immaculate state. Craig Lawton: 'He would have his blazer, tie, shirt, trousers . . . and trainers, where everyone else would have shiny shoes.' Wayne Bullimore: 'We would all have kitbags, but Doc would turn up with his boots in a plastic bag or with one shinpad.' Giuliano Maiorana: 'He would turn up at games with no shoelaces, that kind of thing.' Les Potts remembers him with 'hair sticking out, shirt hanging out' on another trip to Wembley the following season, for the Rumbelows Cup final against Sheffield

Wednesday. 'He wasn't trying to be rebellious or anything like that,' Lawton says. 'Doc was Doc.'

If there are two things Alex Ferguson hates almost as much as losing, they are tardiness and scruffiness – a standard he applied to everyone, including journalists, but particularly to young players. Maiorana suggests that, when looking to the reserves or the youth team, Ferguson was hoping to see 'yes-men – blazer and tie, short back and sides, people who would be there on time, not a hair out of place, and do as they were told'.

That sounds like the total opposite of Doherty, whose one concession to style – such as it was – was a perm that owed far more to Bob Dylan than to Mark Hughes. 'He told me they'd asked him to get his hair cut, so he went and got a perm,' Niall Dunphy says. 'He said that Bryan Robson told him, "I used to have a haircut like that ten years ago." Seriously, it was not a good look, but Aidy thought it was great. He wasn't fussed about looking smart. I think that wound up the coaching staff a bit.'

And yet, for as long as Doherty was fit and firing on all cylinders, Ferguson regarded him as a special case, worthy of indulgence. 'Fergie and Archie Knox loved him,' Jim Leighton says. Jonathan Stanger and Peter Smyth, two of Doherty's peers in that apprentice group, say the same thing: 'Fergie loved him.'

'Talent was the most important thing in Alec's eyes,' Knox says. 'Never mind how the boy looked. The marking card was always, "Is he going to be a footballer?" And Adrian was definitely heading in that direction. He was such a talent.'

*

At the end of the 1989/90 season, shortly before his seven-teenth birthday, Adrian Doherty was summoned to Old Trafford, along with his father, Jimmy, to discuss his future with Alex Ferguson and the chairman, Martin Edwards. They were taken into an office, where Ferguson told Doherty he was hugely excited by his progress and future prospects. With the pressure eased by the FA Cup success, the manager was making long-term plans now and Doherty was integral to them. He was pleased that the boy now seemed more settled in Manchester and hoped he would return to digs in time for the new season. Doherty's apprenticeship, worth £29.50 a week plus bonuses, had another year to run, but, in view of his exceptional talent, the club wanted to replace it with a new five-year profes-sional contract worth upwards of £200 a week, plus a five-figure signing-on fee payable at the end of each sea-son, as well as bonuses for every appearance, every win and separate lump sums to be paid when, not if, he made his debut for club and country. It was an unprecedented offer – the longest and most handsome contract the club had ever offered a player before his seventeenth birthday. That was how highly they regarded him.

'I don't think I want to sign for five years,' the boy told Ferguson.

Jimmy Doherty was taken aback. So were Edwards and Ferguson. 'How long do you want to sign for?' an incredu-lous Ferguson asked.

'A year? Two years?'

'You need to think about this, Adrian,' Ferguson said sternly. 'This is a very good contract. It will give you secur-ity and the best possible chance. There are lads in your team who would give their right arm for a contract like this. You don't turn down a five-year contract at Manchester United.'

There were eighteen-year-olds at the club – among them Ferguson's son Darren – who were still on apprentice contracts. Most would be grateful for a one-year professional deal. Doherty was urged to think about his long-term security. He was adamant he would not sign for five years. They ended up compromising on a three-year contact. Ferguson and Edwards agreed they had never known anything like it, but the boy was worth a special case in more ways than one. He was going to be a star. He just didn't seem to realise it yet.

As they left Old Trafford that day, Jimmy congratulated his son on the new contract and on everything he had done to earn it over his difficult first season in Manchester. He also asked Adrian why he had turned down the longer deal. Adrian simply said – as if it were blindingly obvious – that he could not be sure whether he would want to be doing this in five years, so three years seemed sensible. 'I couldn't believe it when he turned down that contract,' Jimmy says. 'It makes a lot more sense now.'

CHAPTER 14

Old Trafford legend has it that one of the issues Alex Ferguson was so aghast to discover on his arrival at Manchester United was swiftly resolved when he controversially sold Norman Whiteside and Paul McGrath in the space of forty-eight turbulent hours in the summer of 1989. 'I had to get rid of this idea that Manchester United was a drinking club,' Ferguson wrote, in *Six Years at United*, of his decision to sell the pair. 'I knew that if we were to have United meeting the vision and expectation of supporters, as a club of class and style, somewhere in the profile there had to be discipline.'

The battle against the booze, though, was far from an overnight success. As Lee Sharpe puts it in his autobiography, it was difficult for Ferguson to make further inroads into that drinking culture when 'one of the biggest drinkers at that time, an awesome drinker not under any circumstances to be kept pace with, was the manager's great warrior and standard bearer: Bryan Robson, . . . the king of everything at United at that time'. With Ferguson still to establish total authority over the United dressing room, the booze continued to flow freely not just on Saturday nights but on those long afternoons and evenings at the Griffin in Bowdon, the Four Seasons hotel in Hale

Barns and other watering holes across the area. It was the same throughout English football at the time, but new signings were often surprised to see that it remained so at United. Roy Keane has said he was delighted to find 'a serious drinking sub-culture' on his arrival at the club. That was in 1993 and, according to Keane, Robson was still at the heart of it.

As captain, Robson, who states that he 'could drink loads of pints without falling over and making myself look stupid', would organise team-bonding sessions, which were not for the faint-hearted. For the younger players, the stepping stone to Robson's drinking club was – suitably enough – through a reserve-team drinking club. 'We had a Tuesday club or a Wednesday club where we would go down to the Priory Arms in Salford and let off some steam,' the Irish reserve-team defender Derek Brazil says. 'Then on Saturday nights we would go into town.'

Did Adrian Doherty join in? 'Occasionally he did,' Brazil says. 'But he couldn't take it. A couple of drinks and he would be wasted. I remember having to take him back to Brenda's.'

'Brenda's' has assumed such notoriety in Manchester United ex-player circles that the uninitiated might wonder what kind of den of iniquity it was. 'A bit of a madhouse,' say both Marcus Brameld and Michael Gray; 'chaos – and I mean chaos,' says David Johnson; 'truly an animal house,' wrote Lee Sharpe in his book.

In fact, 'Brenda's' was the collective name applied to two adjoining terraced properties on Priory Avenue, Salford, a quiet cobbled cul-de-sac about a minute's walk from the

Cliff. Those two houses served as digs for countless young players who have passed through United down the years – ten or more at a time. Whether they reminisce fondly or with a grimace, nobody forgets their time at Brenda's.

The landlady was the charming Brenda Gosling. Upon finding an uninvited guest on her doorstep on a Sunday afternoon in early 2015, eager to talk to her for his forthcoming book about Adrian Doherty, she said she would rather not contribute. Nothing personal, she said, but she knew United would not want her to be involved. She did, however, remember him moving in there at the start of the 1990/91 season and she mentioned him waltzing her around the room in delight when he saw she had borrowed and ironed some clothes for him. This spared him another of those wardrobe malfunctions after he was called up to the first-team squad at short notice. She smiled with the same fondness that everyone does when they talk about Doherty, but she declined to be interviewed – and was so charming in doing so that for once it was easy to take no for an answer.

Whatever her charm, Gosling seemed a formidable woman – not one who would readily allow her young lodgers to run amok. They were not allowed to drink under her roof. There were curfews if they were going out at night. They were not allowed to smuggle girls back. If there was anarchy in the form of some of the mindless games they dreamed up, then it was not dissimilar to some of the nonsense that would unfold in the dressing rooms at the Cliff when the coaching staff were upstairs – 'the Bong', 'the Lap', 'Shag the Bed' and so on. At United, there was still a culture of wild behaviour whenever authority turned its back, whether the authority in question was Alex Ferguson, Eric Harrison or Brenda Gosling.

In the case of out-of-town players, without families nearby, that amount of free time, away from authority, was far greater. 'I've no doubt it was far more difficult for those of us in digs than the lads who were local, who went home every night and were on a tight rein with their parents,' the Northern Irish forward Colin Telford, who moved into Brenda's after starting his apprenticeship in July 1990, says. 'Although there was a fairly tight rein on us in the digs – and the landladies would let us know – they couldn't keep an eye on us all 24/7.'

Alex Ferguson used to pride himself on having a network of informants – often disapproving Manchester United fans – who would drink in various pubs across Cheshire and Greater Manchester, tipping off his staff if they saw players enjoying themselves a little too much on a night out. It seems reasonable to assume this network did not extend to a snout at Follies wine bar on Whitworth Street, just around the corner from Piccadilly, which became Adrian Doherty's haunt on Monday nights.

'No, I don't think we would have been on Mr Ferguson's radar,' Paul Chi laughs. 'I don't think he would have known it existed. It was a club for women at the weekend – lesbians, I suppose – but they were kind and said we could use it on Monday night.'

This 'we' was a group that called itself the New Troubadour Club, set up by Chi, Chas Rigby and a handful of other Manchester music enthusiasts who were looking for somewhere for local acoustic performers to showcase new material. 'It was a place for singer-songwriters,' Rigby says. 'It was an acoustic venue, no electric. It was dingy, smoky, a perfect place for gigs. We would get maybe ten or fifteen artists a night.'

'It was an exciting new place to be,' Chi says. 'There were a lot of young people. It was probably the only place where, as an up-and-coming artist, you could try out something you had written.'

The artists who performed at the New Troubadour Club included David Gray, who would find fame and fortune with a multi-million-selling album in the late 1990s; Gray's best man, Bryan Glancy, a well-known songwriter whose nickname, 'The Seldom Seen Kid', was used for the title of Elbow's Mercury Prize-winning fourth album in 2008, two years after his death; Henry Normal, a poet who would become a highly successful television writer and producer; and Adrian Doherty, who, unbeknown to his audience, was on the fringes of the first-team squad at Manchester United.

'Oh yes, Adrian played,' Rigby says. 'I don't think he was ever one of the featured artists, but he definitely played. I remember him doing some Bob Dylan songs, but also some of his own.'

Was he good? 'He was always joking, doing it for laughs,' Rigby says. 'He wasn't serious. There were a lot of poets there who were too serious for their own good, arty-farty types. I don't remember Adrian doing poetry, but his songs were funny, original. He would get a laugh. He was one of those guys who, had he carried on playing and singing, would probably have gained a following. He would have a few drinks with us afterwards. He enjoyed the *craic*. He was a breath of fresh air at that place.'

Did they have any idea who he was? 'No, we didn't have a clue,' Rigby says. 'I remember him saying he played a bit of football, but we had no idea, even though Bryan and I were ardent Man United fans. We said, "Come on. What do you do?" "Ah, bit of this, bit of that." A few months went by and I was in the Troubadour and Bryan came in with one of the United yearbooks with a team line-up in it and he said, "Have a look at this. You won't believe it." We told him we had sussed him. He just laughed and said, "You bastards," something like that. But even then he didn't really talk about it. I think his mindset was that, when he was there, he was a performer, not a footballer.'

It was a new season and time for a reshuffle at the Cliff. Adrian Doherty was told on his return to pre-season training in July 1990 that he would be with the reserves while the rest of his year group – along with Ryan Giggs, as he was now officially known, having taken his mother's maiden name following his estrangement from his father, Danny Wilson – stayed with the junior teams. Doherty had leapfrogged some of the previous season's reserves, including Wayne Bullimore, Kieran Toal, Lee Costa and John Shotton. The reserves had an appealing-looking pre-season programme, playing against Kidderminster Harriers' and Barnet's first teams before a reserve-team tournament in Cornwall involving Everton and Liverpool. The A team, meanwhile, were back at Littleton Road, playing against Broadheath Central Club and Upton Athletic Association.

'It's never easy, that,' Toal says. 'It's tough when someone bypasses you and this was the first time it had happened. Later it would happen with Ryan Giggs. But Doc's talent was just so overwhelming, you would have looked a complete idiot if you had moaned about it. You could see things opening up for Doc first-team-wise. There was already Lee Sharpe on the left. On the right-hand side, where Doc played, there was Danny Wallace, who had a few injuries, and Russell Beardsmore. Lovely lad, Russell, good career, but he wasn't going to set the world alight, so I think the first team was crying out for someone like Doc.'

Doherty would come to see his promotion as a mixed blessing. In four of the reserves' seven pre-season matches, he was a substitute, and on three of those occasions he got no further than the bench. Worse, when he and his United team-mates went out to drown their sorrows after an abject performance in the Studio Ten Challenge Trophy in Cornwall, he got himself in trouble – not for drinking but for being seen fraternising with the opposition from Liverpool. The Liverpool reserve-team coach Phil Thompson kept telling him how brilliant he was. That did not go down well with the United coaching staff.

Once the season began for real, the reserve team was once more flooded with senior players in need of a run-out – Jim Leighton, Viv Anderson, Colin Gibson, Ralph Milne, Beardsmore and Sharpe – and Doherty was back down to the A team. There is a recollection among friends and team-mates that Doherty found the going a little tougher during the early stages of the 1990/91 campaign. Perhaps it was something akin to second-season syndrome. Perhaps he was unsettled by the change of accommodation, having left the relative tranquillity of the Mannings' house in Levenshulme, albeit two bus rides away, for Brenda's. Looking back, it is hard to work out why anyone ever imagined that a house full of testosterone-fuelled teenage footballers, with long, empty afternoons and evenings to fill, was a better idea than looking to find the out-of-towners some kind of surrogate-parent arrangement to give them at least a semblance of the family environment enjoyed by the local players. Either way, homesickness was becoming an issue again, but help was on its way.

The number of applications to Manchester's three universities spiralled upwards in the late 1980s and early 1990s as students from all over the country decided it was the place to be. 'I went to Salford,' Gareth Doherty says. 'For me, it was obvious – partly because I supported United, partly because of what was going on with all the bands I liked and of course mainly because Adrian was there. As a family, we had talked about that.'

In his first year at Salford, Gareth lived on Wellington Street, a short walk from his brother's digs on Priory Avenue. 'Adrian wasn't a great one for the phone, so we would just call around to see each other once or twice a week,' Gareth says. 'His digs were just like another student house really – except they had their meals cooked for them and I'm sure they would have their bathroom cleaned. Sometimes we would go for a couple of pints at the Priory Arms. Darren Ferguson, Colin McKee and others would be there too. Adrian took me into the training ground one day, into the canteen, and introduced me to some of the players. Ferguson, McKee and those were good lads, but some of the others looked down their noses at me. One thing I remember is it was the first time I ever had spaghetti bolognese. Adrian was saying, "It's good stuff, man. Try it." And I was saying, "How do you eat it?"

'We hung out a bit, but we weren't in each other pockets. Sometimes we would meet at the launderette for a chat – as weird as that sounds. Sometimes we would go to the cinema at Salford Quays or go into town to watch a band. Mostly he would come over to ours and we would sit around talking with the guys I lived with. He got on pretty well with them. He never talked about football. Just music and anything else. We played darts a lot. Whoever got the lowest score would make tea. Adrian didn't make much tea. Sometimes he would join us if we were going out and he would have a few pints of Guinness. I'm sure the other lads in his digs used to wonder where he went, but then they were probably out at Discotheque Royale or wherever, drinking a lot more.'

Sean Ferry had also joined his cousins in Manchester, but was living further out, in Didsbury. 'The first weekend we were in Manchester, we all met up, went into town, ran into a few United players in Corbieres – Darren Ferguson, Lee Costa and a couple of others – and got talking to them,' Ferry says. 'A few weeks later I bumped into them again, this time in McDonald's, and they were raving about Adrian. "You're Doc's mate, aren't you? He's sensational, you know. He's brilliant. He's something else."'

*

It was panic stations at Brenda's. Darren Ferguson was moving in. Looking back, nobody is quite sure whether the boss's son was coming at his own request, in a bold attempt to silence the tiresome 'Daddy's boy' jibes, or whether Alex Ferguson was doing the football equivalent of an Education Secretary sending their kids to the local comprehensive in order to prove it was not as bad as the critics claimed. As Giuliano Maiorana recalls, 'Everyone was going mad, fretting that he was being sent to spy on us.'

Among team-mates and fans alike, Darren Ferguson's rise through the Manchester United ranks attracted predictable accusations of nepotism, but both he and his father have always felt he was judged far more harshly, not less, because of who he was. 'Darren was in a different fishbowl to the rest of us, with his father being manager,' Lee Costa says. 'We all joked with him about it, but it wasn't an easy situation for him to be in.'

Darren Ferguson proved himself in two ways. The obvious one was by showing himself to be a far more refined player than his twin brother, Jason, who, despite a decent scoring record when he was given a few run-outs in the B team the previous season, concluded he would be better off working elsewhere in the football industry. Another was through a gregarious personality that made him an immensely popular team-mate. He was certainly nobody's idea of the squeaky-clean daddy's boy once they got to know him. 'Darren was a great lad,' Kieran Toal says. 'He would be drinking pints, smoking fags. He loved a night out.'

Living in digs, Darren Ferguson no longer went back to the big family home in Wilmslow with his father after training. He was, more than ever, one of the lads. And when Darren Ferguson was one of the lads, everyone else felt like one of the lads. He was one of the few United players who was capable of getting Adrian Doherty out for a pint or several. Darren Ferguson, Lee Costa, Craig Lawton, Colin McKee, Colin Telford, Marcus Brameld and, later, Pat McGibbon and Keith Gillespie were all players that Doherty got along with. It was probably not coincidence that most of them were of Celtic origin. Doherty would still do his own thing much of the time, such as his trips to the New Troubadour Club, but he began to be seen as an individual rather than a loner.

'We had a good set of lads,' Brameld says. 'Doc was the only one who was into completely different things. I remember him taking us to the students' union on a Tuesday or Wednesday night. We were used to nightclubs where you would get dressed up. "Christ, Doc, what have you brought us here for?" Then we would end up at this random flat. He used to come out with us quite a bit. He would be quiet, always in the background. The other lads were a lot more forceful.'

Darren Ferguson, more than most, was enjoying life in the digs. Then, it was presumed after one night out too many, he was abruptly summoned home. For all the accusations of nepotism, it seems the only special treatment he received was being told he had no choice but to return to the family home when others were being told they had no choice but to stay in digs. And maybe, with hindsight, that was more of an advantage than he or any of them could have appreciated at the time.

*

Almost from the moment Adrian Doherty returned from Strabane a year earlier, there had been a feeling among his contemporaries at the Cliff that he would be the next one off the production line to make his Manchester United debut. Now some of them were beginning to wonder. 'I got the impression Doc was being held back a little bit,' Marcus Brameld says. 'I know he had been in the first-team squad, but I'm not sure if the manager was ever going to put him in. I don't know if maybe Doc's demeanour held him back a little bit.'

Peter Smyth volunteers the same view. 'Doc was ready for it and I've no doubt he would have made a positive impact because, mentally, he was incredibly tough – on the pitch anyway,' Smyth says. 'But off the pitch, he was a little bit . . .'

Unpredictable? 'Exactly,' Smyth says. 'Because for me – and you can ask anybody else – he was definitely on a par with Ryan Giggs in terms of ability, pace, courage, wanting the ball, scoring goals. It's just the other side of it. I got the feeling the manager felt that he couldn't risk this lad, that he thought, "I want to put him in, but I can't because what have I got coming?" You can't play for the first team on Saturday and go busking on Monday, can you?'

What gave Smyth the impression that Alex Ferguson and his staff had gone cold on Doherty? Was something said? 'It's only a feeling,' Smyth says. 'Just because every-thing in that first year, in terms of what we needed to win a match in the youth team, was Giggs left, Doherty right. Then after that, it was still the same philosophy, but it wasn't being pushed into us quite as much.'

By now, Ryan Giggs had left school to begin his apprenticeship. Promotion to the reserves could at times be deceptive, but there was nothing misleading about the fact that he was picked for six consecutive second-team matches between mid-October and early December. That run of games would certainly have added to Giggs's sense of belonging at a time when United were negotiating his first professional contract, but it also reflected the club's growing excitement about a youngster whose few rough edges were being smoothed down by the week. On 29 November, the day he turned seventeen, a five-year contract was put in front of Giggs. He signed it immediately. The full five years, obviously.

When Jim Hunter and other members of the Mourne & District branch of the Manchester United supporters' club arrived in Manchester in early December 1990, they asked Barry Moorhouse, an Old Trafford official, how the boy from Strabane was getting along. Usually Moorhouse was effusive. This time he told them Adrian Doherty was 'on a bit of a downer, a bit homesick,' Hunter says.

The group of travelling United fans were already planning to go to the A team against Liverpool at the Cliff the next morning, before the first team's home game against Leeds United in the afternoon, but the junior fixture had now taken on increased importance. What they saw in the first half left them concerned. 'Adrian looked no more interested in playing football than flying to the moon,' Hunter says. 'The whole team was awful in the first half. Alex Ferguson was watching from his upstairs office, banging on the window. Then Adrian saw us as he came off at half-time and, click, something just changed. He came out for the second half and he was unbelievable.'

United ended up beating Liverpool 5–1 that day. Doherty scored the third and ran the Merseysiders ragged – none more than the usually unflappable Alan Hansen, who was thirty-five years old and two months away from conceding defeat in his battle to overcome a debilitating knee injury. Some wonder whether that morning at the Cliff might have made up his mind. 'I remember Adrian turning him inside out,' Hunter says. 'Hansen was so pissed off.'

Liverpool's misery was completed by a Hansen own goal. Alan Tonge, who was watching on the sidelines while recovering from an injury of his own, remains convinced that Hansen did it out of frustration. 'He absolutely bulleted a header past their keeper,' Tonge says. 'I think he was just so frustrated because our lads were pasting them. Doc was on fire that day. He absolutely murdered them.'

At the end, Hunter asked Phil Thompson what he thought of Doherty's performance. His recollection is that the Liverpool coach replied, 'If he ever leaves United, I'll walk barefoot to Manchester to sign him.'

Afterwards, Doherty thanked his travelling supporters' club for coming and said he would join them at Old Trafford that afternoon for the Leeds game. 'At the match and on the bus, people were asking him for his autograph,' Hunter says. 'He was so shy, but he came out to the supporters' club that evening and then went back to the hotel with us. We had a few drinks.

'I remember one of the lads asking him what he thought

of the Chelsea game a couple of weeks earlier. Adrian genuinely didn't have a clue. He was more interested in talking about reading, playing the guitar. It wasn't a conversation you would have with a footballer. It was books, films, philosophy, music. Everyone then sat down to listen to him play the guitar.'

Adrian Doherty was back in the groove. The autumn blues behind him, he was called up to the first-team squad for a second time for the match against Queens Park Rangers on 19 January. This was the time of the waltz with Brenda Gosling. Again, Manchester United had a plethora of injuries and the seventeen-year-old, along with Neil Whitworth and Darren Ferguson, was called up in case Mark Hughes or others failed a pre-match fitness test. 'The three lads are being brought along as a precaution in case any more of our senior players have to withdraw,' Alex Ferguson told reporters the day before. 'Having said that, I wouldn't hesitate to throw one or two of them in if I have to. They have all proved themselves in the reserve team.'

Whitworth, Ferguson Jr and Doherty ended up watching from the stands at Loftus Road, but it was another step closer to the first team. As he boarded the coach afterwards, Doherty was collared by a young United supporter, Tim Glynne-Jones, who asked if he would be willing to be interviewed for his fanzine *The Shankill Skinhead*. Sure, Doherty said. No problem. He gave Glynne-Jones the telephone number for Brenda's and said they could talk in the week. 'It was a bygone age in terms of getting access to the players,' Glynne-Jones recalls.

When you ask a young footballer what his ambition is, you expect an answer along the lines of 'to win the league' or 'to score in the cup final' or 'to play for my country'.

But Adrian Doherty is different. 'I'd like to finish my book really. It's just an adventure story, but it's kind of half-finished, like. I'm stuck, you know? That's the problem I'm having at the minute. I've written about 75 pages but I can't seem to get no further with it. I suppose I'd like to finish before the year's out.'

(extract from *The Shankhill Skinhead*)

Glynne-Jones has fond memories of his chat with Doherty that day. 'Adrian was very personable,' he says. 'He had a natural confidence about him, but he was just like a normal kid. I had interviewed Lee Sharpe, who had had a bit more publicity and was a bit more worldly, a bit more guarded, but Adrian was natural and easy-going. I asked him how he spoilt himself and he talked about biscuits – chocolate digestives or something – and playing the guitar.'

The interview is accompanied by a panel which lists Doherty's preferred diet – bread and jam, toast, chips, Dolly Mixtures, Toffos and digestives ('very good biscuits') – but he did enthuse about how he was now enjoying Manchester and being looked after at Brenda's. 'Manchester's a good place,' he said. 'There's always plenty to do compared to where I'm from. You know, in Strabane, there's not even a discotheque in the whole town. I like Strabane, but, you know what I mean, you'd be glad to get out of it. I was a bit homesick at the start but I'm not any longer. The digs are excellent. We get excellent meals, *excellent* meals – desserts and everything. Excellent, seriously.'

One line in the interview sticks out. When asked whether it had been a dream come true to join United at the age of fourteen, Doherty replied, 'I wasn't really too bothered one way or the other. I was just lucky to get the chance. [But] I was really excited. You wouldn't refuse anything like that.'

That is not quite the attitude his friends remember back in Strabane, on those evenings when he would train on his own on the school playing fields, but it was certainly in keeping with the off-hand manner in which he would respond whenever anyone tried to talk to him about football after his arrival in Manchester. 'He often gave you the impression he could take it or leave it,' Lee Costa says. 'I have no doubts he wanted it like the rest of us, but he showed it in different ways. His mentality wouldn't have worked for everyone, but it was working for him. On the pitch, he was flying. It was only a matter of time before he played in the first team.'

Adrian Doherty and Ryan Giggs, two seventeen-year-olds with the world at their feet at Manchester United, were used to being pitted against each other. Who was quicker? 'We were about the same,' Giggs says. 'On Monday mornings Eric Harrison would put on sprinting drills, "doggies", and he would always put the two of us against each other because we were the two quickest. One week I would win. The next week Doc would win. He was so quick off the mark. All the lads would be on the sideline, cheering us both on. It would push us. It was competitive. I didn't want to lose.'

Over the past year, it had felt like a race to the first team too. Sometimes one of them would be on the fast track, sometimes the other. The previous spring it had been all about Doherty. Then, through the autumn, it was all about Giggs. Now, in early 1991, the buzz surrounded Doherty again. He was, as Giggs puts it, 'definitely on the brink of making his first-team debut'.

CHAPTER 15

It was love at first sight. From the moment the Old Trafford crowd clapped eyes on him, as he emerged from a
baggy adidas tracksuit and took his first tentative steps in
Manchester United's senior team, they adored him. For
some players, the Theatre of Dreams brings on stagefright,
but for this seventeen-year-old winger, a first-team debut as
a substitute against Everton felt like the start of something
big. Immediately, among those witnessing his wonderful
blend of pace and trickery for the first time, there was a
temptation to liken him to the great George Best.

For the 45,656 in attendance, the afternoon of 2 March
1991 would go down as an 'I was there' moment. With an
injury-ravaged United team heading for a 2–0 defeat, an
otherwise forgettable match assumed an historic dimension when Denis Irwin limped off towards the end of the
first half, replaced by this slip of a lad, all flicks and tricks
and lightning-quick bursts.

Years later he would reflect on his first-team debut as
an anticlimax, as he found himself bogged down on a
cabbage-patch pitch, unable to inspire a struggling team. He
would say he remembered little of the afternoon other than
being given an almighty kick by Everton's former England
defender Dave Watson, intent on giving this upstart the

traditional welcome to the big time. But for those who were watching, there was something about the boy that inspired hope and excitement. Sometimes you can just tell. And you could certainly tell with young Ryan Giggs.

Adrian Doherty was sitting in the Main Stand alongside the injured members of United's first-team squad. Steve Bruce, Bryan Robson, Mark Hughes and the rest of the crocks made for illustrious company, but Doherty wished he could be somewhere else. Busking in the city centre? Quite possibly, but above all he wanted to be out there on the pitch with Ryan Giggs and their fellow teenager Darren Ferguson, who started the game that day. With an injury crisis worsening and a European Cup Winners' Cup tie against Montpellier looming, the Everton fixture had been earmarked as the day when Doherty might get the chance to make the leap into the first team. But no. With wretched timing, he had injured his knee in an A-team match against Carlisle United's reserves a week earlier. And it was still sore. Very sore, in fact.

The *Derry Journal* had dispatched their football reporter Arthur Duffy to Manchester after being tipped off that Doherty, the boy wonder from down the road in Strabane, was in line to make his debut. Duffy had been accompanied on the journey over by a large contingent from the Mourne & District branch of United's supporters' club. They had all arrived in high spirits the previous day, excited at the prospect of seeing their local hero in the United first team, only for the boy himself to inform them that – sod's law – he was injured too. 'No big deal,' he told Duffy. 'It will happen soon enough.'

As the match unfolded, as Ferguson Jr and then Giggs crossed the Rubicon, joining the illustrious list of first-team players for Manchester United, Duffy looked over at Doherty from his seat in the press box. 'He had his finger in his mouth and he looked devastated,' Duffy recalls. 'First it was Darren Ferguson and then it was Ryan Giggs. I was thinking, "What must Adrian be thinking now?" He said to me afterwards, "That should have been me."'

Duffy had travelled to Manchester in the hope of witnessing a proud moment for his region, an uplifting story that would offer his readers rare, if fleeting, respite before turning back to the front pages and the latest on a political situation still fraught with tension. There would have been journalistic merit in the story of Doherty's crushing disappointment – 'Strabane lad misses out on dream debut', 'Adrian curses injury blow', 'Doc suffers United heartbreak' – but Duffy's instincts towards him were protective. As appealing as it might have sounded, that quote, 'That should have been me', never made the pages of the *Derry Journal*. Duffy preferred a more reflective piece in which he detailed Doherty's philosophical mood when they chatted in a greasy-spoon café the day before the match:

To his credit, the youngster appeared unconcerned when I spoke to him last Friday afternoon. 'I've got plenty of time to make my debut,' he insisted. 'I'm kind of annoyed at being injured, but that's the way football goes. I'll get my chance eventually, but I suppose I couldn't have picked a worse time for this to happen.'

Despite his comments, one couldn't help but notice the disappointed look on Adrian's face as Darren Ferguson, the

19-year-old son of team manager Alex, strode out in front of over 40,000 partisan fans on Saturday afternoon at Old Traf-ford to make his full debut. The same concerned look greeted the substitution of regular right-back Denis Irwin and the introduction of another young 'Red Devil' starlet in the form of 17-year-old Ryan Giggs during the same game.

After the match I spoke with him again. 'I thought both did well,' he said confidently. 'They're very good players, you know, and they'll be glad to get their home debuts out of the way. My chance will come. I've got plenty of time. I'm only 17.'

A week earlier at the Cliff, on 23 February, Alex Ferguson and his first-team players had been preparing for a Rumbelows Cup semi-final second leg away to Leeds United while the A team took on Carlisle United reserves. It was one of those Lancashire League fixtures that Adrian Doherty and his team-mates had learned to approach with a certain apprehension. When they faced the A teams of Everton or Liverpool or Manchester City, they were mostly up against players their own age and, as combative as it might have been at times, it was two teams competing as equals. Fixtures against a reserve team from Carlisle, Rochdale or Bury, let alone Marine, tended to pit them against older professionals, often with a chip on their shoulder or a grudge to bear. 'Carlisle: every game, you'd be black and blue,' Peter Smyth says. 'You would just get walloped.'

Some of Adrian Doherty's team-mates, Smyth included, seem to recall that he got walloped that day. It calls to mind a winger in full flow, bringing the ball under control, looking up and accelerating away, gaining pace but never losing mastery of the ball, swerving in and out of opponents like they were Coke cans on the playing fields back in Strabane, the ball tied to his foot with an invisible string – and then BANG.

The version Doherty gave to his friends was rather more mundane. 'I remember him saying it wasn't a bad tackle,' Dee Devenney says. 'He said he was going in for a 50-50 and his knee just went – and whatever happened happened.'

That is precisely how Doherty explained it in a *News of the World* interview two and a half years later. 'It was a simple collision for a 50-50 ball,' he said. 'There was no foul. I heard something go, but nobody realised how bad it was. My knee felt funny when I got up and tried to run. But I did walk off.'

Jim McGregor was in the physiotherapist's room at the Cliff, overlooking the pitch. He was making his preparations for the trip to Leeds, no more than half an eye on what was happening outside, but he saw play had stopped and he was troubled to see a player was lying on the floor, others surrounding him. He was even more alarmed to realise it was that nice Adrian Doherty. 'He was in a heap,' McGregor recalls. 'He wasn't a lad who screamed or shouted at all, so I raced downstairs. I actually ran straight onto the pitch. I looked at the knee and I thought, "I don't like the look of this." I knew there and then that it was a serious sort of injury.'

The C-word entered McGregor's mind: cruciate. It is the word every football medic dreads, the word that leaves players terrified. The cruciate ligaments are those that both stabilise the knee and enable a wide range of flexion. McGregor had witnessed plenty of cruciate injuries down the years. He had seen Dennis Stevens, 'a super footballer', suffer one at Oldham Athletic in the 1960s. At Everton he had seen Geoff Nulty collapse in agony following a tackle by Jimmy Case in a Merseyside derby in 1980. Nulty never played again. Doherty's, too, McGregor says, looked like an injury to the cruciate ligament. It was clearly not on the Nulty scale, but it was a cause for concern.

'If it's bad,' McGregor says, 'it's obvious immediately. You can diagnose it straight away. Don't forget there are different degrees of damage. You can strain a ligament, you can tear a ligament or you can rupture a ligament. There's the anterior cruciate ligament and the posterior cruciate ligament. You can still get immediate laxity with a rupture. With Adrian, that day, there was far too much forward movement in the knee and you think, "He's damaged a cruciate." We took him off immediately.'

This is where McGregor's recollections become sketchy. He cannot remember whether he or anyone else took Doherty to hospital that afternoon. Either way there would be little that could be done at this stage. There would be no scans and no immediate decisions to operate, as there often are these days. The swelling would have to go down first. Doherty was sent home with instructions to report to McGregor in the treatment room at the Cliff first thing on Monday morning.

Adrian Doherty dumps his kitbag at his digs and hobbles the short distance to his brother Gareth's house on

Wellington Street, his knee troubling him every step of the way. He knocks on the door. Gareth answers.

'How'd it go, man?'

'I've done my knee.'

'Is it bad?'

'Not sure yet. Bloody sore, though.'

'Are you going to be missing games?'

'Could be out for a few weeks. Don't know yet.'

'Jeez, man. That's bad timing.'

Gareth invites Adrian in. They shoot the breeze – talk of football, talk of music, talk of Strabane. They have something to eat, something cheap and unimaginative, as student etiquette dictates. They sit around, playing darts, watching television. *Grandstand* is on in the background. Liverpool, stunned by Kenny Dalglish's resignation the previous day, fall to a shock 3–1 defeat at Luton Town and are replaced at the top of the table by Arsenal. To Gareth and his housemates, this is a big deal. Adrian? Not so much. They ask if United won at the Cliff this morning. He has no idea. He is vague enough about details when he has played the full ninety minutes, never mind when he has limped off injured.

The Doherty boys call home to Strabane. Adrian tells his father about the injury. 'Is it serious?' Jimmy asks. 'Are you OK?'

'Not sure yet. Bloody sore, though.'

Adrian Doherty would come to reflect that his injury came at 'the worst possible time'. Seventeen-year-olds, even those as extraordinarily gifted as Ryan Giggs and himself, tend not to be thrust into the Manchester United first team without an injury crisis like the one that was sweeping the Cliff once more in early 1991. He had been in excellent form, knocking on the first-team door again. With so many senior players injured, with a heavy fixture schedule exacerbated by progress in the Rumbelows Cup and the European Cup Winners' Cup, Doherty, Giggs and Darren Ferguson had been in the manager's thoughts for the league matches against Sheffield United and Everton, perhaps even to make up the numbers on the substitutes' bench for the European tie against Montpellier.

Giggs had been training on and off with the first-team squad for months and was in blistering form before Christmas, but he has previously admitted that he 'hadn't been playing particularly well for the youth team or the reserves' prior to his call-up for the matches against Sheffield United (as an unused member of the travelling squad) and Everton. He, like Ferguson Jr, benefited from the injury crisis. So too, over the next few weeks, would Mark Bosnich, Neil Whitworth and Paul Wratten, all of them making their first senior appearances for United. The door to the first-team squad was wide open and Doherty was out of action. Yes, the injury really had come at a bad time.

Others have questioned whether Alex Ferguson was ever really going to hand a senior debut to Adrian Doherty, a scruffy seventeen-year-old who liked to spend his Saturday afternoons busking. It is time to ask the man himself. He responds by letter. In a glowing testimony – which, for reasons to be explained later, surprised Doherty's family – the former Manchester United manager makes clear that he was indeed ready to play the teenager in the first team.

'Adrian was not your typical football-mad lad,' Ferguson writes. 'He was a quiet boy at ease in his own company, preferring to spend his free time engrossed in more artistic activities such as writing poetry and playing his guitar. He loved his music, with Bob Dylan a particular favourite, and was known throughout the club as "The Doc".

'On the pitch he was a fast and skilful player who was excellent with both feet. Adrian was a complete natural with a football. It came easily to him. Sadly just before Adrian was to make his debut, whilst playing in an A-team fixture, his knee gave way and he sustained a serious injury.'

In view of what happened next, that final sentence is important. Not just because it confirms that Ferguson was ready to select Doherty at first-team level but because the former manager states when the 'serious injury' was sustained. That is how Jim McGregor remembers it too. And yet a review of Doherty's medical records leaves you to wonder whether anyone realised how serious it was.

As for what happened next, we know Adrian Doherty was asked to report at the Cliff at 9.30 a.m. on the Monday to see Jim McGregor. In English football at that time, any injury beyond the obvious – a broken leg, a dislocated shoulder, a broken nose – tended to fall under the responsibility of the club physio. McGregor was a qualified physiotherapist, unlike some of the 'bucket-and-sponge merchants' at other clubs. But as the former Manchester City midfielder Paul Lake ruefully observed in his autobiography, *I'm Not Really Here*, reflecting on the mishandling of the knee injury that ended his hugely promising career, the culture at most football clubs in that era was for medical teams to be 'incredibly short-staffed . . . with one part-time doctor and one physio tasked with overseeing 40 players'.

McGregor certainly had his hands full at the start of that week. There was Denis Irwin and Bryan Robson, who would be passed fit for the match at Sheffield United the following evening, and there was Mike Phelan, Lee Sharpe and Mark Hughes, who would not. By the end of the week there was also Neil Webb and there was Robson again, both of them having picked up injuries in the 2–1 defeat at Bramall Lane. Since McGregor's prime responsibility was to try to help the senior players get fit, in the midst of another United injury crisis, even a youngster as highly regarded as Doherty is likely to have found himself some way down the queue for the treatment table.

Doherty told the *Derry Journal* it had been 'boring' turning up at the Cliff at 9.30 a.m. for treatment all week. By that point he had learned that 'it's not going to clear up as quickly as I first thought'. He said it was 'sore now and again after treatment', that he was 'hoping to be fit for our [FA Youth Cup] quarter-final match with Southampton but I'm not sure if I will'.

Doherty liked McGregor. All the players did. The Scot had an easy charm and an ability to make them feel at ease. He knew about films, books and music. Doherty saw him as someone he could open up to, however slightly. He even told McGregor about *The Adventures of Humphrey and Bodegard*.

Among the first-team players, there was still a mystique around Doherty. They all knew he was a nice lad, but they could not begin to fathom out what was going on inside his head. If they were going to be seeing more of him over the seasons to come, they wanted to know more. They asked him what he did with his time when he went back to digs. So he told them: 'Playing the guitar, reading, writing, that sort of thing.' This was a triple-whammy. They knew he played the guitar. They even had a suspicion that he was a reader, which was considered eccentric enough. But writing? What on earth does a seventeen-year-old Manchester United footballer write about? Not dressing-room secrets, they hoped. Egged on by McGregor, he told them about *The Adventures of Humphrey and Bodegard*. As he said to Arthur Duffy with great amusement later in the week, 'I think Mark Hughes thinks I'm an absolute idiot.'

The *Derry Journal* certainly got their money's worth out of Duffy's trip to Manchester. First there was the interview with Adrian Doherty, coinciding with the first major setback of his career. In some ways, the soft-focus stuff is more interesting. He discusses his writing ('I always enjoyed writing stories at school, so after I started to get wages I bought a typewriter and started writing a story'), his uncomprehending team-mates ('some of the first-team players, like Mark Hughes, take the mickey out of me and slag me about my book') and the grey silky shirt that looked uncharacteristically flash for Doherty ('I got it for £1 in a class second-hand shop. You don't get bargains like that in Strabane, you know').

Doherty also touched on the homesickness he had endured in those difficult early days in Manchester. 'I found it very hard at first,' he told Duffy. 'I even went into Alex Ferguson and told him I didn't want to play football any more. I just wanted to go home. He gave me a few weeks off and asked me to phone him. Mr Ferguson was right. Now everything's great. It took a bit of getting used to, but it was a choice between being a YTP worker in Strabane or an apprentice professional with Manchester United. Which would you go for?'

Duffy also got a few words on Doherty from Paddy Crerand, the 1968 European Cup-winning midfielder whose father hailed from County Tyrone. 'It's a pity he's injured,' Crerand told him. 'I thought he may have figured in the Sheffield United game last week or possibly against Everton. He's like a slightly taller version of Jimmy Johnstone. He's really exciting to watch on the right wing and I've no doubt in my mind that he's a definite first-teamer.'

Duffy was not finished yet. On the Monday lunchtime he ventured over to the Cliff, told Alex Ferguson of his interest in young Doherty and, in those days when interviews were sought and granted without fear or favour, he asked whether it might be possible for a quick chat.

Talking at length about young players was not usually Ferguson's modus operandi. But, to Duffy's delight, the United manager went for it. Maybe it struck a chord with something he had been thinking since giving Ryan Giggs his debut forty-eight hours earlier, or maybe it was something he had felt about Doherty for a while. Either way, he ended up giving Duffy just the interview he wanted.

'I don't like giving out information on their progress because, nine times out of ten, the headlines make the youngsters out to be something they're not,' Ferguson said. 'Irish lads, in particular, can be crucified with newspaper reporters making them out to be the next George

Gareth and Adrian wearing identical
T-shirts. It was the seventies, after all.

A young Adrian wearing his Sunday
best for his First Holy Communion,
with big brother Gareth for company.

Manchester United supporters club, Ballycolman branch. Back row: Aidy Devenney,
Gareth Doherty, Sean Ferry. Front row: Adrian Doherty, Stephen Devenney.

Left: Looking cute in a school photograph taken at St Mary's Boys R.C. Primary School, Strabane.

Below: Adrian gets to grips with baby brother Peter as Gareth and Ciara smile for the camera.

Above: Wearing his Manchester United pyjamas while doing homework. He was no fan of crusts, it seems.

Right: If the cap fits … But Adrian rarely felt at ease during his days in the Northern Ireland youth set-up.

Lining up for the Northern Ireland schoolboy team to face Brazil at Windsor Park in 1988. Adrian is front row, second left, flanked by Brendan Rodgers and Peter Smyth.

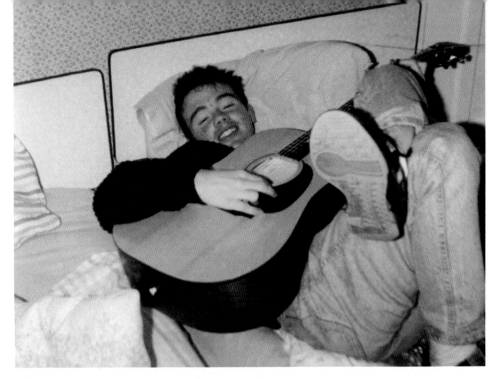

After beginning his Manchester United apprenticeship, Adrian bought a guitar to alleviate the boredom in digs. It was the best investment he ever made.

Panic over. Adrian has found his blazer and is ready to set off for United's FA Youth Cup tie at Burnley, January 1990.

'Get your hair cut,' the United coaches said. So Adrian did. Bryan Robson told him: 'I had a haircut like that ten years ago.'

Above: Manchester United line up before the FA Youth Cup semi-final against Tottenham at White Hart Lane in April 1990. Back row (left to right): Mark Bosnich, Ryan Wilson (soon to be Ryan Giggs), Darren Ferguson, Paul Sixsmith, Jason Lydiate, Sean McAuley. Front row (left to right): Mark Gordon, Craig Lawton, Lee Costa, Alan Tonge, Adrian Doherty.

Right: Looking lean and athletic and pushing for a first-team call-up in a reserve game against Nottingham Forest at the City Ground, September 1990.

The end is nigh: an unhappy post-injury run-out in Manchester United's A team game against Manchester City, March 1993. 'He looked like he didn't want to be there,' Mick Winters says.

Team-mates say no full-back could keep pace with 'The Doc' before the injury. But here, struggling to regain his old acceleration, he cannot find a way past Manchester City's Richard Edghill.

Left: Horsing around in All Saints Park, Manchester, in early 1992.

Right: With Leo Cussons (left) in Enschede, Holland, in the mid-1990s, by which time Adrian's football ambitions had been forgotten and his focus had moved entirely to music and poetry.

Dressed up and ready for work as a day porter at Brennan's Yard Hotel, Galway, in 1996.

Playing the guitar at Rob and Alison Jones's wedding reception in 1997. 'He was a show-stopper,' Alison says, 'one of life's little geniuses.'

Adrian deep in thought in Manchester, working on his latest composition.

Best. It's a hard reputation to live up to, but then again stories like that catch the eye. Whether they come from Cork or Belfast, it's always the same and, to be honest, I'm fed up with it. That's one of the reasons why we don't like to talk about youngsters. We prefer them to be able to speak for themselves with their performances for the first team when they break through.'

Duffy understood exactly what Ferguson was saying – he agreed with it – but he wanted a sense of where Doherty figured at this stage of his career. He had seen another seventeen-year-old, Giggs, make his debut two days earlier, so was it reasonable to expect the boy from Strabane to follow suit?

'Adrian has got great potential and could go all the way,' Ferguson said. 'However, he's still got a bit of growing to do and I'd like to see his muscles develop more. He came here as a scrawny little kid but has gained a few more inches and put on a bit more weight since he became full-time almost two years ago. He's now an influential youth-team player and has turned out for the reserves on a few occasions. He's a terrific prospect and, now that he's happy and settled here, it's up to us to ripen that potential and get the best out of him.

'I'm sure he'll make it. He's got years ahead of him. He's developed from a shy, modest youngster into a lively seventeen-year-old. We expect him to maintain the commitment and drive which we try to instil in all our apprentices. It's during this time [the late teenage years] that they come of age. For many it's make-or-break time and it's during this period that a lot depends on the player's attitude. Adrian appears to have a good attitude. He's injured at the moment and I fully expect him to be out of action for the reserves and youth squad for two or three weeks. He got a whack on a knee during a game last Saturday and has a knee ligament problem – nothing too serious.'

That was the reassuring thing for Adrian Doherty: they kept telling him it was not serious. If it was, he would have been sent to the club doctor and then to the surgeon by now. There was still talk of him getting back for that FA Youth Cup quarter-final tie at Southampton on 22 March, so how bad could it be?

'He wasn't too down about it,' Gareth Doherty recalls. 'He didn't think it was the end of the world. I think he thought, "Two or three weeks and I'll be grand." It seemed to me that, because he was only seventeen, it wouldn't matter even if he was out for a few weeks or even months. So what? He'd get in the first team next season. It definitely didn't seem like, "This is it. This is serious."'

CHAPTER 16

The first mystery about the injury that would wreck Adrian Doherty's career surrounds the initial diagnosis. His family's recollection is that the dreaded word 'cruciate' was mentioned from a fairly early stage. This is backed up by Jim McGregor, the Manchester United physio at the time, but it is not reflected in the small file of medical documents the club's solicitor, Maurice Watkins, sent the family in 2003. In those documents, there is no mention of the word 'cruciate' until an MRI scan on 25 July 1991, five months after that fateful day at the Cliff, revealed a proximal tear of the anterior cruciate. That also happens to be the first mention of the word 'scan'.

It was, of course, a different era. 'Nowadays everything is scanned,' McGregor says. 'I laugh uproariously now when I hear someone has a slight calf strain, but they "won't know the precise extent of the injury until he has had a scan". Jesus Christ, we had to diagnose the injuries and let the manager know – practically immediately – how long the lad would be out.'

As McGregor said previously, there are different degrees of cruciate damage, whether to the anterior or the posterior ligament, ranging from a strain to a tear to a rupture. Given that Doherty was able to walk off the pitch, walk around to his brother's house later that day, walk to and around the Cliff each day and was passed fit to play in a few exhibition matches at the end of the season, it would seem plausible that, if he did indeed suffer cruciate ligament damage on 23 February 1991, then the initial damage was on the less serious end of the scale.

The strange thing in Doherty's case is that the 'serious injury' sustained in an A-team match, as described by Sir Alex Ferguson years later, was not regarded with any great concern at the time. It would be tempting to give United's medical team the benefit of the doubt and conclude that perhaps McGregor or Ferguson was confusing the injury against Carlisle United reserves with the one Doherty sustained in a disastrous comeback attempt later in the year. But that later incident was at Littleton Road – not at the Cliff, where McGregor recalls the cruciate ligament damage happening – and not in an A-team game shortly before he was due to make his debut, which is how Ferguson remembers the injury. All the indications suggest that the problem arose with the injury Doherty suffered on 23 February 1991. Yet beyond any hospital visit on the day – presumed, not documented – there is no record of an assessment by a doctor, let alone the club's consultant orthopaedic surgeon, for another seventeen days.

On 12 March, after a fortnight of physiotherapy, Adrian Doherty was referred by Manchester United's club doctor, Francis McHugh, to Jonathan Noble, a consultant orthopaedic surgeon, who was based at the Bupa hospital in nearby Whalley Range. According to a letter sent to the Doherty family in February 2003 by Maurice Watkins, who was then the club's solicitor, Noble diagnosed a sprain of the medial collateral ligament and his recommendation was for an active rehabilitation programme rather than surgical intervention. The next update came after a review on 21 March 1991, at which point Doherty was told that things were looking much better.

On 22 March, the day after that encouraging review – whether by McHugh or Noble, it is unclear – United were away to Southampton in the FA Youth Cup quarter-final. Tony Park has the team sheet that was printed and distributed shortly before kick-off at the Dell that night. Curiously, Doherty's name is on it. But when the teams emerged, it was Raphael Burke, a first-year apprentice, wearing the United No. 7 shirt. Had Doherty been included in the travelling party, only to withdraw on the day of the game? Had he even been named in the starting line-up that night, only to break down in the warm-up? Nobody – friends, family, team-mates, coaches, physio – has any recollection of that. Burke says it is not the kind of thing he would remember almost a quarter of a century later. In the absence of any further information, it seems safest and most reasonable to put the team sheet mystery down to a misunderstanding.

Someone has got their hands on a camcorder, so Adrian Doherty and his mates are having a bit of fun. On 15 March he is to be found in the lounge at his brother's digs on Wellington Street. Mick Winters, visiting from Strabane, is the man behind the camera. Adrian takes a sip of tea as he accepts the challenge of heading a football against a wall a hundred times without allowing it to drop. These are not loopy, up-and-down headers. This is a hundred headers, back and forth, in less than a minute – a header every 0.6 seconds, including the bounce-back. It does not look physically possible to do it quicker than that. At times the action is reminiscent of Woody Woodpecker attacking a tree trunk. 'It's not prime-time TV, boys, but it just shows you the magic is still there,' Adrian says as he approaches the hundred. 'I haven't touched a ball for three weeks.'

Two days later, on St Patrick's Day, they are in Albert Square in Manchester city centre, outside the town hall. This time Adrian is behind the camera as he tries to convince a passer-by – ginger hair, big beard, thick glasses – that he is a news reporter. 'Professor Beatnik,' he calls to the passer-by, 'could you please give us a few words on the current state of what's been happening to you in the last few weeks and any plans for the future?' The 'professor', who is nothing of the sort, looks horrified for a moment, fearing he is going to be the lead item on that night's *Granada Reports*, and then explodes into laughter, telling the off-duty footballer, 'You're a f***ing barmpot.'

Back at Wellington Street the next evening, Adrian Doherty, wearing an oversized shirt and a pair of sunglasses with only one arm, picks up his guitar, takes an unconvincing drag on a cigarette, adopts his performing persona – mid-Atlantic accent, curled lip – and starts to strum away at his latest composition:

> *Let the games begin*
> *Let the swiftest runner win*
> *Let the music start*
> *Let the notes pierce through hearts*

Let confusion and chaos spring forth
From the south right up to the north
Let the smoke rise from below
Let the waters rise and overflow

Let the thunder roar
Let the rain from the heavens pour

'A song that's rather pessimistic,' Doherty says of that particular number, but he is more upbeat as he begins another rendition of 'The Times They Are a-Changin''. His singing style, for better or worse, is intentionally Dylan-esque, not least in its earnestness. 'He was a Dylan sort of a singer,' Winters reflects after revisiting the footage. 'He had an unusual voice, that whole Lou Reed thing. Maybe some people would think he couldn't sing, but I would say it was more an unusual voice.'

There is also at one point a mickey-taking exchange with his brother Gareth, whom he describes, to camera, as 'a legend in his own lifetime'. 'The man behind the camera is a legend in someone else's lifetime,' Gareth replies. Adrian takes a moment to consider his response. 'I'll be a legend in the next lifetime,' he says.

Two and a half months after damaging ligaments in his right knee, Adrian Doherty was back on the pitch in a Manchester United shirt, unexpectedly called up for the Blue Stars youth tournament in Zurich. He and his family were encouraged that he had been passed fit, although there is no mention, in his medical records, of any assessment by a doctor around this time. The matches were just forty minutes long, but in barely twenty-four hours Doherty started four games (being substituted in two of them) and then came on as a substitute in the final, in which United were beaten by Spartak Moscow.

A fortnight later United were due to send a team to the Caribbean to play two end-of-season friendly matches against Trinidad and Tobago. Doherty asked if he could be excused, citing his sore knee, which he felt needed rest, and, more naively, his need to attend a christening, having been asked to be godfather for Frank and Geraldine Manning's baby daughter Samantha. His request was rejected. After a ten-hour flight, he was injured in the first match, on a hard pitch, and left Trinidad complaining that his knee was not right. There is no record of his having been assessed on his return to Manchester.

Ask any Manchester United supporters for their defining memory of the European Cup Winners' Cup triumph in Rotterdam in May 1991 and they are likely to offer one of two things: Mark Hughes's winning goal and Alex Ferguson conducting the post-match celebrations as the jubilant fans sang 'Always Look on the Bright Side of Life'.

Ask any United reserve-team or youth-team player of that era for his abiding memory and his reply is likely to be rather different. 'Rotterdam? Jesus Christ,' Kieron Toal says. 'It was like a court case after that.'

The first-team squad, coaching staff and club directors flew from Manchester to Amsterdam on the eve of the game and were taken to their hotel in Rotterdam. The reserves and youth-team players, Adrian Doherty among them, flew in the following morning and were taken into

Amsterdam to spend the day at leisure, unsupervised, before a scheduled meet-up for an early-evening bus transfer to Rotterdam for the match. Big mistake.

'We were having lunch on this riverboat,' Toal says, 'and the guy at the front of the boat, who might have been from Amstel or something, shouted, "Who wants a beer?" Well, you can guess what everyone says to that. And it went from there.'

One of the players present says that just about everything you could imagine happening with a group of drunken lads in Amsterdam – 'proper stag-do stuff' – happened that day. Anne Frank's house and the Rijksmuseum were not on the agenda. The trouble peaked on the bus transfer to Rotterdam, when a heated argument between Alan McReavie and Ralph Milne developed into a brawl that left the latter with a cut face. Cans of beer were thrown in the melee. Some of the younger players were sick on the bus. The driver refused to go any further until police arrived to escort them to De Kuip.

Word got back to Alex Ferguson, inevitably, and a full-scale inquest ensued, a low note on which to end the season after United's victory over Barcelona in the final. McReavie and Milne were released on free transfers – although both were out of contract anyway – and just about every player present was reprimanded, many of them fined. Sore knee or not, it would have been an inopportune time for Doherty to ask if he could skip the end-of-season trip to Trinidad in order to go to a christening and rest a knee that, at least according to the club's medical staff, was no cause for great concern.

*

The local-boy-done-good walked on stage at Strabane's hottest entertainment venue, the Melmount Centre. 'It's Doc!' someone shouted. Adrian Doherty was wearing a long-sleeved T-shirt with the slogan 'MONKEY MAGIC: WARRIOR AND MARTYR' on the back. He never did shake off his affection for *Monkey*.

Followed onto the stage by an awkward-looking Gerard Mullan – hiding behind black shades, carrying a tambourine – Doherty slung his guitar over his shoulder and spoke into the microphone. 'Hello, Strabane,' he said as he started to pluck away. 'We'd like to play a few songs that we think youse might like, or . . .' The crowd laughed supportively. 'This our theme tune.'

> *We want to clear up any doubt*
> *What we're all about*
> *We just want to hear you scream and shout*
> *Cos we are the Drunken Louts*

The Drunken Louts had been spawned only hours earlier, when Doherty heard Mick Winters lamenting the lack of a warm-up act for his band the Infidels at that night's gig. Doherty volunteered himself and Mullan. 'I told him: a) we haven't got any songs and b) we can't sing,' Mullan recalls. 'Adrian said, "That's fine. We'll work on it."'

They went outside, Doherty carrying his guitar as always. 'He said, "Think up some words for some songs,"' Mullan says. 'The first one we came up with was called "The Make-It-Up-As-You-Go-Along Song". Another one went something like, "Cootchie cootchie cootchie coo, cootchie cootchie cootchie coo", so you can get an idea of the way this is going. It was tongue in cheek, trying to make the audience laugh. Incredibly, we got a great reception and people were asking, "When are you on again?"'

There are three striking things about the video recording of that performance at the Melmount Centre in late June 1991. Firstly, despite having turned eighteen a fortnight earlier, Doherty looks far less like a budding footballer or singer-songwriter than a sweet, innocent child. Secondly, there are no obvious signs of discomfort with his knee; if he is in pain, he is playing through it. Thirdly, while clearly desperate to engage the audience, he is not taking it remotely seriously. The songs he and Mullan 'performed' that night were made up on the spot, or shortly beforehand, and were intentionally lowbrow. Yet back in Manchester he was writing songs and poems as a serious pursuit – some of them surreally absurd, others showing an intellectual depth. He did not perform any of that stuff. That was serious. The Drunken Louts, quite evidently, was not.

Doherty's persona changed when, midway through their eleven-minute gig, he performed a cover of 'Knockin' on Heaven's Door', again trying to mimic Bob Dylan. Later he joined the Infidels on stage to perform 'All Along the Watchtower'. He did not always hit the right notes – or even try to – but he knew what he was doing and there was a real energy to his performance. What is more, he loved it. 'He was so happy doing that,' Winters says. 'Even though he was shy, he got a great buzz from it.'

Mullan cringes at reminders of the Drunken Louts,

but Doherty's sister, Ciara, remembers that evening with great fondness. 'My friend Rachel and I were watching and thinking, "Wow, this is mad," because they were all going nuts on stage and really enjoying it,' she says. 'I remember seeing another side of Adrian that night and being really proud of him.'

According to Gareth Doherty, 'further crimes against music were committed' over the next few months, not just up the road in Castlederg but even in Manchester. 'We would just be in stitches,' Mullan says. 'The only thing Adrian would take seriously was his Dylan stuff. The rest of it was just for a laugh – "Bad Stranger", "The Shake Song". I can't remember where we did the last one in Manchester, the farewell gig, but we gave them some eggs to throw at us at the end.'

Adrian Doherty returned to Manchester for pre-season training in July. On 24 July, following an assessment, Dr McHugh referred him to Jonathan Noble once more, saying that while the youngster had worked very hard on his remedial exercise programme over the summer, he was still having problems with his right knee. McHugh noted that an instability in the knee was followed by a perceived 'shift' if Doherty attempted to turn sharply. Noble saw Doherty the following day and it was at this point, according to the medical records, that an MRI scan was taken, revealing a proximal tear of the anterior cruciate ligament. Noble spelt out the pros and cons of arthroscopy – examination or treatment of the injury via the insertion of a scope through a small incision – but concluded that for now it would be wrong to rush into such a course of action, given the risks involved.

So there it was: a proximal tear of the anterior cruciate ligament in Doherty's right knee. Not disastrous, according to Noble's assessment, but certainly bad news. Had it been there all along? Had the injury evolved? Had something gone amiss? Noble was hopeful there was still no cause for surgery, but he did raise the concern, in correspondence with McHugh, that the injury placed a definite question mark over Doherty's long-term future in professional football.

By 4 September, there was no sign of improvement, so Noble gave the green light for the arthroscopy, which he carried out with Doherty under anaesthetic. A tear of the medial meniscus was discovered and resected. The diagnosis of a torn anterior cruciate ligament was repeated, but still reconstructive surgery was felt to be a last resort.

Was it standard practice that, upon finding a proximal tear of the anterior cruciate ligament five months after the incident, no surgical reconstruction was recommended? Noble declined to be interviewed for this book, but Joe McClelland, the Belfast-based surgeon who would eventually operate on Doherty, says Noble's approach was 'very much par for the course in those days'. Surgery was considered a risk, though there was also the danger, McClelland says, that 'the longer these injuries went on, the more likely you were to have other damage to the knee joint.'

Jim McGregor – a physiotherapist, not a surgeon, it should be said – says he is 'surprised' when told that no operation took place until almost twelve months after the initial injury, but he backs up Noble's and McClelland's assessment that the discovery of a torn cruciate ligament did not automatically lead to surgery. 'In those days quite a lot of surgeons weren't keen to operate immediately,' McGregor says. 'The surgeon must have looked at Adrian's knee and thought perhaps with doing his weights and his knee exercises, it would be all right.'

The worst thing about being injured was those long mornings in the claustrophobic gym at the Cliff doing those tedious strengthening exercises – your quadriceps, your hamstrings – while team-mates were kicking balls around the training pitch, building up towards their next match. The grim, lonely, interminable afternoons in digs were the same as ever, but now there was not even a reward at the end of the week. 'It was even harder being in that environment, in digs, when you were injured,' Craig Lawton says. 'Half of the lads would be off to a reserve game on the Saturday. Others would be off with the A or B team. You would be left on your own. You would be in the gym all week with nothing to show for it.'

As Ben Thornley says, recalling his own grim battle with a cruciate ligament injury a few years later, 'the gym at the Cliff didn't have any views because the windows were right at the top and you couldn't see out of them. There's not a lot of air in there and you're in there on your own and the end is just nowhere in sight and you just feel . . . rubbish.'

Adrian Doherty hated it. He longed to get away from the training ground, back to the digs to read or write, or to go into town, but he must have been doing something right with his rehabilitation. According to his medical file, by 10 October he was back into graded training and things were felt to be progressing 'quite well' as he gradually stepped up his recovery programme with a view to getting back on the pitch and trying to make up for an awful lot of lost time.

There are two things Ian Brunton distinctly remembers about watching Manchester United's B team take on Marine Youth on 7 December 1991. He remembers that Paul Scholes, a first-year apprentice, scored four goals. And he remembers it was the game when Adrian Doherty made his long-awaited comeback from injury – with catastrophic results.

'We had heard a rumour that Doherty would be playing and I was delighted that his woes were apparently behind him and he was back playing football,' Brunton says. 'But even though United won and a little lad called Scholes scored four, I recall thinking Doherty was well off the pace of the game when it kicked off. He looked a shadow of the player I had seen previously. That is not unusual with a player in his first game after a very long layoff, but I also thought his running style wasn't the same. I thought his gait had changed.'

Disaster struck. Doherty's knee gave way again and he hobbled off in agony, this time in no doubt that something very serious had happened. He felt helpless. Nine and a half months had passed since he was first injured. He had heard one diagnosis after another. Already there had been worries that, with the summer signing Andrei Kanchelskis proving a revelation on the right wing and Ryan Giggs now firmly established on the left, the door to the first-team squad was closing. There had also been concerns that the damage to his knee might rob him of his explosive pace and that he might not be the same player again. Doherty had spent long, torturous mornings in the treatment room and the gym, doing his rehab work – and for what? Another setback? More months of misery? Would he ever get back to fitness? He was not just back to square one. He was in a far, far worse position than he had been before. The light at the end of the tunnel had been that of an oncoming train.

Brian McGillion, by now among the Strabane exiles studying in Manchester, remembers that as a dark night. 'He told me he was going out,' McGillion says. 'I told him I didn't think it was a good idea, the mood he was in. He said, "Look, I'm going out. You're either coming with me or you're not." I thought if I didn't go out with him, he would go out into town on his own and I didn't want that to happen. So I went with him.

'We went to some posh bar on Deansgate. We were fish out of water, both of us. He wasn't there for the *craic*. He just wanted to get away from the football crowd or anyone who would mention football to him. Any time I tried to talk about it, he looked like he was ready to walk out. He already had a big issue coming back, worrying that he was going to lose a yard of pace or whatever, and now this had happened. He was very despondent. It was the only time I remember him being like that in his life, but, to me, that was a turning point because I could just see the frustration coming out of him.'

This time there were no shades of grey with the diagnosis or the recommended course of action. On 18 December an arthroscopy showed damage to the anterior cruciate ligament in the right knee. Jonathan Noble was now unequivocal in recommending a surgical reconstruction of the knee, but procedure demanded a second opinion and, since Doherty was due to return home for Christmas, the decision was made to refer him to Joe McClelland, in Belfast. Adrian Doherty headed home with Noble's words ringing in his ears:

Unless it is attended to surgically, you will never play significant football again, probably even at a recreational level.

CHAPTER 17

'You feel worthless,' Gary Neville says. 'You feel like you have no value. You feel embarrassed to speak to your team-mates who are out there fighting for the club every week. You're going to the gym to do another hour on the bike and it's a lonely, lonely place.

'I can't think of any other profession or walk of life where you have to go to work every day when you're not physically able to do your job. I was out injured for over a year towards the end of my Manchester United career. At the training ground, all the players would park around the back of the building. After two or three months out, I started parking around the front just so I wouldn't have to talk to anyone, just to get away from being asked 300 times a day, "How is it? Is it getting better?" Now, if that's how I felt at thirty-two, as the captain of Manchester United, having been there sixteen years, having made 500-plus appearances, with my family all around me, and I was parking in a different car park so I could avoid my team-mates, I can only imagine what it must be like for a young player away from home in that situation. And if it's in your development years, where you've got younger players catching up with you, overtaking you, that must be a very lonely situation. Did Adrian Doherty feel that? I can't say because he was a couple of years above me and I didn't know him well, but I do know it's extremely hard to keep your spirits up in that situation.'

Just as he recalls the first time he clapped eyes on Doherty, daunted by his brilliance during an FA Youth Cup game, Neville remembers the day that news swept the Cliff of what seemed like another brutal blow to the winger's hopes. 'There was a really sombre atmosphere around the place when that injury reoccurred,' the former Manchester United and England defender says. 'It really reverberated around the club when someone did their cruciate. It was the most feared injury in football at the time. Once the reoccurrence happened, you knew Adrian would be lucky a) to get back to the standard he was before, b) to get to the standard that was good enough to make a career at Manchester United and c) possibly to make any career as a professional footballer.'

Neville's assessment calls to mind three different players and three different characters who have suffered cruciate knee ligament damage in the cause of Manchester United during the Premier League era. The third group would include the talented young winger Ben Thornley, who had an extremely bright future until disaster struck in a reserve match against Blackburn Rovers in April 1994. Thornley recovered sufficiently to have a professional career, but played just 264 minutes of Premier League football over his final four seasons with United before dropping down via Huddersfield Town, Aberdeen, Blackpool and Bury to non-league level by the time he was twenty-eight. The second group would include Wes Brown, who, arguably, went from a brilliant defender to a solid one after damaging cruciate ligaments for the second time at the age of twenty-three. And leading the first group, those who got back to their best, would be Roy Keane, who damaged his anterior cruciate ligament in September 1997 but returned for the start of the following season, in which he, in inspirational style, led United on the greatest campaign in their history. As for whether this simply came down to Keane's determination to beat the injury at all costs, this is a man who subsequently claimed to have been 'out on the piss every night' during his rehabilitation and 'doing stuff I shouldn't have been doing – not just dancing, but daft stuff like jumping over hedges and cars'. Keane was an incredible force as a footballer, but it was also his good fortune that by 1997 expertise surrounding cruciate ligament injuries and, accordingly, the success rate with surgery had increased considerably. Adrian Doherty was not so lucky.

There is no doubt Adrian Doherty, like Roy Keane, found himself 'doing stuff I shouldn't have been doing' to try to lessen the sense of desolation that Gary Neville describes. An awful lot of players would relate to that. In a *News of the World* interview in August 1993, Doherty mentioned that, after his injury, he 'got interested in other things – like drink'. Of his long, miserable fight against injury, he said, 'In the end, I got fed up with the whole thing. My head went a bit. I didn't think my career was over, but I was possibly a bit stupid.'

As several of his team-mates put it, Doherty 'liked a pint of Guinness'. He was an outsider in so many ways at Manchester United, but, by developing a taste for the black stuff, he found greater acceptance among his team-mates. For as long as he was showing his face every now and then, having a few pints with the other lads at the Priory Arms or even in town, he would not get the misfit treatment.

Ultimately, though, Doherty's idea of a great night out – go to a spit-and-sawdust pub, see a band, enjoy the *craic*, get the guitar out – was rather different to theirs. 'He wouldn't come out to nightclubs or bars if the rest of the lads were going out on a Saturday night,' Craig Lawton says. 'He would go some-where where there was live music playing.'

Doherty was already regarded by all at the Cliff as 'dif-ferent' – different clothes, different accent, different interests, different friends. And because he let his hair down in different ways and in different circles, away from the herd, there was a tendency to view his 'refuelling' hab-its differently too, particularly when framed retrospectively in the context of his failure to return from injury.

According to his team-mate Colin Telford, one of the few United players with whom he made a genuine connec-tion, Doherty liked to 'go out on his own for a couple of pints sometimes', accompanied only by whatever he was reading or writing at the time. Telford understood that his team-mate was simply looking to get away from the foot-ball crowd, to get a bit of peace and quiet and to unwind. But at a club where a persistent drinking culture in the early 1990s was collective – 'team bonding sessions that [Bryan Robson] would clear with the manager,' according to Lee Sharpe, 'having lunch at two o'clock, drinking all day, ending up in some pub or club' – others found it odd that Doherty should leave the digs on his own and walk into a pub or get the bus into town, guitar over his shoulder, whether he was going to Manchester Central Library, the Corn Exchange, the New Troubadour Club, an unfamiliar pub or anywhere else. 'He would walk to Lower Broughton Road and jump on the bus,' Telford says. 'He would be back at digs before 9 p.m., in his room, and you wouldn't hear from him.'

In the course of extensive interviews, on and off the record, with Doherty's friends and associates from Strabane, Manchester or any of the places where he lived subsequently, the most extreme story anyone could come up with about alcohol was this amused recollection from Telford. 'He rang me at the digs one night to tell me he had managed to drink ten pints of Guinness for the first time in his life,' Telford says with, considerable affection. 'Then he told me he was going to hang out with some tramps and chat to them, which, as far as I know, he did.'

Drinking ten pints in a night is not behaviour that dieticians or indeed Alex Ferguson would have recommended, but neither would it have put him among United's premier boozers even in the post-McGrath era. 'There was still a drinking culture at the time,' Telford says. 'The rest of us were all going out drinking together, chasing women. From memory, Doc would have come out with us once or twice, but he wasn't one for the disco bars.'

As for whether going out on his own, away from his team-mates, meant Doherty was some kind of forlorn loner, drowning his sorrows, that is not how his closer friends at United remember him. 'Definitely not,' Keith Gillespie says. 'You do have ups and downs, particularly when you've had bad injury problems and you're away from home, but Doc wasn't the depressed type. He was happy-go-lucky. He was a laid-back character.'

'I never remember him expressing any frustration,' Telford says. 'He was having fun. He was a funny wee bollix. I think, in his head, he was having the best time ever.'

On 2 January 1992 Adrian Doherty travelled to Belfast with his father to be examined by Joe McClelland. The surgeon noted there was still puffiness around the knee and recommended that Doherty come back for further assessment a couple of weeks later. In the meantime, he spelt out to the young Manchester United footballer that the injury was extremely serious and that, even in the event of an operation, there was genuine doubt about his prospects of a full recovery.

'I remember him as a very pleasant young man who struck me as being very motivated to get back to playing football again,' McClelland says. 'My feeling at the time was that, with the injury he had, it was going to be difficult for him to get back to the sort of level of professional football he had been at.'

The operation took place at McClelland's Belfast surgery on 17 February 1992, six days short of a year since Doherty first suffered ligament damage in his right knee. Upon removing the stitches eleven days later, McClelland noted that the wounds were healing nicely and that it appeared so far to be a fairly uneventful recovery, but that there was little indication as to how stable or strong the knee would feel in six months' time. Meanwhile, Doherty was sent back to Strabane, not Manchester, with a warning that the road back towards fitness – or some semblance of fitness – would be a long and difficult one. Alex Ferguson told the *Derry Journal* that Doherty could stay at home for as long as he wished.

The instructions, whether from Jonathan Noble or Jim McGregor in Manchester or from McClelland in Belfast, were always about building up strength in the muscles around the knee. But how was Doherty to do that without a gym or professional supervision? The Doherty family did not have a gym at home, or indeed room for one, so Adrian's father, Jimmy, went out to a local hardware store to get some sandbags to help with the resistance work. 'Can you believe that?' he says. 'How prehistoric can you get?'

Giuliano Maiorana, Doherty's fellow cruciate ligament victim, also recalls resorting to improvisation in his rehab. 'My dad used to buy Italian papers and we read an article about this Italian skier who had done her cruciate and they were explaining in the paper the things you should do to strengthen your knees afterwards,' he says. 'I used to do those exercises all the time, just with this article out of the paper. Copying exercises from something you'd read in the paper. That's something you would do if you played on a Sunday morning, isn't it?'

The letter sent by Maurice Watkins to the Doherty family states that, following further examination by McClelland, Adrian returned to Manchester to commence a supervised rehabilitation programme on 1 April 1992. McClelland's observation to Noble was that the operation had gone well.

Jim McGregor's recollection is less positive, though he was not willing, years later, to support Jimmy Doherty's suspicion that the operation was a failure. 'It wasn't a success,' McGregor, United's former physiotherapist, says. 'All I would say is that it wasn't a success.'

Gary Neville spoke of how an eighteen-month battle against career-threatening injury made him feel 'worthless', like he had 'no value'. Neville's life was dominated by football and by his role as an emblem of the club he adored. Adrian Doherty was not like that. The take-it-or-leave-it attitude to which he and others have referred might have been exaggerated considerably, but it seems clear the combination of a laid-back character and a rare depth and breadth of other interests – both social and intellectual – helped to lessen the anguish that would be felt by any teenager in his situation.

Instead of being on the fast track to the United first team, Doherty was on a treadmill, going nowhere. In a literal sense, he was not even on a treadmill. Apart from the few weeks leading up to that ill-fated comeback attempt, his daily routine had taken him little further than the weights machines in the gym, doing the same exercises day after day.

Doherty claimed in that *News of the World* interview in 1993 to have got 'fed up with the whole thing'. It would be entirely understandable if, far more than Neville, he felt 'worthless'. So if he felt worthless as a footballer, how was he to retain a sense of value as a human being? By going out and having a few drinks, having a laugh, telling himself and others that there were more important things than football? Yes. By sitting in his bedroom at the digs, reading and writing? Yes. He might by now have abandoned *The Adventures of Humphrey and Bodegard*, but that 1991/2 season was when, with his football ambitions so seriously damaged, he threw himself into his most prolific period of writing songs and poetry – some of them dark, most of them whimsical, clever and in some cases very amusing. If you were to try to bestow autobiographical meaning on his poem 'The Lost Soul' and his song 'Desolation', which speak of turmoil, then it would be wrong to dismiss the soaring, jocular optimism of 'By the Powers', 'An Oblivious History' and others. His songs and poems do not come across as those of someone writing about the wretchedness of his plight, but rather of someone writing to escape that wretchedness. Adrian Doherty was determined not to be defined by his job or by the injury that had put his career in such grave peril. He knew he was far more than that.

By the Powers

By the powers that have been bestowed upon my gracious head
There is nothing I cannot do, there is no talent I do not possess
No problem I cannot remedy, no distance I cannot travel
No task I cannot accomplish, no enigma I cannot unravel

I possess immaculate prowess in saying that which should be left
  unsaid
I can walk upon the waters, I can communicate with the dead
I can do anything which seems impossible, I am perpetually
  inspired
I can catch bullets in my teeth whenever they're getting fired

So just to tell you the truth, I am just an all-round good guy
And I can't even help being so fabulous, no matter how hard I try

Oh, of all the great and renowned men all down through the
centuries
Never before or never again will the world see anyone quite like
me, quite like me.

Leo Cussons laughs, almost uncontrollably, upon being informed that Adrian Doherty's team-mates at Manchester United describe him as quiet and shy. 'Really? Oh my god!' he says. 'You could say a lot of things about him, but . . . quiet? Hahaha. What a dark horse. Oh my god.'

So how would Cussons describe the professional footballer whom he and others on the Manchester music scene came to know as 'McHillbilly' as they played in a short-lived band called the Mad Hatters? 'Brilliant,' he says. 'I don't know anything about football, so I can't comment on that, but he was one of those extraordinarily talented individuals you come across very rarely in life.'

Cussons cannot put a month or even a year to when he first met Doherty, a couple of years his junior, at an open-mic night. He suspects it was late 1991. Doherty performed a couple of songs, Cussons congratulated him and the pair of them got talking, initially about their shared admiration for Bob Dylan and Tom Waits before moving on to their literary and philosophical interests. 'And he was one of the most fascinating, brilliant people I had ever met,' Cussons says.

Sooner or later, between conversations that covered subjects as diverse as Dante, Edgar Allan Poe, Carlos Castaneda, the Koran, transcendentalism and the meaning of life, they talked about more basic stuff like what they were doing in Manchester. Cussons was a well-travelled aspiring musician from the Isle of Man, a descendant of the family who owned the company that manufactured Imperial Leather soap, and says he was in Manchester to 'seek fame and fortune – that Dick Whittington thing'. Doherty mentioned his background in Strabane and hesitantly revealed he was a professional footballer for Manchester United. He used a stage name, McHillbilly, because it would not go down well at work if people found out. In town, he would be McHillbilly or, in informal circumstances, Aidan rather than Adrian. Aidan was not much of a stage name, in truth; half of his team-mates at United called him that anyway, as an alternative to 'Doc', deeming 'Adrian' too much of a mouthful.

The pair of them met each week at the New Troubadour Club and would both join the list of aspiring artists for the open-mic sessions. Cussons would do his stuff and then Doherty would do his – again almost always sticking to the less serious end of his ever-increasing repertoire – and then they would stick around afterwards, play some pool and have a few drinks with Chas Rigby and 'Seldom Seen Kid' Bryan Glancy.

One week Cussons and Doherty decided two heads were better than one. They called themselves the Mad Hatters – and then they got a third member for good measure. 'Yes, a guy called Vimto,' Cussons says with a laugh. 'He was a fair bit older than us and he was near enough a tramp, but he was quite a good musician so he came along too.

'I've got one or two recordings somewhere – and that's not even the good stuff. Aidan was enormously talented, you know. Things like 'Barley and Oats', another one about mice. They're astonishingly original and clever. It was close to genius, some of it.'

Doherty loved songwriting. He also loved performing and how it felt to transmit his energy to an audience. When his football career looked so promising back in early 1991, he told both the *Derry Journal* and *The Shankill Skinhead* of the buzz he had felt when playing in the FA Youth Cup games at Old Trafford rather than the usual Lancashire League fixtures at the Cliff or Littleton Road. 'I love the crowd,' he said. 'I think it makes me feel better.'

Now it was a different kind of crowd that Doherty was entertaining in order to get that feeling. 'We would walk into a pub and ask if we could play and very often they would say yes we could,' Cussons says.

You mean obscure little pubs, off the beaten track? 'No, the exact opposite,' Cussons says. 'We used to haunt all around that part of Manchester where there's the art-house and the Palace Theatre, basically that whole stretch up to the university back. We used to go into pubs there and Aidan would sing – not cover versions, his own songs – and people would go completely wild. He would be standing there with his guitar and they would just love it.'

Some might call Doherty's approach unconventional, eccentric or even destructive as he threw himself into his music, his poetry and his other pursuits, drinking more than the odd pint of Guinness along the way, at a time when his football career was unravelling. Having considered the alternative, which was to throw himself, physically and emotionally, into what seemed an increasingly forlorn bid to salvage a career that was bringing no end of anguish, others might conclude that his approach was quite inspirational. Rather than be left feeling worthless, Adrian Doherty, at a time of rising misery in his professional life, managed to find enjoyment, appreciation and, critically, self-worth elsewhere.

CHAPTER 18

Gareth Doherty awoke with a start. Someone was trying to climb through the bedroom window of his student house in Salford. Oh f***. What should he do? He looked around in a panic. Oh f***. And then he heard his brother's voice. 'Sorry to wake you, man,' Adrian Doherty whispered. 'Can I borrow your suitcase?'

A suitcase? In the middle of the night? Adrian was bluntly told to come back in the morning. 'No, I need it now,' he said. 'I'm heading to New York. The bus goes in a few hours.'

When he awoke again a few hours later on 13 May 1992, his twenty-first birthday, Gareth Doherty wondered if he had dreamed it. But no, his suitcase really had gone and so too, it seemed, had his brother. What the hell was going on?

'It's a wee bit hazy with the passage of time,' Brian McGillion says, 'but we were out in Manchester one night and I was saying I had to be up early because I had to get the bus to London for a university trip to the Bank of England. Shortly after that, Adrian says, "Peedge [McGillion's nickname], can I get a lift with youse?" "Why? Where are you going?" "I was thinking about . . . Do you fancy coming to America with me?" "What do you mean? When are

219

you going?" "I'm going to go tomorrow. I was thinking I could take that bus down to London with youse boys. What do you reckon?" I laughed and thought nothing more of it.'

McGillion was astonished to see Adrian Doherty boarding the bus the next morning, borrowed suitcase and all. 'He was still trying to get me to go with him,' McGillion recalls. 'I remember saying to him, "Why are you going? What are you going to do?" "Why not, Peedge? Why not go?" He got off the bus, made his way to the airport and I assume he bought a ticket there. And I think really it was just to get away from everything that was happening – the football, the injury, the rehabilitation. It was just an escape.'

'No, no, it wasn't that. We went to New York to try to get signed up,' Lee Cussons says. 'We weren't there as tourists. It was – seriously – to get signed up. We were thinking the audiences would be more appreciative in New York than they were in Manchester. I know that sounds terribly naive, but, looking back, I think they were. There was a certain wow factor.

'Aidan had built quite a good reputation in Manchester, but we had played in one or two bars in the Northern Quarter and not been asked back, so he decided we would be appreciated more in New York. We had talked about it in theory, so it wasn't *totally* spontaneous, but then that one night he just said: "Let's do this tomorrow."

'And yes, that's right, there was this tour bus going down to London and he insisted he was going to get that and make his own way. And this was going to be very complicated because I couldn't leave for another couple of days, we didn't have any accommodation – we were going to try and stay with friends of mine – and we didn't have mobile phones, so I didn't know how on earth we were going to make it work. I managed to get him a number for a friend of mine in New York and off he went, although, Aidan being Aidan, he actually ended up arriving later than me despite setting off three days earlier.'

How come? 'He called from London – either Heathrow or Gatwick – and he said he had bought his ticket but the flight wasn't until the next day or maybe even the day after that,' Cussons says. 'And it involved some kind of change-over at Shannon, in Ireland, so I'm pretty sure he ended up spending a night there too. I don't mean in hotels; as far as I know he spent these two or three nights in the airports themselves. And then of course there was that business with the shoes.'

The 'business with the shoes' has become another of the Adrian Doherty legends. Everyone remembers that his arrival in New York was in some way held up by the state of his trainers, to which somebody somewhere took fierce exception. Everyone is in agreement that, as a consequence of being stripped of his battered old trainers, he ended up replacing them with a pair of steel-toecapped boots – 'the ugliest boots I've ever seen,' according to his cousin Karen Ferry – which he insisted on wearing, to the hilarity of friends and team-mates alike, for at least a couple of years thereafter.

What nobody is quite sure of is where those steel-toecapped boots came from. Leo Cussons thinks Doherty was given them after someone – possibly the caretaker at one of the New York apartment blocks where they stayed – took pity on him due to the condition of his trainers. Karen Ferry thinks her cousin might have found them abandoned in a subway station in New York. The most popular, appealing version is that officials at Shannon Airport objected to Doherty's scruffy appearance and, after a rigorous cross-examination, including a call to Old Trafford to verify his claim that he was a Manchester United footballer, only allowed him onto American soil on the condition that he replaced the trainers with some footwear from lost property. Take your pick.

As for 'Vimto', he was not part of the 'Mad Hatters take Manhattan' trip – 'probably because he was pretty much a tramp,' Cussons says. A shame, really. He might have got some new footwear out of it.

Adrian Doherty's parents were alarmed when he excitedly called them, a few weeks off his nineteenth birthday, to tell them he was on his way to New York. This, after all, was a time when, Manhattan was still notorious as a hotbed of crime. Who was he going with? His friend Leo. Where would he stay? Leo knows some people. Is this arranged? No, but it will be fine. Did he have a contact number in New York? He had one somewhere, but he would call to let them know he was safe once he had found his bearings. Would he get in touch with his cousin Karen, in Boston, when he got there? Yes, good idea. What was he going to do for money? He had money in his UK bank account and a few dollar bills, but he wasn't sure; maybe they could look into some way of getting some of that money to him, perhaps via Karen. What was he planning to do in New York? Play a few gigs, go to gigs, hang out in Greenwich Village, East Village, all that great stuff. What about his career at Manchester United? It was the summer; he was just going on holiday, same as all the other lads would be. How long would he be in New York? He didn't know yet. 'We're worried, Adrian. We don't think this is a good idea.' 'It will be cool, trust me.'

21 May 1992

Sorry for not phoning (if I haven't managed to get through by now). The phones in New York are very awkward. Having a really good time. I'm staying in East Village, which is near Greenwich Village. Plan to phone Karen tonight + to go Friday to spend week or so there. New York very busy + strange – an experience. The sun shines brightly most of the time – people are more friendly than expected. Everything is good + if you could send that money on to Karen, would be most grateful. Cost of things is more than I thought – but well worth it. To go here is totally different than anything else. Have been down Macdougal St – all those places – v. groovy.

Multigym expensive. Alcohol cheap. Some people are offensive. Others fun heaps.

Leo Cussons confesses he does not how long he and Adrian Doherty (alias S. McHillbilly) spent in New York in the summer of 1992. Upwards of three weeks, possibly around four, no more than six, he suggests. They had the time of their lives, even if many of the memories seem to blur into one. 'It was wonderful,' he says. 'It was that whole East Village music scene we had read about from the 1960s. We would sit around in bars, talking about music, and Aidan would be writing songs. He loved it there.

'We were staying in all these different places, crashing on people's floors, sleeping on sofas. We started off staying with some friends I had met while travelling in Europe a few years earlier. Then we would stay somewhere else. Everyone used to congregate around this square in the East Village and each night there would be a different place to go, a different place to play. And we would go out and play in the East Village.'

What level are we talking about? Playing in bars? Busking in the street? 'Everything,' he says. 'We would play in the street, at open-mic events, at this place called Gargoyle Mechanique, which is quite well known in the East Village, and various other places, the names of which escape me.

'You had all these people desperately trying to succeed, desperately trying to get attention, and some of them were very talented. Some had great big record labels, Capitol Records and so on, and they were touring, and these were the ones who were coming up and saying – mostly to Aidan, I have to say – "That was amazing, that was amazing." I got on well with people out there, but, like in Manchester, Aidan was very clearly the star. I was just his sidekick. Everywhere he went, he had an impact. People loved listening to him. And not just in New York but apparently in Boston too.'

It was just like the movies. The police sirens were blaring, the lights were flashing red and blue. The handcuffs were out. On his first night in Boston, Adrian Doherty found himself sitting in the back of a patrol car, heading to the police station.

He was there for hours that night, waiting with his cousin Karen Ferry. Their driver had been pulled over by highway patrol and found to be over the drink-drive limit. Eventually the driver emerged, to be told by Doherty, 'That was brilliant. Is it like this every night?'

It had been a few years since Ferry had seen her cousin, but, she says, 'he was exactly the same Adrian as back in Strabane, even the same haircut. My room-mates loved him.'

Doherty had come to Boston alone, leaving Leo Cussons in the East Village. 'He brought his guitar with him,' Ferry says. 'In the daytime I was working, so he used to take off to Harvard Square. He loved it there, with all the buskers on the street. He always came across so shy, but he had the confidence to go into these bars, listen to the musicians and ask if he could go on and sing or play with them. And they would let him. Some of them asked him to come back the next day. He would always come home for dinner, though. We always said he must have smelt the potatoes being peeled.'

Karen Ferry had heard from her brother Sean about Doherty's football exploits, but was only loosely aware at the time that his progress at Manchester United had been interrupted by a knee injury. She remembers being given short shrift when she tried to ask how it was going. 'He didn't want to talk about football,' she says. 'It was all music with him. That seemed to be his number one thing.'

*

After the home comforts of Boston (the odd brush with the law aside), it was back to the raw creative energy of New York's East Village. Adrian Doherty and Leo Cussons had explored Greenwich Village too – 'v. groovy', as the postcard said – but they had found it to be overrun by tourists.

They played in Brooklyn too. It was not just in bars or in the streets, but at parties, in people's flats or gardens. Cussons recalls joints being smoked and passed around – 'pure weed'. Did the off-duty footballer partake? 'No, he definitely didn't do drugs,' Cussons says. 'He would drink, certainly, but not drugs. He would sometimes try to smoke cigarettes, but for some reason his lungs wouldn't take it.'

As a professional footballer, Doherty's 'otherness' made him an outsider in a conformist society. In the East Village, the only way to fit in was to be different, quirky, original and eccentric. And there was no doubt that, as McHillbilly, he was all of those things. He was not Bob Dylan, but he was turning heads and drawing plaudits.

'He didn't have a great or smooth playing style, but he just had this energy and huge talent that people really responded to,' Cussons says. 'He was like this fireball. And he had an extraordinary ability to write songs. He really made an impact. He would be doing this thing which was almost a rap, half-shouting, and people would respond to him.'

Along with his parents, brothers and sister, Doherty's friends from Strabane talk of receiving postcards in which he raved about his trip. 'I remember him saying he loved the East Village,' Mick Winters says. 'The whole experience really floated his boat. He loved the poetry, the music and the performing.'

Dee Devenney, Kevin Doherty and Niall Dunphy all recall stories about their friend walking, oblivious as ever, through dangerous areas of the Bronx. And they remember receiving postcards in which he mentioned the names of some of the characters he had encountered, such as – always the same names – Evil Jim Friendly and Jimmy Teaspoon.

'I don't know how many of these bands that were there at the time made it, but they seemed very talented to me,' Cussons says. 'But so was Aidan. There were a lot of people there who were making a living and he was having as big an impact as any of them. He wasn't what you would call a technical singer or guitarist, but the words he wrote were brilliant and a lot of people there recognised that.

'One of the guys on the scene at that time, in these same circles, was called Paleface. He hasn't made it big-time but he has been able to make a good living out of it. He was one of those who was very impressed by Aidan. He might remember Aidan – if you could track him down.'

Paleface (real name unknown) is an American singer-songwriter who, while somewhat underexposed commercially, was a major mover in the East Village music scene of that time. It was there, in 1990, that he took under his wing the artist who would come to be known as Beck. Paleface and Beck were room-mates and went to open-mic nights together. Indeed, Beck credits him as being a great inspiration in a career that has brought multiple awards and platinum albums. Paleface, teetotal now, confesses to having almost drunk himself to death by partying too hard through the 1990s. The chances of him remembering Adrian Doherty, who was on the East Village scene for a month or so in the summer of 1992, seemed rather remote.

'Yes, I do remember him,' Paleface says by telephone. 'I often can't remember who I played with last week, but I remember him – although I remember him as McHillbilly. That's right, isn't it?'

Wow. It is. What do you remember? 'I remember his music and I remember liking it,' he says. 'His stuff was different. And at the time, things were changing in the city. All the old stuff was going out. There were all these little pop-up places to play. You could play two or three in one night. You would go there and play and then you would go to the next one and the next. The audiences were also looking for something at that time, which happens sometimes in New York. He used to make a good impression.

'My favourite memory of him isn't actually connected with his music. A group of us found a contemporary art party to crash somewhere on Eighth Avenue. The guy who was running the party was quizzing us about who we were and what we were doing there. And Adrian/McHillbilly – in this thick accent of his – started singing the scarecrow song, "If I Only Had a Brain". It was a classic moment. He had a lot of balls to do that. We were very soon escorted out of the party.'

Did he, as Leo Cussons insists, have a genuine flair for it? 'Yes, I'd say so,' Paleface says. 'He never got to the stage of giving me a CD or anything, but I enjoyed hanging out with him and enjoyed his music. He was one of the good artists. People move on so fast, so I don't think I would have remembered him if he wasn't one of those artists who made an impact music-wise.'

There were traces of 'Evil Jim Friendly' found on Google – last heard of playing bass guitar for a New York artist named Billy Syndrome – but he could not be contacted directly. As for 'Jimmy Teaspoon', that pseudonym appears to have been dropped before he had time to leave a digital footprint. More is the pity.

At some point in June 1992, Adrian Doherty recognised it was time to return to England. Pre-season training at Manchester United was looming and, those expensive multigym visits notwithstanding, a month in New York was unlikely to have done wonders for his recovery from the knee injury. 'Football hardly came up in conversation at all because I didn't have any interest in it and I don't think he had any interest in talking about it,' Leo Cussons says. 'He was just throwing everything into his music.'

They did not get signed, but Cussons still feels they might have made a breakthrough had they tried a different approach. 'Aidan was talented enough to get signed up,' he says. 'If you could have controlled that talent or tamed it, so that he had been just a little bit softer and so that people would be thinking, "Oh, so he's not *totally* crazy," then someone might well have said, "I can take this and work with it and publish these songs." And in fact, if we had managed it better and if I hadn't been a complete moron at the time, the smart thing for me to do would have been to help his music because he was a great talent.'

New York was an escape in some respects, but it had

been worth it. If you can make it there, you can make it anywhere, as the old song goes. They had not 'made it' – the Mad Hatters did not quite take Manhattan – but they had had so much fun trying. Now it was back to the humdrum of life as a professional footballer at Manchester United.

CHAPTER 19

On the treatment table in a crowded Manchester United dressing room, Ryan Giggs was receiving a rub-down in front of a film crew. 'Here I am, massaging the superstar's calf, if that's what you'd call it,' the physio Jim McGregor declared. 'I've seen a larger muscle . . . on a wee sparrow.' Giggs smiled and performed a mock Mr Universe pose. At that moment, Adrian Doherty walked in looking forlorn, wearing a baggy brown shirt and carrying a piece of kit, which he laid down on a bench. Whether conscious of the camera crew or not, he turned around and, scratching his head, walked out again. If Giggs was very much the young superstar as United closed in on their first league championship in more than a quarter of a century, his fellow prodigy from the youth team was, more than ever, the odd man out.

That vignette appears five minutes into *Captain's Log*, Steve Bruce's video diary of the final weeks of the glorious spring of 1993, in which United became champions of England for the first time since 1967. One might be tempted to dismiss it as an irrelevance had it not been flagged up by Doherty's brother Gareth, who says he had never seen Adrian looking so lonely as he appeared during that unintended cameo. 'It's heartbreaking because Giggs, the superstar, is there getting massaged and Adrian has gone from being one of the two stars of the youth team to being a shadow,' Gareth says. 'He looks like a ghost in that clip.'

That is in keeping with Phil Neville's recollections. Neville was a sixteen-year-old looking forward to beginning his apprenticeship later that year, but he was already a familiar face around the dressing rooms at the Cliff. His main memories of Doherty are of him 'ghosting in and out of rooms'. Unlike his older brother, Neville never saw Doherty play prior to the injury, but he was aware of the expectation and excitement that had surrounded him just a couple of years earlier. 'Back then there were three young players everyone used to talk about – Ryan Wilson, as he was at the time, Jules Maiorana and Adrian Doherty,' Neville says. 'But from when I joined the club, because I'm that bit younger, all I really remember of Doc is him coming in and looking sad. He looked gutted. When you get an injury like he had, at that age, it must be so, so hard.'

Others remember Adrian Doherty's final season at United differently. 'In digs, you would wake up in the morning and the first thing you would hear is him singing in his room,' the Northern Irish defender Pat McGibbon says. 'He would be singing all day. That was one of the things about Doc. To have been so close to the first team and then the way things worked out, that must have been very disappointing for him, but he was always singing. He always seemed happy.'

Doherty's hardships, though, were not lost on the young man whom McGregor quite rightly called 'the superstar'. 'It was tough for Doc,' Giggs says. 'You could see pretty quickly it was going to be a struggle with his rehab and with the complications he had with the injury. Especially with being the type of player he was – quick and dynamic – and with that type of injury, you could see he was going to find it hard to get back from it.'

Did the pair ever talk in later times? 'We were both quiet, to be honest,' Giggs says. 'It was probably painful when we tried to have a conversation. "How's it going?" "OK. How's it going with you?" "OK." I remember seeing him out in Manchester in the day once. I was shopping and he was walking along the street on the other side and we had a quick chat. I don't think anyone at the club was really close to him, but everyone liked him. He didn't have a bad bone in his body.'

For his first eighteen months at Manchester United, Adrian Doherty, along with Ryan Giggs, had been a rare ray of sunshine at a club where storm clouds appeared a constant feature. The only clouds over the Cliff now were those threatening to darken Doherty's days unless he could somehow keep feelings of self-pity at bay.

At first, in the year or so after his injury, the buzz around Doherty had quietened to a hum. Now it had been reduced to a terribly awkward silence and the excited chatter around the club was all about Gary Neville, John O'Kane, Chris Casper, Nicky Butt, David Beckham, Paul Scholes, Keith Gillespie, Ben Thornley, Robbie Savage and others. These were the players who, along with Giggs, delivered United's long-awaited FA Youth Cup triumph in May 1992. After so many false dawns, this, at last, promised to be a golden generation for United. As the club's then reserve-team coach Bryan 'Pop' Robson puts it, 'It was such an outstanding group that anybody else outside of it, either before or after, would be swept out of the way.'

One by one, those youngsters were allowed to dip their toes into the world of first-team football. Between September 1992 and January 1993, Gary Neville, Beckham, Butt and Gillespie all made their senior debuts. This was the big time to which Doherty had been so close a couple of years earlier. It was usually just a fleeting taste, an opportunity to sample the thrill and the pressures of playing for United and to intensify their focus on their long-term progression. O'Kane, Casper, Scholes and Thornley would all have to wait a little longer, but, to Doherty, it was increasingly clear which way this was going.

'Especially coming from Northern Ireland myself, I knew all about Doc, but all the lads in our year knew what a great prospect he had been, how he had been in the first-team squad at sixteen and how badly the injury had knocked him back,' Gillespie says. 'He was still pretty happy-go-lucky in general, just getting on with things, but rehab can be very tedious. We would look into the gym and he would be doing his leg weights every day. It's not exactly fun. And the truth of the matter is that, in the time he had been out, we had come along and overtaken him. I'm sure he realised that. If you're injured for a long time at that age, younger players get ahead of you. That's just what happens.'

In January 1993, when Doherty was finally approaching a comeback, Gillespie, a fellow right-winger as well as a fellow countryman, made his first-team debut in an FA Cup tie against Bury at Old Trafford. Gillespie took the opportunity, scoring the second goal in a 2–0 win. Now it was his turn for the inevitable 'new George Best treatment'. His breakthrough, along with talk of recasting young Beckham as a right-sided midfielder, served to underline the increasing hopelessness of Doherty's position as a nineteen-year-old winger who, after such a long layoff, was struggling to regain the speed, never mind the confidence, that had been his hallmark. Such scenarios can turn even the nicest young footballer bitter and cynical, but Gillespie encountered none of that from Doherty. 'Doc was delighted for me,' he recalls. 'There was no jealousy. That shows the character of the guy.'

The final season of Adrian Doherty's Manchester United career had begun in depressingly familiar circumstances as he was sent for reviews at the hands of Jonathan Noble, the club's orthopaedic surgeon, on 11 August 1992 and again a month later. The medical records note the surgeon's profound, persistent concern about Doherty's struggle to extend his knee fully. He was reminded of the importance of the muscle rehabilitation programme. It was the same exercises every day. Eighteen months on from the initial injury and there was still no real improvement.

There was another blow for Doherty when his friend and fellow Brenda's inmate Colin Telford departed for Raith Rovers in September 1992. 'Doc was struggling at the time I left,' Telford recalls. 'The injury wasn't going away. And while he kept having setbacks, breaking down, there were all these exceptional younger players starting to come through. It must have been extremely difficult for him. Maybe it was worse for him after I left because he wasn't close to many of the other lads. I lost contact with him, but to be honest I lost contact with pretty much everyone else at United too because, after the injury problems I had, I couldn't wait to get away. It wasn't a bed of roses there, you know, especially when you were injured.'

David Johnson, three years Doherty's junior, was the latest unhappy member of the cruciate ligament club at the Cliff. He spent time in digs with Doherty, but above all he remembers their long, lonely mornings together in the gym. 'It was me, Doc and Jules Maiorana. We had all done our cruciates,' Johnson says. 'It was just the three of us with Jim McGregor day after day, doing our rehab, doing our weights. It's amazing looking back when you see the facilities they have now. Back then we never even had a swimming pool. I was limited to pushing weights. I was with Michael Clegg [the former United defender, who later became strength and conditioning coach at Sunderland] recently. He said he remembered me smashing my legs on that machine every day trying to lift the heaviest weights I could, as high as I could. You wouldn't dream of doing that now.'

What was Doherty like in the gym? 'Doc just got on with it,' Johnson says. 'He didn't come in late or miss his treatment. But he had the worst injuries. Everyone knew how good he was. Everyone knew there was Ryan Giggs and there was also Adrian Doherty, who was going to be the same kind of amazing player once he got fit. But we never got to see him play.'

Demos

S. McHillbilly: Bizarre black humour from a quite unique act. McHillbilly sounds like a psychopathic singing version of

John Cole, the BBC political correspondent. Add a touch of John Hegley, Wild Man Fischer and Loudon Wainwright III, and you're still in the dark. I liked the rap number 'Waiting to Cross the Road'.

(*City Life* magazine, November 1992)

Adrian Doherty never bothered to keep newspaper cuttings detailing his football exploits, but he kept that one. He was delighted with it, apparently. John Hegley is a performance poet and comedian; Wild Man Fischer was an eccentric and somewhat unhinged American songwriter, known for his early collaborations with Frank Zappa; Loudon Wainwright III, father of the arguably more famous Rufus, is an American songwriter and humorist. Doherty would never be mistaken for Bob Dylan, but he was playing, recording and performing for his own pleasure and satisfaction. If anybody else enjoyed it, that was a bonus.

As winter came, Adrian Doherty was finally given the go-ahead to leave the claustrophobic gym behind and return to the training pitches. It was progress at last, but nobody would try to suggest that in physical terms, let alone mentally, he was over the damage. 'The knee still wasn't straightening 100 per cent,' Jim McGregor says. 'He couldn't get a full extension. I remember putting my hand under his knee when it was supposed to be straight and saying to him, "If only we could get those five degrees in your knee." But because we couldn't get that, he still lacked a bit of power.'

Whatever the surgeon, McGregor or Doherty tried to

do, that extension just would not come. The chances of him regaining full mobility, speed and power seemed remote, but the time had come, at last, for him to pull on a pair of football boots again and do some running. David Johnson recalls that Doherty now ran with a slight limp. Then came the more serious test of whether the knee could withstand the twisting and turning that are basic requirements for a footballer. That was what had gone so horribly wrong with his comeback attempt the previous winter. The next step was to start ball-work – first a simple give-and-go, control-and-pass, building up to trying to strike a ball with some semblance of the aggression, confidence and power that had once come so naturally. Then, slowly, it would be back to full training with the reserve-team squad, now under the unfamiliar charge of Jim Ryan and Bryan 'Pop' Robson. Only once all of those significant physical hurdles were overcome could Doherty think about whether he was up to the rigours of another comeback in the Lancashire League.

Doherty made his return in a B-team match against Blackburn Rovers on 30 January 1993 – almost two years after his initial injury and thirteen months after that ill-fated comeback attempt against Marine's youth team. He was nineteen now and, when his name finally reappeared on the noticeboard with the weekend's team selections, his relief was tempered by another indication of how far he had fallen behind. The future of Manchester United was to be found that afternoon at the Cliff, where John O'Kane, Gary Neville, Chris Casper, Phil Neville, Keith Gillespie, Nicky Butt, David Beckham, Paul Scholes and Ben Thornley featured in the A team's

7–1 victory over Tranmere Rovers; Doherty, by contrast, was going to Blackburn with the B team with first-year apprentices such as Colin Murdock, Michael Appleton and Terry Cooke. If the players who would come to be known as the Class of '92 were in the A team, awaiting elevation, then Doherty, of the Class of '90, was in the B team with players from the lesser-known Class of '93. He lasted the full ninety minutes of a 2–2 draw, but it was described as a hesitant, rather than triumphant, return to action.

Two weeks later there was another inglorious outing for the B team, a 1–0 defeat away to Wigan Athletic A. Promotion to the A team followed for a home match against Rochdale reserves, but only as a second-half substitute in a line-up that included Gary Neville, Beckham and Butt. It was a similar story a week later, appearing as a substitute in the A team's 6–1 victory over Chester City. He came on in place of Scholes in the second half, but, much like a 36-year-old Bryan Robson, he must have felt out of place among a team full of young players who had grown up together through the apprentice ranks and who, in so many cases, would continue to flourish together in the first team. Doherty's first few steps back to competitive action were faltering, rather than fearless. As the other Bryan Robson – 'Pop', the reserve-team coach – puts it, he seemed 'withdrawn, nervous, so handicapped by the injuries'.

Gareth Doherty recalls that this period saw the emergence of 'a different Adrian, much calmer, much more mature'. He had moved out of Brenda's and into a flat in Cheetham

Hill, a couple of miles further out from the Cliff. This was when he began to cycle to training on a battered old bike, his team-mates gawping with bemused wonder from their flash cars as they passed him on the final stretch up Lower Broughton Road.

Later in the season he would move again, this time to Longsight, a rough-and-ready area a couple of miles south-east of Manchester city centre. He would cycle to meet his older brother in Rusholme or Hulme, but these days his social life did not go much beyond their regular afternoon sessions playing pool in the Gamecock, a pub remembered most fondly for the handwritten sign near the entrance, warning, 'No smackheads allowed.'

Gary McHugh, another Strabane exile studying in Manchester, remembers meeting Adrian and one of his mates for a drink one evening. 'We had been sitting there for a while when Adrian got up and went to the toilet and this mate of his, a student, a big lad from Sligo, turned to me and said, "I couldn't do that man's job,"' McHugh recalls. 'I figured Adrian must have told this lad something that wasn't entirely true, so I said, "What do you think he does?" He said, "He's a ratcatcher." I was in stitches. When I told him Adrian was a professional footballer at Manchester United, he couldn't believe it. He had known him for almost two years. To me, that typifies the kind of fella Adrian was. He wanted to be known and judged on his personality and who he was, rather than the job he did.'

Adrian's sense of humour remained intact, but his appetite for a night out was not what it had been a few months earlier. 'We would sometimes try to get him to join us on a night out, but he wasn't interested,' Gareth says. 'He might have a pint of Guinness, but that was that. He suddenly seemed mature – more mature than I was, as his older brother.'

That sounds like a very different Adrian Doherty to the 'fireball' Leo Cussons witnessed in New York the previous summer. Cussons had moved to London and Doherty had put the 'McHillbilly' persona, with all it entailed, to one side. He was re-evaluating, reassessing, looking to recapture whatever it was that had deserted him.

The Lost Soul

Lacking a sacred spark
I forage in the dark.
Woodenly I play my part
Yet persist, still, to act.

The spark came bright and pure.
Would to God it still were!
For life holds much allure,
When one's bright, when one's pure

Gone is my secret spark.
Its music did depart!
Lax and numb falls my heart,
Wanting its vital part.

The spark lost its lustre
First, from fuss and bluster
Vain learning did dust the
Sheen off its bright lustre

Whence has my sacred spark
Got to? Will it come back?
Can it its steps retract?
Life hurts! For its sad lack

Of. Devils play with it!
Vice runs away with it!
Still, I would save it yet.
This soul, then, pray for it!

Lacking a sacred spark,
I rummage in the dark.
In vain, do play my part
Till I can get it back.

CHAPTER 20

There is a danger in supposing that every poem and every song is based on the writer's own feelings or experiences, but 'The Lost Soul' is one poem that feels as if it might be based on what Adrian Doherty was going through in the two years after his Manchester United career took such a dramatic turn for the worse. His father, Jimmy, has often wondered what his son meant by the missing 'sacred spark'. Was it the loss of his enthusiasm for football or was it the loss of something deeper, such as his self-confidence or perhaps his faith, which had been so central to his life before he moved to Manchester? The 'Devils' that he mentions – are they the 'Red Devils' of Manchester United? Or was 'The Lost Soul' completely unrelated to how he, an individual generally described as happy-go-lucky, was feeling?

Adrian Doherty was certainly looking for something more in his life. On top of the countless hours spent writing music, poems and stories, his hunger for knowledge led him to read voraciously. Theology fascinated him. He lapsed as a Catholic early in his time in Manchester, but he had continued to explore the subject of religion with an intellectual rigour. 'He liked to know about things,' Geraldine Manning, his landlady in Levenshulme, says. 'I was always surprised he didn't get into Buddhism or something like that because that would have been his thing. He read books about it, but he read about everything.'

'He would spend hours and hours at Manchester [Central] Library,' Frank Manning says. 'If he wanted to find out about something, he would just go and find out.'

As Gerard Mullan relayed earlier, Doherty would read about anything and everything. He became intrigued by the writings of Carlos Castaneda, such as *The Teachings of Don Juan*, which told of the Peruvian-American author's experience of shamanism, whereby the practitioner reached altered states of mind through meditation. This would send Doherty off on another voyage of discovery, scouring the library or the bookshops at the Corn Exchange to find out more about shamanism, which would in turn lead him to something else. That is how Adrian Doherty liked to learn. It was a never-ending search for information and, increasingly, answers.

Doherty had always liked the idea of meditation. Everything he read made him like the idea more. He would try it in his room at Brenda's in the afternoons and evenings. It made him feel relaxed and unencumbered by the misery and hopelessness of life at the Cliff. He read about different kinds of meditation, about the philosophical conflict between religion and science, about Zoroastrianism, Gnosticism and Kabbalah. In his eagerness to learn more, he joined an esoteric group in Manchester, where he could discuss these subjects with others. One recurring theme was the pursuit of gnosis, or spiritual knowledge. This in turn led him to find out more about the quest for enlightenment. It did not just take his mind off what was happening in his football career. It unlocked doors in his mind. And every time he opened a door, Adrian Doherty wanted to find out where it would lead him.

'He went along to one of these esoteric groups and to a gnostic group,' Leo Cussons says. 'He was just eager to find out more about religion and where it came from. A lot of it was about the beginnings and roots of different religions. He wasn't into every aspect of it, by any means. There was plenty of it that he didn't care for at all, but the subject as a whole fascinated him. What really appealed to him was a) finding out more about religion and b) this business of trying to reach a higher level of consciousness, which I suppose is what these days is referred to as mindfulness.'

Thomas Woodward is an instructor at a gnostic group in west London. One of the first things he tells me is that there have been 'many different splinter groups, all with different variations in what they teach and how they teach it', and that the one to which Adrian Doherty belonged in Manchester in the early 1990s has disappeared, pretty much without trace. 'In a broader sense, gnosis speaks about the history of humanity and some of the great mysteries, dating back to Greek and Roman mythology,' Woodward says. 'It also focuses on how, although we like to think the human race is very advanced, we lack values when it comes to morality. Part of the teaching is that, if we want to change the planet for the better, we have to begin with ourselves.'

Gnosis is also described as a means of training the consciousness to develop discipline and psychological stability.

Students are taught to transform an undisciplined mind into a disciplined mind and to work – not least through meditation – towards reducing afflictive emotional states and to cultivating beneficial ones.

'There are definitely Buddhist principles involved,' Alison Jones, who met Doherty through his involvement in gnostic groups in Manchester and, later, in Galway, says. 'It suited Adrian. It gave him the ability to try to understand aspects of his psychology. He would look at things like impatience and frustration and what causes them. It's about self-discovery and trying to live in the moment – that "mindfulness" that people talk about nowadays.'

'A lot of it is about offering an alternative way of living,' Woodward says. 'It's about rejecting the values of materialism and selfishness and the negative emotions that grow out of them and trying to restore more moral values.'

Football was changing. The 1992/3 season was the first of the Premier League era. Alex Ferguson was among those who were highly sceptical about the rebranding, asking whether there was 'anything different about the new set-up except the fancy name', but it can now be seen as the beginning of a period in which the financial dynamics of the game shifted dramatically, causing attitudes in boardrooms and dressing rooms to do likewise. Money had always been a significant factor in English football, but, thanks to the first of many huge Premier League broadcasting deals, with BSkyB, it was about to become an obsession. Transfer fees, wages and ticket prices were all about to escalate. So were commercial opportunities for clubs and players alike. Suddenly agents were no longer the preserve of the elite player. Nor were the latest sports cars and designer gear. If there was something cheesy about BSkyB's 'Whole New Ball Game' advert, it nonetheless succeeded in bestowing a hitherto unimagined glamour and sexiness upon the game and its players. Suddenly we were being urged to regard footballers as pin-ups with bare torsos, floppy hair, Porsches and mock-Tudor mansions. In the eyes of someone like Adrian Doherty, even without his increased distaste for materialism, the absurd vainglory of the football industry had just reached new levels.

Lee Sharpe had already been cast as pin-up material. So too Ryan Giggs, whom Ferguson was so desperate to stop going down the 'George Best route' as regards some of the off-the-field distractions that were increasingly enticing to Sharpe. But this heightened image-awareness among young footballers was not restricted to Sharpe, Giggs or indeed David Beckham, the young Londoner who had always been ribbed by the local lads for spending too much time in front of the mirror and too much money on designer labels. Footballers in general were so much more image-conscious now, particularly the younger ones. Doherty's preference for an Aran jumper, tracksuit bottoms and battered trainers had always earned him strange looks at the Cliff. Now, as his sense of style became ever more eccentric, even extending to what one team-mate recalls as the type of luminous satchel a paperboy would use, he seemed more of an outsider than ever.

'To us as footballers, Doc seemed different because he wasn't bothered about fashion and he never had any cares in the world,' David Johnson, who lodged with him at

Brenda's, says. 'Maybe that says more about footballers than it does about him. When you're an apprentice, especially at Manchester United, a lot of the lads would come in wearing smart gear – not flash, but smart new tracksuits, new boots, new trainers, that typical footballer thing of everyone trying to keep up with the latest thing. David Beckham was immaculate 24/7. He would save every penny he had to buy a shirt that would cost a fortune. He read *FHM*. Doc had no interest in that. He would sit there reading books – big wow – and he would always wear the same clothes and trainers. Becks and John O'Kane would drive to training in their new cars even if they only lived around the corner. I used to walk and I would get there before they had turned on the engine. Doc would come in on a bike – an old bike. I think he had got it off the kit man or something. I'm not even sure it had gears.'

'For me, Doc's outlook and his values were refreshing,' Pat McGibbon says. 'He never placed value on things that other people would. Cars and flash clothes wouldn't interest him at all. He certainly wouldn't have been in it for the fame.'

Robbie Savage, who by now was a second-year apprentice, would probably have been considered the antithesis of Doherty when they lived at Brenda's. If the Welshman was bubbly, loud, outgoing and unashamedly image-conscious, even in the days before his blond, surfer-dude hairstyle, then Doherty was quiet, introverted and would probably have feared he would be dazzled if he looked inside Savage's wardrobe.

'The Doc was almost . . . hippy-like,' Savage says. 'He was a free spirit, completely opposite to the modern-day footballer. As apprentices, on £29.50 a week, we would try to save up for the best branded labels. Most players, when they got their first professional contract, a car was the first thing they would buy. Or clothes. Doc would spend his money going to markets or getting something for his guitar. Even if he had had loads of money, a huge contract, he would have been no different. He was happy just sitting in his room listening to music, writing songs, playing the guitar. His room was his sanctuary. I used to love hearing him strumming away. What a lovely boy and, I have to say, what a player. He was an unbelievable talent. It was just such a shame he got injured.'

The Adrian Doherty enigma means there are three conflicting schools of thought as to how he handled the anguish of his painful final season at Manchester United.

The most common perception, among several friends and team-mates alike, was that he was so happy-go-lucky, so laid-back about everything, not least football, that he seemed unworried by the way his career was unravelling. An alternative view proposes that he succumbed to understandable frustration and, as a consequence, lost focus. His liking for a night out was common to both of those theories, though what some would see as drowning his sorrows was interpreted by others as more consistent with a desire to find fun even in adversity. The opinion held by some of those closest to him is somewhere between those two extremes – that after all he had endured, Doherty was no longer quite as able to shrug off the frustrations, but he was determined not to be consumed by them.

If at times you get people proposing two or even all

three different theories about Doherty's state of mind in those final months at United, it probably suggests it varied between anguish, ambivalence and a studied stoicism. He was, after all, seeking a different approach – a sense of equanimity that would enable him somehow to rise above the frustrations and futilities of his football career.

'Quite often people come to gnosis in search of inner strength, if they're dissatisfied or going through a rough patch,' Thomas Woodward says. 'As well as having the teachings from an intellectual point of view, it helps people cope with difficulties.'

Even at the best of times, he had not always warmed to life at United and to the more unpleasant, isolating aspects of the atmosphere at the Cliff and at the digs. 'I'm not saying he didn't love the game like the rest of us, but he was totally different in his outlook,' Lee Costa, who had played alongside him in the youth team and lived with him at Brenda Gosling's digs, says. 'He was the type of boy who, if someone had come up to him and said: "You can never play football again," he would have looked them in the eye and said: "OK, what's next in life then?"'

Quite clearly there was a part of him that was almost counting down the days on the contract. His friend Brian McGillion suggests that, in his final season at Old Trafford, Doherty 'began to make that break in his own mind and probably began to feel he was just clocking in and clocking out each day until it was officially over'.

A popular phrase among his team-mates is 'happy-go-lucky', but happiness does not come so easily when you are down on your luck. There was no more laid-back character at the Cliff, but nor in some regards was there anyone more earnest. Phil Neville is correct in suggesting Doherty appeared sad and 'gutted' as he went through his daily rehabilitation programme in more and more desperate circumstances, but his brother, Gary Neville, opts for adjectives which say more about the Doherty enigma – 'warm and engaging' but 'quiet and shy'; 'meek and mild' but 'placid and deep'.

Would gnosis, with its emphasis on anti-materialism and the suppression of ego, be compatible with a career in professional sport? 'It wouldn't be incompatible with a football career,' Woodward says. 'We're not expected to live like monks. Gnosis is down to earth. It's about taking the most effective tools out of all the religious teachings across the world and trying to restore more moral, spiritual values in the way you look at life. At the heart of it is always a commitment to look at your own life and try to make positive, lasting changes. Meditation can be one part of that.'

Perhaps meditation was behind what Gareth Doherty recalls as that 'different Adrian, much calmer, much more mature' in the final months of his United career. 'I don't want to give the impression that he completely changed or became in any way solemn,' Gareth says. 'He was still the same person, with the same sense of humour, and he would still have a laugh with us, but he had been through a very tough time at United and, looking back, I would say he was making a very conscious effort to be strong mentally.'

It takes something special, usually involving free beer, to entice three students from their beds on a Saturday morning and into deepest Moss Side. On 6 March 1993, for Sean Ferry, Mick Winters and Paul Vaughan, it was the prospect of watching an A-team match between Manchester City and Manchester United. It was a surprisingly star-studded United team – including Clayton Blackmore, Danny Wallace and the club captain, Bryan Robson – but, for the three students from Strabane, it was all about Adrian Doherty.

Vaughan was excited by the opportunity to watch Doherty in action for the first time since he illuminated Old Trafford in that FA Youth Cup tie three years earlier. Ferry's overriding feeling was nervousness for his cousin, whom he had seen hobble off the pitch during the ill-fated comeback attempt against Marine's youth team fifteen months earlier. Ferry had spent the past years dreaming of watching his cousin play alongside Robson in a United shirt, but, from what he knew, this did not feel like the time or the place. Winters had his camera with him, hoping to take some pictures to add to his portfolio for his photography course. In his admittedly football-ignorant mind, he imagined he would capture the emotion of a moment when his friend scored and celebrated a goal, letting out the frustrations of the past two years. As it transpired, the pictures he took that Saturday lunchtime tell an altogether different story.

In one picture, the ball at his feet, Doherty is looking to use his famed acceleration to take the outside route past Richard Edghill, but the next shot shows him struggling to build up the speed and strength to get past the City full-back. In another sequence of pictures he trots over to take a corner, but then is seen to have deferred to Colin McKee and to have turned his back on the ball. In another, he is standing near the edge of the penalty area, hands on hips, looking like he wishes he could be somewhere – anywhere – else. Perhaps the aspiring photojournalist in Winters would have wished to round off his day's work with a shot of Doherty trudging off the field, disconsolate, when he was substituted in the second half. But, understanding what was being played out in front of him, Winters lowered his lens in sympathy.

'The others would know far more than I did from a football point of view,' Winters says. 'I just remember thinking he didn't look engaged at all. He looked like he didn't want to be there. I felt sorry for him.'

'I remember saying to "Bean" [Ferry] that it wasn't Adrian out there,' Vaughan says. 'What I meant was that it wasn't the Adrian I had seen before the injury. On one hand, you're thinking, "Well it's only his fourth or fifth game back," but then you're thinking maybe it's a build-up of different things. Has he lost speed? Has he lost heart? Has he lost motivation or courage or belief? Might he be not physically or psychologically able to do what he was doing before the injury?'

Gareth Doherty was away that weekend and upset by the bulletins he received from his friends, as well as by the critical self-assessment that followed from his brother. 'I know Adrian was disappointed by how he played that day,' Gareth says. 'He was struggling for sharpness, but so would any player be after being out for two years with a career-threatening injury. I just felt you couldn't rush into a judgement on his future prospects. Even now, never mind then, it would take a long time to get back up to speed, physically and psychologically, after an injury like that. My real thought was that he needed to give it time himself. But the only way he was going to do that was if he knew the club would give him time. I don't think he really had that feeling at United after the injury.'

Even at this low point, struggling to recapture the speed, dynamism and confidence of old, Doherty was still good enough to shine while training in the company of David Beckham, Paul Scholes et al. Chris Casper, another member of the Class of '92, remembers being turned inside out by him in training. 'I still don't know how he did that,' the former England Under-21 defender says. 'That had never ever happened to me before. He was still incredibly quick and skilful. He was probably half a yard off where he had been when I watched him as a schoolboy – you wouldn't expect him to have been back up to full speed – but I thought he was coming to the end of his rehab. I thought he was on his way back.'

Those whose opinion mattered did not share that view. Despite scoring in the B team's 4–0 win over Blackpool's A team on 20 March, it would have been pushing it to imagine that Doherty's subsequent elevation to the reserve team was based on renewed confidence in his prospects. Alex Ferguson and the coaches had begun to view the reserve team as a no-man's-land between the title-chasing first team and the all-conquering A team. By now, though, Doherty was reduced to clutching at straws. And, as far as football was concerned, this was his first straw for some time.

On 31 March Doherty was named in the reserve-team

squad for a game against Newcastle United. Keith Gillespie was preferred on the right wing, with Doherty a substitute. It was a similar story against Bolton Wanderers reserves on 7 April, when Doherty came on as substitute for Dion Dublin in a 2–2 draw. Six days later came a long-awaited start in the reserve team away to Stoke City when he was drafted into the starting line-up after the late withdrawal of Bryan Robson. At last it was a chance to remind people of the potential that was so abundant at seventeen but seemed to have drained away now that he was nineteen, in the final weeks of his contract. Doherty grasped this opportunity, helping to set up two goals for Dublin in a 3–3 draw. The following day he told both his older brother, Gareth, and his father that he had finally, for the first time in what seemed like an age, felt some of the old sharpness and confidence coming back. Perhaps – perhaps – there was a chink of light at the end of the long, dark tunnel in which he had spent the previous two years. There were still four reserve-team matches left. That might mean four more chances to try to make some kind of case to be offered an extension to the contract that had at times felt like a millstone around his neck. Little did he know as he left the field at the Victoria Ground that evening that his Manchester United career was effectively over.

CHAPTER 21

Adrian Doherty was on the scrapheap. They were expanding the facilities at the Cliff and in the car park there was a skip piled high with rubble. Doherty had climbed up into the skip, onto the rubble, and was talking into a camera for his and – as he saw it – his father's amusement. 'Well,' he announced. 'You did warn me, Da, and, look, here I am on the scrapheap at Manchester United.'

Mick Winters, the man behind the camera, found it hilarious. 'I couldn't believe what I was seeing,' he says. 'There he was, in the car park at Man United's training ground, in a skip, surrounded with rubble, sat in all of this masonry. It was a bit of a joke that he was doing for his dad, who had warned him he needed to think about the future because could end up on the scrapheap if United let him go.'

Nobody can find that footage now. Jimmy Doherty does not know whether to laugh or cry at the reminder. He opts for laughter. 'It was typical Adrian, tongue in cheek,' he says. 'He liked wordplay and he wasn't afraid to have a joke at his own expense.'

The painful, unavoidable truth was that Adrian Doherty was indeed heading towards the scrapheap as far as a career at Manchester United was concerned. That three-year contract he had signed back in the heady summer of 1990 was in its final weeks. His knee was still causing him trouble. Even if he were to recover full fitness and full speed, it had been two years since the initial injury. The writing was on the wall. The end was nigh.

Gareth Doherty cannot forget the day his brother came to tell him his Manchester United career was over. It was a time of great excitement for United's supporters, with the club finally closing in on that elusive league title, but there was to be no place in this new golden era for Adrian. His contract was not being renewed, he told Gareth. He was 'cut loose', as his father puts it. United officials have maintained it was not quite as merciless or as one-sided as that, but, to the Doherty family, what happened over those two years, culminating in his release, felt and still feels brutal.

'He didn't say much, but he looked shocked,' Gareth says. 'Not angry, though. I was the angry one. I was saying, "I can't believe they're doing that. You deserve better than that. They should have stood by you and given you the chance to get fit and prove yourself." One of the guys we were with said, "Well that's the way it works. Nobody is bigger than the club." I got really angry with him on Adrian's behalf. When it's your brother or your mate, then he's bigger than the club in your eyes. Adrian just said to me, "Forget about it, man."'

Did Adrian really want to stay at United? 'I think he would have done if he had felt wanted,' Gareth says. 'But it had been a long time since he had felt wanted, so that has an effect. I think he was still under the impression they would offer him something, though. I'm not saying he would definitely have stayed, but he seemed surprised they had let him go like that. Just before that, there was that reserve game against Stoke and he felt he might have been getting a wee bit of sharpness and confidence back. That was the last game he played. After an injury like he had, it's going to take you six months, minimum, maybe twenty or thirty games, to get back. You might never get it back, but to make a decision to cast a young player aside like that, when he's only played something like five games after almost two years out, is . . . well, it's plain wrong in my opinion. Not just because he's my brother but because I think you don't treat someone like that when they've got injured playing for the club, when there are question marks about the injury and when he has spent so long trying to get fit again.'

Craig Lawton can relate to that sense of feeling cut adrift by Manchester United. The Welsh midfielder suffered the same fate a year later, released after spending almost an entire season on the sidelines with groin and hernia problems. 'Sometimes, as a young player, you feel like a piece of meat in a bag,' Lawton says. 'I had been on the fringes of the first-team squad, getting on the bench at QPR, and then I was injured for almost the whole of the next season. I played five or six reserve games towards the end of the season and then I was told I was being released.

'The only conversations I had were with Alex Ferguson in the car park at the Cliff. He just said, "We've had a think about your contract and we're not going to take you on. We've got other lads coming through." There's not a lot you can say. Don't get me wrong. The group of lads who were coming through behind us really were exceptional, the best imaginable, but the fact of the matter is, as a young player at a club like Manchester United, you can't afford to get injured for a long time.

'I would have thought that even a twelve-month contract, with the wages we were on at the time, wouldn't have been any kind of burden for a club like Manchester United. It was the same with Doc. Five or six games towards the end of the season isn't enough to give someone a chance to get fit again when you've been out for so long. Even three months at the start of the next season would have been an opportunity to get fit and prove yourself, but no. "We're not going to take you on." It's a harsh world.

'Then you think, "What do I do now? Who do I contact?" You need more help and support than we ever got at the time. I had been there at the same club as an apprentice and then as a pro, so I had never needed an agent. I gave the PFA [Professional Footballers' Association] a call, but both the PFA and the club themselves could have done a lot better than they did at the time, particularly to those who had been long-term injured. It shouldn't just be a cut-off where you either get a contract or you're left to fend for yourself. There's a lot more guidance and expertise that a young player needs once he has gone through that rehabilitation after a long injury. I think it's different now. I hope so anyway.'

Giuliano Maiorana feels even more aggrieved about the circumstances of his release from Manchester United in 1994, which, like Doherty's and Lawton's, came in the midst of a battle to overcome long-term injury. 'Football clubs don't give a shit about you,' Maiorana says. 'You're there, then you get injured and then, unless you're an established player, they give up on you. I said that to [Alex] Ferguson: "I f***ed up my knee playing for this club and they just chuck you on the scrapheap." It's disgusting. People were asking, "What happened to that Giuliano Maiorana?" Nobody knew. A lot of people didn't even know I had been injured. I just disappeared. There was no mention of me in the papers when I left, no statement explaining the situation. At the end of the day, you're just a piece of meat. If you make it, great, fair play, you deserve everything you get. If you don't, you're scarred. I didn't get any help from United. The PFA weren't much better. I was furious when Ferguson told me. Apparently I went outside and started kicking the bins. I don't even remember that. I just know I saw red.'

Only Sir Alex Ferguson knows the precise details of his parting of the ways with Adrian Doherty, but it seems safe to assume the nineteen-year-old did not 'see red' or take out his frustration on the bins outside. Rather than be interviewed for this book, Ferguson preferred to restrict himself to the sentiments – warm sentiments, it must be said – he expressed in a letter. He wrote that, after the injury sustained in February 1991, 'just before he was to make his debut', Doherty 'did return to the field and played a few games, but sadly it was clear that he would never be able to play top-flight football'.

Ferguson's letter implies that he and Manchester United made an assessment based on the legacy of the knee injury. That was certainly the version given to Doherty and his father when they sought an explanation a few weeks later and were referred to Sir Bobby Charlton in his largely ceremonial capacity as a club director. They were also referred to another orthopaedic surgeon, Anthony Banks, for a second opinion on the knee. 'He looked at the knee and diagnosed it as a damaged cruciate ligament,' Jimmy Doherty says of the meeting with Banks. 'He said it wouldn't stand up to top-level football again. That only seemed to take ten minutes. Adrian looked at me and said, "Did you come all this way to hear that, just for ten minutes?"'

There was something Jimmy Doherty wanted United to do. He asked whether the club would issue a statement explaining the circumstances behind Adrian's release. Already, back in Strabane, there was inevitable speculation that 'there must be more to it' than the devastating injury everyone knew about. Whether Adrian had any future as a footballer or not, Jimmy felt it would help his son if there was an official statement that would enable, for example, the *Manchester Evening News* or even the *Derry Journal* to explain what had happened. That statement was not forthcoming. Adrian shrugged, struggling to see what difference it would make, but Jimmy was deeply disappointed by the lack of communication over his son's release.

Adrian Doherty never revealed the circumstances of his release – or any conversation with Ferguson on the subject – in the years that followed, but neither his elder brother nor anyone else recalls witnessing any trace of resentment. 'I don't remember Aidy ever being angry or frustrated about *anything*, including what happened at

United,' his friend Niall Dunphy says. Dee Devenney agrees: 'I honestly think he was OK with it. Not OK with getting injured, but he did quite quickly come to terms with the fact that he might not play professional football again. I think, after everything that had happened, he had lost the love for it. The dream had gone and it wasn't the be-all and end-all for him any more. Probably there was always a regret that it hadn't turned out better, but, being the kind of character he was, it helped him that, with his music and his reading and writing, he didn't have all his eggs in one basket with football.'

Any bitterness was quelled not just by his good nature but by a tendency, perhaps gained or enhanced through gnosis, to suppress what ego he might have had and to accept personal setbacks with humility. If, by 'reducing afflictive emotional states and cultivating beneficial ones', he became more able to handle a desperate, hopeless situation with a calmness that staggered his friends and family, let alone his team-mates, it is easy to understand why, as his long-term professional ambitions disintegrated, he found gnostic instruction helpful.

'Collectively we were all gutted for him that it didn't work out,' Kevin Doherty says. 'Anyone that knew or cared about Adrian shared that disappointment – not disappointment in him but disappointment for him. The injury had damaged what could have been a brilliant career for him, but I've always felt he came to terms with it and dealt with it in a phenomenally adult way.'

On 2 May 1993, Manchester United were confirmed as champions of England for the first time since 1967. The entire first-team squad, along with wives, partners and friends, piled round to Steve Bruce's house for a celebration that continued until 6 a.m. Some of the players were still worse for wear when they pitched up at Old Trafford barely twelve hours later to take on Blackburn Rovers. For once, Alex Ferguson was happy to turn a blind eye. It was less a sporting contest than a coronation. United won 3–1, adrenalin overriding the previous night's excesses, but the enduring memories are of an atmosphere that reflected an outpouring of joyous relief. 'The emotion that night was incredible,' Brian McGillion says. 'It was people who had been going for forty years, kissing each other, hugging each other, tears streaming down their faces. I was privileged to be there.'

The consensus among family, friends and team-mates is that Adrian Doherty was not there that night. The feeling is that he was already back in Strabane. 'The strange thing is I don't actually remember Doc leaving,' Keith Gillespie says. 'It seems he just slipped out of the back door. And then he was gone.'

CHAPTER 22

Adrian Doherty was drifting – drifting out of Manchester United, out of professional football, towards the type of anonymity he had at times craved. On one hand, his release by United had left him isolated, his future uncertain. On the other, he felt free. As always, a Bob Dylan lyric captured the complexity of the situation. To paraphrase a line from 'Chimes of Freedom', was he now condemned to drift or would he else be kept from drifting?

Instinct and impulse, as well as medical advice, told him to move away from football and start afresh. The past four years, particularly the past two, had drained him of the ambition to be what others wanted and expected him to be. Plus his knee felt terrible. Some imagined he would swallow his disappointment, dust himself down and prepare to drop down to a smaller club – 'You'll bounce back, Aidy', 'You'll prove them wrong.' But Doherty was not interested in proving people wrong. He wanted inner peace, not to be fuelled by feelings of revenge or self-justification. If his appetite for football had been drained at United, and if his knee was giving him such trouble in any case, then why on earth would he go begging in an effort to earn a trial at Stoke, Burnley, Preston or Crewe or wherever? To go cap in hand is all part of the fun when you are an amateur musician, but not when you are a former Manchester United footballer. If something came up, he might think about it – if it was a big club, then certainly – but if not? Well, there were more important things in life.

Besides, the telephone did not ring. Of the four professional players who were released by United in the summer of 1993, Russell Beardsmore, George Switzer and Ian Wilkinson were quickly fixed up with moves to Bournemouth, Darlington and Stockport County respectively. Jimmy Doherty had asked both United and the Professional Footballers' Association for any enquiries about his son's services to be directed to him in the first instance. If any Premier League or Football League clubs asked United that summer about a player who had been so widely coveted prior to his injury, Jimmy does not recall hearing about it.

For Adrian Doherty, there was no decision to make. Football had turned its back on him and, with every day that went by, he felt happier to respond in kind. Sod it. Catch yourself on. Daft wee game, anyway.

Gareth Doherty was amazed at the way his brother had accepted his release by Manchester United, but how could he really be this calm? 'I tried to talk to him about it, but when Adrian said he didn't want to talk about something, you knew there was no point pushing it,' Gareth says. 'If it was me in those circumstances, I would definitely have felt angry and bitter. Adrian didn't react like that. He didn't want any fuss or sympathy. I'm sure deep down there was some sense of relief to be out of football and that environment. Football wasn't the be-all and end-all for him. But I also think he must have felt a bit lost at times that summer. Anyone would in those circumstances.'

Adrian Doherty's family and friends do not know why he ended up moving to Preston in the summer of 1993. Gerard Mullan is one of several who suspect it was driven by impulse: 'A lot of the time he would just put a pin in the map and say, "Off I go."'

That is consistent with the explanation Doherty gave both to friends he made in Preston and to the *News of the World* reporter who interviewed him later that summer. In that interview, he simply said, 'I fancied a change. I just wanted to move to another place. I went to Preston, but I could have chosen anywhere. The name just sounded good.'

If it takes a certain type of character to make such an explanation sound even vaguely credible, then Adrian Doherty is probably the one, as his parents admit.

> Geraldine: There was no reason for some of his decisions.
>
> Jimmy: He was spontaneous. Maybe too spontaneous [laughs].
>
> Geraldine: He didn't seem to plan anything. He would just get a notion. And if he got a notion, he would just go on ahead and do it. I've always wondered whether that came from being tied down at United. Because when he got his freedom, he just made the most of it.

Gareth Doherty says his brother's overwhelming priority that summer was to get away from Manchester in search of a fresh start. Whatever Adrian's fondness for Strabane and his friends and family there, it was not a viable option. 'He didn't want to move back here and get a hundred questions about Manchester United every time he walked out of the door,' Gareth says.

Preston, though? It made little sense. Most of his English-based friends were based in Manchester, Liverpool and Leeds. Gareth Doherty and Dee Devenney were going to Berlin for the summer to work and tried to persuade him to go with them. Leo Cussons had moved to London. Preston held no obvious attraction. It was neither here nor there. It was nowhere, particularly given that he did not drive. It would make him more remote, which might have been the idea in certain respects, but a large town in the bustling north-west of England, with a population of more than 100,000, was not quite an oasis of tranquillity. It really does seem largely to have been as spontaneous, impulsive and random as he suggested. Want a new start? Stick a pin in a map. Have guitar, books and ugly steel-toecapped boots, will travel.

By late July 1993, Adrian Doherty had moved into a rented flat in Preston and was looking for work – pub work, outdoor work, factory work, nothing too taxing for now. He was spending long afternoons and evenings reading and writing. He had found a local guitar group, meeting at the New Britannia pub on Wednesday evenings, and a regular open-mic night at the Lamb. It was not quite New York's East Village, though, or even Manchester's New Troubadour Club. And it was only as the football season drew nearer, and he put some distance between himself and the miserable end to his Manchester United career, that he wondered whether he should give it one last shot.

His father told him Tony O'Doherty, from Derry City, had been in touch. O'Doherty was shocked to hear Adrian was not fixed up with a club and – a long shot – had asked if he might fancy a fresh start with Derry.

Every instinct told him to say no. He had moved to Preston. He did not want to move back to Strabane and face the music every time he left the house ('There goes Adrian Doherty, the lad who used to be at Manchester United'). His knee was still not right and perhaps never would be. Why would he want to be back in Derry, playing in the League of Ireland? What was the point?

A couple of days later, his father got in touch again, saying Derry were being very persistent and were willing to be flexible to find an arrangement that would suit him. They wanted him to come along, train with them, play a couple of pre-season games and see how he felt. If he wanted to carry on living in Preston, he could just fly over for the games at weekends. They were extremely keen. It was not every day they got the chance to sign a player like Adrian Doherty.

He thought about it. Professional football had left him cold, but this was not professional football. This, for better or worse, was the League of Ireland. It was Derry City, the club his father had played for in the 1960s, the club that had offered a safe haven when Adrian returned from Manchester, homesick, in the autumn of 1989. Maybe it was worth a go. What was the worst that could happen? He would turn up, train, play in a pre-season game and say no thank you. On the other hand, he might actually enjoy it. If he could get his spark back and build up his fitness and his confidence, it might be exactly what he needed. At least this way he would know whether he still had the appetite to play football.

Roy Coyle is a legend of Northern Irish football. A ferocious wing-half, who briefly played alongside George Best in the national team in the early 1970s, he is lauded as the most successful manager in Irish League history, having led Linfield to no fewer than thirty-one trophies, but by the summer of 1993 he was finding life far less comfortable at Derry City, which, for political reasons, competed south of the border in the League of Ireland.

Adrian Doherty represented a challenge, but one that captivated Coyle, who says he was 'amazed' to be able to take a player of such calibre on trial. Upon learning that Doherty was available, he made a call to Alex Ferguson. Coyle does not divulge much of that conversation beyond the Manchester United manager's description of Doherty as a 'rare talent'. A rare talent who would need to be handled with great care, certainly, but one who, if he could get fit, focused and motivated, would thrive at almost any level – and would be a sensation in the League of Ireland.

Coyle also spoke to Eddie Coulter, the scout who played an important part in Doherty's move to United. Coulter knew only too well that things had not gone to plan in Manchester, but his message was unequivocal. 'I told Eddie I was thinking about signing Adrian,' Coyle says. 'Eddie told me, "Don't think about it. Just sign him." '

First impressions go a long way in football. Roy Coyle's perception of Adrian Doherty was of a wonderfully gifted footballer who was arriving on trial at Derry City with a certain amount of baggage – albeit not in a literal sense. 'He turned up with one of the smallest suitcases I've ever seen,' Coyle says. 'It must have been a foot and a half long and six inches wide and it contained his life's belongings.'

Derry's players, of course, knew about Doherty. Some, such as the defender Peter Hutton and the reserve goalkeeper Michael Nash, had played with him in his early teens. Among others, Adrian Doherty was a name that aroused a certain intrigue. Schoolboy prodigy, professional contract with Manchester United . . . and then what? Injury or not, why had he not been fixed up in England if he was so good? What was the story with this kid?

Doherty's appearance at that first training session added to the sense of curiosity. Footballers were not supposed to look like this – scruffy, unkempt, old trainers, boots in a plastic bag, a hole in his baggy jumper – particularly not footballers who, they speculated, had been earning hundreds of pounds a week at United. To judge by the buzz around the club, they were expecting a superstar. Derry City's historian and former goalkeeper Eddie Mahon remembers Doherty as 'very ethereal – almost not of this world. His interests were on a higher plane than playing football. I would describe Adrian as a hippy. "Hey, man" and whatever else. And I say that in an affectionate way.'

Hippy or not, what happened next followed exactly the same pattern as when he pitched up at Moorfield, the same as when he had his trials with Northern Ireland schoolboys, Nottingham Forest, Arsenal and United and every time he stepped up a level in training at the Cliff. 'Once he had his boots on, it was a completely different story,' Nash, who had seen it all before, says. 'The first impressions were blown out of the water.'

From that first training session, it was clear to Coyle and his players that Doherty still had it. His touch was sublime. His pace might not have been what it was before, but, even with a mangled knee, it was still frightening. 'I was in awe of him,' Coyle says. 'The other players' eyes were popping out. "What have we got here? What's he doing here? This boy shouldn't be here." Players aren't stupid. But they couldn't understand what he was doing here. He was far too good for this level.'

Nash was heartened by what he was seeing. 'Adrian was just so much better than everyone else,' the goalkeeper says. 'He still had the pace, the touch and the eye for goal. Off the field, maybe things were a bit different for him now, but when he was on the training field, playing his game, his appetite still seemed to be there.'

Hutton had worried Derry might prove too much of a comedown for Doherty, but his initial concerns were eased by those first few training sessions. 'I knew there had been a period where things hadn't gone as well as we had all hoped for him,' Hutton says. 'The fact he was back in Derry told you that. He should have been terrorising defences in the Premier League. We knew the situation with his knee and the unfortunate circumstances. But we were still looking at a real talent. We were probably thinking that even if he only had half that ability he would still be a very precious commodity for us. A lot of people thought he wasn't going to play again at any level, so it was encouraging that he was willing to give it a go. He never flinched anything. He was always there, training hard.'

From a selfish point of view, Coyle wanted Doherty to sign for Derry. But as a football man, he felt there was another conversation they needed to have. 'I spoke to him about his ability and about trying to get back to England,' Coyle says. 'I told him he had time on his side to do that. I told him, "With the life you could have with that talent you've got, it would be a terrible sin to be playing at this level, Adrian." But it was like I was looking into a void. It was going over his head. I thought, "Deep down, this lad doesn't want to go back." He just wanted to play part-time and go through life doing what he wanted to do.'

Both Doherty's and English football's loss, as Coyle saw it, was Derry City's gain. The player was not yet willing to commit to a contract, but he agreed to play in a testimonial match away to Cliftonville.

Two and a half years earlier Arthur Duffy, of the *Derry Journal*, had been listening to Alex Ferguson enthuse about the rare promise of a seventeen-year-old who was regarded as the most talented young Northern Irish footballer for years. Now the same kid was back at the Brandywell and was being feted, however cautiously, as the returning hero. Duffy says he was 'astounded' by the turn of events, but he was also as inquisitive as his job demanded. The cynic in Duffy told him this was too good to be true, but the buzz from the dressing room, ahead of a planned run-out for the trialist at Cliftonville, told him he might be pleasantly surprised.

If there was once an unwritten rule among football writers that they should avoid calling a spade a spade when covering their local team for their local paper, then Arthur

Duffy was not one to follow it. He was scathing of Derry City's performance in their 0–0 draw away to Cliftonville. He called Paul Trainor and Mark Ennis 'totally out of touch', accused Paul Carlyle of 'throwing in the towel early' and did not hesitate to call the team's display 'dreadful' and 'insipid'. And this, it should be noted, was only a testimonial match.

One player escaped Duffy's ire: 'The only spark of inspiration to emanate from the field of play was the performance of Adrian Doherty'; 'his blistering pace and tricks on the ball were regularly applauded by the attendance of 2,000'; 'in the 56th minute Doherty's quick turn of foot carried him into the Cliftonville penalty area'; 'Doherty's skill and trickery'; 'surrounded by three defenders, the 20-year-old jinked his way out of trouble before setting up defender Paul McLaughlin'.

Doherty recognised and spoke to Duffy afterwards. 'I'm glad to get the run-out,' he told the *Derry Journal* reporter. 'I'm not match-fit yet, but hopefully it will not take me too long to achieve that. Originally I was going to play for twenty minutes, but I felt good and managed to continue for the entire second half. I'm happy about that.'

Could he really see himself signing a contract with Derry? 'I've spoken to Roy Coyle and Tony O'Doherty and I expect to have further discussions with them,' he said. 'If everything goes OK, I don't see why not. I'm just happy to be back playing football again. If I can agree a contract with Derry, then I'd be happy to stay, although I still have commitments in England and I've fully informed Roy Coyle of my position.'

Better was to follow from Doherty on his competitive

debut four days later as Derry scraped past Finn Harps in a League Cup second-round tie. 'Undoubtedly Derry's best player on Sunday,' Duffy wrote of the young winger. 'Showed that he has pace and tremendous dribbling ability and should be a big asset in this year's league campaign'.

Coyle, according to Duffy, was 'very anxious' to secure Adrian to a contract – 'and that includes flying the player in for matches at weekends'. That began to feel like a deal-clincher. Adrian Doherty, going against his initial judgement, put pen to paper on a one-month contract. It seemed the right thing to do.

Arthur Duffy was not the only journalist whose interest was piqued by the Adrian Doherty story. Martin Leach, of the *News of the World*, had heard on the grapevine that the one-time great hope of Old Trafford, a peer of Ryan Giggs, was about to make his debut in the League of Ireland. What a riches-to-rags tale. What's the real story? he thought. He made a call to Derry City. Would Doherty be willing to do an interview? Of course he would. Not because he had any desire to see his name writ large in the press, but because he never said no to anyone. Doherty's father, Jimmy, was concerned when he heard of the interview planned with Britain's most notorious tabloid, but Adrian said he had nothing to hide, nothing to be ashamed of. If he had any ambitions of making it as a footballer back in England – and he was far from certain that he did, even if his appetite had unexpectedly been whetted – then this might at least help to put his name out there. Beyond that, it might help to answer some of the questions and address some of the misconceptions that were already beginning to build up around his departure from Manchester United. Yes, he would do the interview, he said. He spoke to Leach by telephone and they touched on all manner of subjects. Jimmy and Geraldine Doherty worried about how the interview might be presented. Adrian told them it would be fine.

'GIGGS AND ME!' screamed the headline across a double-page spread. 'By the whizzkid whose Manchester United career was ruined by injury.' The main picture across the page was of Giggs. There were two smaller pictures of Doherty. Giggs was mentioned by name in the opening paragraph. Doherty was not. That was the reality now. His story could only be told by reference to how far he had fallen in relation to Giggs:

> *The lad who aimed to wing to the top with Ryan Giggs is fighting his way off the scrapheap – at 20.*
>
> *While Giggs thrills Sky TV viewers in today's Norwich vs Manchester United battle, Adrian Doherty is back home in the Northern Ireland town of Strabane trying to revive his career with Derry City.*
>
> *Superkid Giggs will be starting the defence of Manchester United's league championship; former whizzkid Doherty will be involved in Derry City's Irish League Cup clash with Finn Hearts [sic], a far cry from the heady days of Old Trafford.*
>
> *Giggs and Doherty used to be talked about in the same breath – boy wonders on opposite flanks who would bring the glory back to United.*
>
> *Now the chasm between them is so vast, Adrian can only shrug and say: 'To be honest, I never even think about what might have been for me.*

'Ryan is doing brilliantly. A superstar. And he couldn't be playing for a better team. Me? That's the way it goes. The sun is still shining.'

(*News of the World*, 15 August 1993)

The Doherty family were disappointed by the article. They felt the contrast with Giggs made Adrian look like a failure. Any journalist would say it was an obvious angle to take – the story of two teenage prodigies whose careers had taken wildly different courses over the previous two and a half years. If anything, it looks as if Leach, perhaps out of sympathy with or fondness for his interviewee, went surprisingly soft by *News of the World* standards. Over the course of the interview, Doherty mentioned drinking and losing interest in football. It might have been tempting – wrong, but tempting – for Leach to go for the easy, if misleading, *'Booze wrecked my Old Trafford dream'* line, but instead he went for the Giggs contrast.

Strikingly, there is not a trace of bitterness in the interview. There is barely even a note of regret. Not for the first time, Doherty comes across as off-hand about the whole football experience. What also comes through clearly is that, as well as suffering from homesickness in those early months in Manchester, he struggled to deal with his rehabilitation from that wretched injury. Of the moment itself, he said, 'I heard something go, but nobody realised how bad it was.' There is then another line, where Leach writes, 'Amazingly, Adrian was allowed to play on for a while without surgery because "they didn't think it needed an operation".'

This was Doherty's one opportunity to tell his side of

the story, but he was not the type to point the finger or indeed to make excuses. At the risk of inviting accusations that he was the master of his own downfall in Manchester, he focused more on his own mistakes than on those he might have felt were made by others.

'I'll give it my best shot for Derry. I have to. I can't do anything else. Football is the only thing I can do.'

That was pure modesty. There were plenty of other things Adrian Doherty could do – poetry and songwriting, to name just two – but for now, against his initial instinct, he was prepared to give football one more chance in the red-and-white stripes of Derry City. If that meant flying back and forth between Manchester and Belfast, compromising his chances of holding down work in Preston, and spending an inordinate amount of time on buses, then so be it. Drifting could wait just a little longer.

CHAPTER 23

There is something special about the first day of the football season. It is that excitable feeling, whether for a fan walking into his or her home ground or a player entering the team's dressing room, that there is magic in the air, that this year will somehow be different, a new beginning.

On 21 August 1993, optimism filled both the stands and the dressing room at the Brandywell. Ahead of the opening League of Ireland fixture against Cobh Ramblers, Derry City had made two of the most eye-catching signings imaginable – two of the most gifted raw talents in Northern Ireland, both sons of former Derry players, both of them felt to be returning to their spiritual home. The first was Liam Coyle, the local lad who was back at the club he illuminated in his youth, only to be forced into retirement in May 1990, at the age of twenty-two, by a knee injury. Coyle had employed a faith-healer to help him recover fitness and had enjoyed an astonishing renaissance at Omagh Town during the 1992/3 season. Somehow, Derry had managed to lure him back on the eve of the new season for a measly £10,000 transfer fee. The story of Coyle's recovery from injury only increased the excitement surrounding Adrian Doherty, whose skills and speed had been legendary in his schooldays and who was now seemingly ready, after four years at Manchester United, to resurrect his career back at Derry.

'There was a lot of excitement about the Brandywell,' Coyle says. 'It was big news in Derry when Adrian and I signed. I was back from Omagh and we all thought Adrian was going to be here for a long time. If he could get fit, he would be the best player in Ireland.'

For one beautiful moment, Adrian Doherty felt seventeen again. Seventy minutes into a tight game, with the scoresheet blank, he sensed that things were opening up. He set off on a run from the touchline towards the Cobh Ramblers goal. The run, like Liam Coyle's pass, was perfectly timed and now Doherty was clear, his speed taking him clear of the visiting defence. 'With two towering centre-halves at his heels, the youngster exuded confidence and calmness to check back, pick his spot and chip the ball into the net,' Arthur Duffy wrote in the *Derry Journal*, calling it a 'magnificent goal'.

The thing that sticks in Duffy's mind about Doherty's goal that afternoon is the cathartic fervour with which he greeted it. 'He celebrated like mad,' the journalist says. 'That surprised me, the way he ran around celebrating, and that's when I thought it might actually be the moment that kickstarts his career.'

Duffy was full of enthusiasm for Doherty once again in the paper that Tuesday, saying that the twenty-year-old impressed with his 'skill, vision and pace' and was 'guaranteed to thrill' the Brandywell crowd over the months ahead. He was not alone in feeling that excitement. 'The two of us walked off together at the end and we were the talk of the place,' Coyle says. 'I had set up Adrian's goal and then he set me up to make it 2–0. We had a good little partnership going. He was still quick and he was so good at coming off the wing and finding space. The two of us were similar in some respects. We were both quiet, both from small towns and we both played to entertain people and make people happy. We had quite a lot in common.'

Coyle wondered, though, if there might also be one significant difference between them. 'I needed it,' he says. 'I needed to play football because I thought it was the only thing I could do. I was prepared to suffer with my knee. I didn't care about the pain because I knew I would be lost without football. Did Adrian need football in the same way? I wasn't so sure.'

For Peter Doherty, it was a thrill to be able to watch his brother in action and to have him home for the odd night or two before he headed back to Preston between matches. 'To me, watching that day, I still thought he was brilliant,' Peter says. 'Even though people were saying he wasn't as fast as he used to be, he was still faster than pretty much anyone I had seen playing for Derry City. He scored a great goal and everyone thought it was going to be lift-off for him. But I think now, looking back, his heart wasn't in it.'

In the eyes of his friends in Strabane, Adrian Doherty never really changed. He became far more outgoing in some respects, more introspective in others, but he was always the same kid who hardly stopped grinning or laughing when he was with them.

Peter Hutton recognised a change, though, from the

shy boy he had encountered in the Derry and District team and the Northern Ireland Under-16 team to the twenty-year-old who stood before him now. 'I hadn't seen him in those in-between years,' Hutton recalls of his new team-mate at Derry City. 'He seemed a different person when he came back. He was more . . . eccentric, at least by football standards. He seemed to enjoy his music more than his football. We would meet up at the hotel and he would start playing piano, his own songs, something like "You Canna Hang a Chicken by Teatime". [So close, Peter. It was actually 'Gotta Kill a Chicken by Tuesday'.] He loved his music, singing and busking. He had a life. I also remember he was generous to a fault.

'I'm sure those years living away from home would have affected him, being at supposedly the biggest club in the world, with that weight of expectation, and then having the disappointment of the injury and not living up to expectations – his own and everybody else's. I think he was trying to find out if he still had the same hunger for the game. Physically, was he still up to it? Mentally, was he still up to it? Being honest, his hunger had probably waned. He had been through a hell of a lot. He never ever spoke of his time at Manchester United. He was just focusing on the current time.'

Adrian Doherty only ever liked to focus on the present. Long-term planning just wasn't his thing. At Derry City they had been delighted by his impact against Cliftonville and Finn Harps and now in the opening League of Ireland fixture against Cobh Ramblers. Doherty, despite the thrill of that moment against Cobh Ramblers, was far less convinced. 'I always had the feeling, chatting to him, it was just going to be short-term,' his cousin Sean Ferry says. 'I think he had fallen out of love with the game. He thought he was doing Derry a favour, giving it a go.'

Doherty was back in Preston in midweek, as per the original agreement, while his team-mates laboured to a 0–0 draw with Monaghan United. Then he was back home – if Strabane was still home – to return to the start-ing line-up as Derry lost 1–0 at home to the League of Ireland champions Cork City. This time Arthur Duffy was considerably less impressed. 'Never at the races,' he wrote about Doherty in his player ratings in the *Derry Journal*, awarding him a mark of five out of ten.

Two days later, on Bank Holiday Monday, there was a friendly match across town at Institute, who, unlike Derry, were affiliated to the Irish League – north of the border – rather than the League of Ireland in the south. Doherty played in a 3–1 win for Derry, but already, ten days after scoring on his league debut, everyone could see this mar-riage of convenience was fizzling out. 'He told me he didn't really fancy it,' Liam Coyle says. 'He didn't feel like he could go on.'

'If you're playing in a team like that, you don't want pas-sengers,' Peter Hutton says. 'A few of the senior pros were thinking, "If he's not up for it, then he's not up for it." Some of the younger lads, like myself, were keen for him to play himself back into form because we knew what an unbelievable player he had been in his youth. As for whether he would recreate that, we were hoping more than anything that that would be the case.'

Roy Coyle's hopes were fading too. Doherty conveyed

the same unhappy message to the manager and his assistant Tony O'Doherty: this is not working out. They had seen the enthusiasm drain from his game since the goal against Cobh Ramblers, but they still felt they should persevere for now, such was his talent. They urged him to give it another couple of games and see how he felt.

Maybe it would have been different, even if only in the short term, had Doherty not joined a club in a state of turmoil. 'We were going through real upheaval,' Liam Coyle says. 'There were a lot of problems, with unrest between the players and the management. It started to show on the pitch. I think Adrian maybe saw that and thought, "I'm not going to be involved in this." Roy Coyle lasted only a few games after that.'

Adrian Doherty lasted only another one.

In the press box at Tolka Park, Arthur Duffy shook his head in disgust. He had just witnessed a capitulation. Three points had been there for the taking for Derry City after their opponents, Shelbourne, had a player sent off at o–o early in the second half. Yet Roy Coyle's team had collapsed, conceding two late goals to a team with ten men. 'Derry City's good name in League of Ireland football was disgraced at Tolka Park,' Duffy wrote in his match report in the *Derry Journal*, adding that this new-look team was 'carrying more passengers than Ulsterbus'.

It was a neat line and, while there are few more damning labels in football parlance than 'passenger', someone who needs to be carried by his team-mates, it was one that reflected the journalist's anger at Derry's performance that afternoon. Duffy awarded Gary Lennox, Mark Ennis and

Adrian Doherty ratings of three out of ten, saying that they 'appear to have thrown in the towel after only four games'.

In Doherty's case, it was true. He should not have played at Shelbourne. He should have followed his gut feeling and quit after Cork City or Institute. Or he should have quit while he was ahead, after scoring against Cobh Ramblers. How had he allowed himself to reach the stage where he was a waste of a shirt, a bloody passenger, in the League of Ireland? It had been a big mistake.

He made up his mind on the long bus journey home that it was indeed time to throw in the towel – not just on Derry City but on his football career. He did not want this and, in one way, it felt like a relief to reach that decision once and for all. But it would be hard to feel unburdened, hard to feel liberated, when sitting on a packed bus, hours from home, on roads full of potholes, when you are in the company of players whom you feel you have let down.

Among those who were on that bus back from Dublin, there are mixed recollections as to the manner in which Adrian Doherty broke the news. Roy Coyle does not remember a definitive decision or announcement being made or communicated at that stage, but says that word filtered forward from the back of the bus that Doherty was 'on a downer' after the game. Duffy remembers that Doherty was 'not a happy bunny'. Liam Coyle simply recalls Doherty informing him he had reached the end of the road as a footballer. 'We were sitting on the bus and he told me he was going away,' Liam Coyle says. 'I said: "Are you serious?" He told me the pain was too much and he was going to stop. He wasn't enjoying it. I remember him saying, "I just want to play the guitar and enjoy myself." And because he was so likeable and because of the difficulties he had had with his knee and coming from Manchester United and so on, which was a big step down, I think everybody sort of understood.'

Few understood that context more clearly than Arthur Duffy, who had seen Adrian Doherty in Manchester two and a half years earlier, so oblivious to the fact that the knee injury that had put him out of contention for a United debut that weekend would have such catastrophic consequences. The journalist had followed Doherty's football career with an increasing sense of woe and now it had reached its sad denouement on a bus somewhere on that interminable journey back from Tolka Park.

'He just didn't want this any longer,' Duffy says. 'I felt for him. I really did. It's a long slog, the League of Ireland, especially for Derry City. You jumped on the bus, leaving at noon for a 7.30 p.m. kick-off and you might not be back until two or three in the morning. It wouldn't have been an issue for someone like Peter Hutton, because he loved it, but a young lad like Adrian, who had come from Manchester United, didn't want to be getting picked up in Strabane, sitting on his backside for hours, getting paid a pittance. I think the other lads would have thought, "This guy was about to play for Manchester United. This is hardly going to be a good substitute." It must have felt like a real fall from grace for him.'

Hutton agrees. 'In the hotels, you could see he was thinking, "What am I doing here?" There's a lot of time to kill. He had changed, but it was almost like back to the young boy, where he's thinking, "I'm away here and I don't

want to be. I'm here physically, but I'm not mentally here."
I know some of the lads tried to entice him to think about
carrying on. But Adrian was very strong in that regard.
Once he made his mind up, there was no changing it.'

Roy Coyle, an old-school manager, did not find it so
easy to see things from the player's point of view. 'It
angered me a little,' he says. 'No, I wouldn't say "angered".
I would say it disappointed me that, with the gift he had,
he had chosen a different way of life. I would have loved
that challenge to get inside his head. But I never saw him
again. I don't think he ever played football again.'

It was back-page news in the *Derry Journal* that Tuesday.
Arthur Duffy, having been party to that unburdening on
the bus journey back from Dublin, had his story and both
Adrian Doherty and Roy Coyle were content for him to
run with it. 'DOHERTY'S BRANDYWELL BOMB-
SHELL,' read the back-page headline, telling readers that
the former Manchester United winger, whose arrival a
month earlier had caused such a flurry of excitement, had
'sensationally quit the Brandywell club'. Explaining his
decision, Doherty thanked Coyle and the club for their
understanding. Rather than sounding downcast, he seemed
relieved to be turning his back on football. 'Even before I
was released by United, my heart wasn't in the game any
more,' the twenty-year-old said. 'To be honest, I hoped a
season at Derry would help me get my hunger back, but
that hasn't happened. I'm sorry, but I don't see my future
in football any more.'

At the end of the interview, Duffy and Doherty shook
hands. Duffy had seen players come and go from the

Brandywell, but never had he seen one of such talent appear so fleetingly. 'He had great talent, but we only saw very brief glimpses of it,' the journalist says. 'If there was a pub-quiz question about fathers and sons who played for Derry City, then Jimmy and Adrian Doherty are ones that a lot of people might not get because Adrian wasn't here long enough to make an impact. He went quietly. He just slipped away.'

It had been a little over four years since Adrian Doherty began his apprenticeship at Manchester United. In terms of first-team appearances, his career statistics amounted to none for United and, excluding friendly matches, four for Derry City. Then there are the handful of caps he won for Northern Ireland at schoolboy and Under-16 level. It was a meagre return, not just for the talent he had, but for the anguish that football had caused him.

You might imagine that someone like his former Moorfield team-mate Peter Hutton, who set an all-time appearance record for Derry and went on to manage the club, would bristle at the thought of a career unfulfilled, but he takes the opposite view of the Adrian Doherty story.

'Some people might have found it bewildering, but I didn't,' Hutton says. 'When he came back from England, after the injury, people assumed he would play football at the best level he could, but I admired the fact he didn't just follow the norm. He did what he wanted to do. He had probably earned a few pounds, but materialistic things didn't bother him at all. He was trying to find out what made him tick.

'In those early years he was so focused on his football and

so dedicated. I do believe he wanted to be the best he could possibly be. Then there was the injury and maybe after that he worked out it wasn't really for him. Or maybe his time in Manchester changed his outlook towards football, I don't know. Maybe he was still soul-searching to find out what it was he really wanted to do. That's a credit to him. He could have just gone along with trying to keep people happy, but maybe, as he grew up in Manchester, he realised the only person he needed to keep happy was himself.'

CHAPTER 24

The manager told you where to stand and what to do. You took your position and stood poised with your team-mates. Then there was a huge noise, the action started and it was up to you to perform. You could not let your team down. Speed, focus and good technique were essential. One after another, they were coming at you, little chocolates, ready to be counted or inspected or arranged or decorated or packed before they moved onto the next belt to continue their journey through the factory.

The workers at Beech's Fine Chocolates in Preston were free to talk among themselves as long as they concentrated on the job in hand. Some of them were talking about the latest plot twist in *EastEnders*. It involved a new character called Aidan Brosnan, played by an early 1990s pin-up named Sean Maguire. Brosnan was a softly spoken young Irish footballer who suffered a career-ending knee injury, found his life going off the rails, culminating in alcohol and drug abuse, and then, in keeping with Albert Square's tradition for the least festive type of melodrama, attempted suicide on Christmas Day, watched by a television audience of twenty-three million.

One of the girls suggested that Brosnan sounded like one of their co-workers – that quiet young Irish lad. And wasn't he called Aidan too? 'Hey, Aidan,' she called. 'Don't suppose you play football, do you?'

'Not since I left Manchester United.'

'Oh, Aidan,' she said. 'What are you like?'

From the Theatre of Dreams to strawberry creams, it must have been quite a comedown for Adrian Doherty. But at least the Beech's factory – tucked, unusually these days, on a side street in a busy area of Preston – offered him a fresh start. Nobody knew him and nobody would judge him. It was a friendly, welcoming place.

It still is, to judge by the warmth with which a stranger with a notepad is greeted on a November day in 2014, asking the receptionist whether any of the workers on the factory floor were likely to remember Adrian Doherty, a guy who was employed there more than two decades earlier. She takes down the details. 'If anyone remembers, it will be Marilyn,' she says. 'I'll be back in a moment.'

A minute later, Marilyn appears. Yes, she remembers Adrian and she is happy to help. The only difficulty is that she is mid-shift, so we will have to catch up later.

'A lot of people have come and gone here, but I knew who you meant as soon as I heard the name,' she says when she calls that evening. 'We knew he had been a footballer. That's how we found out, because we were all talking about that storyline in *EastEnders* about an Irish lad who had been a footballer and got an injury. Someone asked him if he played football and he said something about Manchester United. At the time, none of us believed him. He had been here a while by then, so we just thought he was messing around. We thought nothing more of it.'

To be precise, they thought nothing more of it until a few weeks later, when a guy named Cliff Kellett started a short-term contract at the chocolate factory. Kellett was – and is – a huge Manchester United supporter. He was the type of fan who knew the names of all the reserve-team and youth-team players. And he certainly knew all about Adrian Doherty.

'I'd been working there a few weeks when I heard some-one mention Adrian Doherty,' Kellett says. 'Then I heard his accent and I thought, "It couldn't be, could it?" I said to him, "Are you by any chance Adrian Doherty the ex-Red?" He said he was. I said, "What on earth are you doing in Preston?" He said he just put a pin in the map and decided to come here. I couldn't believe it. I'd read about him in programmes, where they were raving about him, and here I was working with him in a chocolate factory in Preston. I was starstruck.'

Kellett asked his colleagues if they realised they were working alongside a former Manchester United wonder-boy. Again, the claim was ignored. They thought the new guy was in on this weird joke. So the next day Kellett returned with a couple of his United yearbooks, contain-ing photographs of Doherty in team line-ups alongside Ryan Giggs. 'It was only then that we realised it was true,' Marilyn says.

Kellett was desperate to find out more – not just about the sequence of events that had brought Doherty to Beech's but about his time at Old Trafford. 'I wanted to hear about all the players and everything else, but Adrian never wanted to say much about it,' he says. 'He certainly wouldn't bring the subject up himself. I remember him saying it had been between him and Ryan Giggs to get into the first team first and then the injury happened. He said it was in the past and he was getting on with his life. He didn't seem gutted about how things had worked out for him. He was just a really nice, quiet lad. He seemed to be quite happy simply to have moved to Preston and to be doing something different with his life. That was what he wanted.'

The natural thing in any workplace would be for a revelation such as Doherty's to be followed by a series of interrogations. But nobody at Beech's got much out of him where football was concerned. 'He didn't really speak about it,' Marilyn says. 'It must have been a big blow to him. Well it would be, wouldn't it, when you think of doing something you love, earning all that money, and then you end up in a factory, slogging your guts out. He had that talent and it was snatched from him. He always came across happy enough, but that must have been hard for him.'

How much would he have earned? 'Not much,' Marilyn says. 'Probably £60 a week in those days. Maybe £80 a week. He would have been "chucking", mainly – moving chocolate from one place to another, taking chocolate off the belts. I think he found it fine, though. It has always been a friendly place to work.'

Frank and Geraldine Manning went to visit their former lodger in Preston. 'He was just happy,' Geraldine says. 'I think he was happier in Preston than he had been for a long time. No money, but money didn't mean anything to him. As long as he could pay his rent and have a bit of fun and somewhere to play his songs and write his poems, that was all he needed.'

Beethoven and I

La la la la la la
La la la la la la
Two super musicians, expert and clever
Beethoven and I, forever and ever
Oh the melodies, oh the melodies
Like the stillest lake, like the voluptuous breeze
La la la la la la
La la la la la la
Two excellent creators, hard to separate
Beethoven and I, who's more and less great?
Oh the melodies, oh the melodies
Like the stillest lake, like the voluptuous breeze
Listen
La la la la la la
La la la la la la
Beethoven's ghost appeared to me one night
It bowed and said: 'Hail the champion outright'
Oh the melodies, think I shaded it on the melodies
Like the stillest lake, like the voluptuous breeze
Listen
La la la la la la
La la la la la la

Gareth Doherty was tickled by the idea of his brother working in a chocolate factory. In the autumn of 1993, he and Gary McHugh went to Preston to help Adrian decorate the flat he had just started renting. 'We were calling him Willy Wonka,' Gareth says, 'but he pointed out to us that he was more of an Oompa Loompa, so the Oompa Loompa song got a few renditions while we worked.'

The decorating was a three-man job, but Gareth remembers that his brother did most of the work. 'Then it suddenly dawned on Gary and me that there weren't any beds in the flat, so we ended up sleeping on these foam sheets Adrian had on the floor,' Gareth says. 'He wasn't a man for luxury and he liked to sleep on the floor himself anyway. He stayed with me in Salford for a week and slept on the floor in my room then too.

'He did seem genuinely content in what he was doing. He liked the chocolate factory. He said he started off with a white hat and then when he reached a certain level he would get a red hat. I used to ask him how the job was going – "No word on you getting that red hat yet?" – and he didn't mind if we slagged him about it because that's how we all grew up together with all our mates. My da remembers Adrian phoning him one day to say he had got his red hat and he was dead chuffed about it.'

Leo Cussons has a similar recollection from his visits to Preston. 'He told me that some days he would take it upon himself to clean the machines at the factory,' he says. 'Then of course he wrote a song about cleaning the machine, but I remember him telling me his manager there was totally amazed with the way he cleaned it. I don't know what they were paying him – not a great deal,

I suspect – but he would basically refurbish the whole thing.

'To me, Preston seemed fairly bleak at that time. For most people, going to work in a factory would be very difficult, especially where he had come from, but he would turn it into an amazing story, writing songs about it. That's amazing when you think about it. How many of us can actually really do that? And what I take from my friendship with Adrian is that. You make something of every moment. The people who were there and shared these moments with him will remember that.'

For all Adrian Doherty's eagerness to enjoy the novel and comical aspects of his new job – drawing inspiration for songs and poems, playing at open-mic nights, busking in the town centre on a Saturday afternoon – working in a chocolate factory was hardly a soft landing after professional football.

'It was one of those jobs where you work your hours, all day, and then as soon as the factory doors open, you "do one",' Cliff Kellett says. 'I've worked outside all my life, so I found it very tough working in a factory. It was just chucking chocolate, checking they weren't leaking out of the packaging, that sort of thing. It was brain-dead work in a way, but it was tough. I was only there seven weeks. It was friendly, but it's not a part of my life I've been desperate to go back to.'

Kellett did bump into Doherty once more – a couple of years later, he thinks. He was walking through Preston town centre one evening, when he heard someone calling his name. They had a brief chat, of which he recalls little beyond Doherty's claim that he preferred Manchester City to United nowadays. Kellett is 99 per cent certain his old friend was joking.

Truly and Utterly

Truly and Utterly were going together
Going down the road in the stormy weather
Truly and Utterly they look like potatoes
But together they look so much better

Said Truly to Utterly:
'Utterly who are you?'
Said Utterly to Truly:
'Truly I thought you knew'

Truly and Utterly, they lived as lovers
Beneath a roof held up by pillars
They wore matching dungarees and collars
Just to be different from others

Said Utterly to Truly:
'Truly we're outstanding'
Said Truly to Utterly:
'Yes Utterly dumbfounding'

Truly and Utterly received some callers
Friends, relatives and someones or others
Truly to all coffee must offer
And Utterly fetch it, as is proper

Greet Utterly and Truly
Utterly in unison
Truly to whomever:
'We're glad you're visiting.'

Adrian Doherty spent two and a half years in Preston. For the first twelve months, there were still semi-regular meet-ups with the Strabane exiles studying in Manchester, Liverpool and Leeds. Niall Dunphy remembers that at one get-together in Manchester, Doherty was still wearing *those* boots, to widespread hilarity. One thing that sticks in Dunphy's mind is that Doherty talked of having briefly tried training on his own with a view to playing football again at amateur level, but had called that off because 'every time he worked up to a full sprint, his knee kept giving way'.

People's lives were changing. Upon graduating, Kevin Doherty began work, accounting and auditing, in Leeds. Dee Devenney went to work and live in Berlin. Sean Ferry and Brian McGillion went back to Strabane. There was no longer that Strabane enclave stretching across the M62 corridor. 'We met up in Manchester from time to time, but at that point most of the conversations I had with Adrian would have been when we were both back in Strabane at Christmas or whatever,' Kevin Doherty says. 'We would catch up, take a walk down into town, that sort of thing, talk about what we were both doing, him about life in Preston. He would try to talk to me about the merits of poetry and he would quote things and try to convince me to read Rimbaud. I told him he was flogging a dead horse with me and poetry, but that was what he liked talking about. He seemed content.'

It all sounds rather humdrum after the turbulent times

in Manchester and the trip to New York. 'I think he just became a quieter, more private person,' Kevin Doherty says. 'Yes, there had probably been a time where he was doing some of the things the rest of us had been doing when he was focused on far higher goals in his teens, but he moved beyond that and settled down a lot more.'

'I went to Preston to see him once or twice,' Gerard Mullan says. 'We just met up in the town centre. I remember we went to some café, had a bite to eat, walked around, went for maybe one or two drinks and then went home. I think it was a greasy-spoon café we went to. He liked that kind of thing now and again.'

Gareth Doherty visited his brother during the 1994 World Cup. 'Adrian didn't watch much TV, but he had invested in a wee portable in his kitchen and he had even bought himself a bed,' he says. 'We stayed up and watched the Brazil–Sweden semi-final. Adrian said he had watched bits and pieces of the World Cup and we talked about different players we liked – Romário, Stoichkov, Baggio. I don't know if he only watched this particular game because I was there, because he was never a big one for watching whole games even before he went to United.'

'He didn't talk about football,' Marilyn says, back at the Beech's Fine Chocolates factory. 'He talked about other things – music, what it must be like to have an out-of-body experience. I remember him writing songs. He once got drunk at our works do and sang one of them. It was a funny, jokey song. He had an eye for the ladies, if I remember rightly. I can't remember much else. I'm sorry. He kept himself to himself.'

*

He did go back, in case you were wondering. Adrian Doherty was not so distressed by the Manchester United experience – or by any subsequent sense of regret – that he cut himself off entirely.

He hitchhiked into Manchester from Preston and, rather than head straight home afterwards, he decided on the spur of the moment to get one of those trusty buses to Lower Broughton Road, from where he made the short walk to Priory Avenue to drop in on Brenda Gosling and the lads.

By now the roll call of inmates had changed and there were some unfamiliar faces – it always was a revolving door at Brenda's – but Doherty was delighted to see his former landlady and, among others, Pat McGibbon. 'He was the same as ever,' McGibbon says. 'We didn't really talk about football. It was mainly about music. "Are you still playing the guitar?" "Aye, still doing a wee bit." As I recall, he was working in a chocolate factory in Preston.'

Did he seem happy? 'He did, yes,' McGibbon says. 'He was just singing away, the same as ever. That was the thing with Doc. He always seemed happy.'

CHAPTER 25

Is it, as Alfred, Lord Tennyson put it, better to have loved and lost than never to have loved at all? What about living your dreams of football stardom and then having them taken away from you? What about spending years of your life chasing the dream of becoming a professional footballer, climbing towards the pinnacle, being on the verge of the Manchester United first team, and then seeing your ambitions shattered by injury, leaving you to try to rebuild your life, with the pain in your knee a constant reminder of what might have been? Is it better to have lived that dream, however briefly, than not? Perhaps it is a little easier these days, if you have the financial security that can come of even a single professional contract in some cases, but there are not too many ex-footballers in their forties now, having missed out on the Premier League gravy train, who would endorse the life of the nearly man.

'People don't appreciate what that's like,' says Giuliano Maiorana, who made a handful of appearances in United's first team in the late 1980s before succumbing, like Adrian Doherty, to the dreaded cruciate knee ligament injury. 'Sometimes I try to tell myself I've had experiences that others can only dream of, but, being honest, that's not how it feels when you've been so close to it and then had it taken away.

'You don't want the memories. I remember saying that if I had had a chip in my brain that I could have taken out, so I didn't have any memory of playing for Man United, I would have taken it out. I meant that. Because all your life, from playing football aged five or six, you've gone to bed thinking about football, thinking about trying to do different things on the pitch, what you did well, what you didn't. Then you get injured and you can't play any more, because your knee is knackered, but your brain is still conditioned to think football. I would be trying to sleep, but my brain was flooded with football. When you don't want to think about football, you go out. But because it's football, the biggest sport in the world, it doesn't matter if you look right or left. Unless you lock yourself in your room, you see football. It doesn't matter if you drive or walk, you see football tops, kids with a football, goalposts. You turn on the news – football. You pick up the paper – football. It's in your face all the time. You can't get away from it and it just reminds you what you could be doing. I went to see a lady to get help and when I explained what I'd been through, she said she thought I was coping remarkably well under the circumstances. Doc might not have had the same experience as me, but that was my experience. I took until I was in my thirties, married with a family, to come to terms with it. I struggled, I'm telling you.'

Adrian Doherty's friends knew it was not a good idea to ask him about football. 'From the moment he finished at Derry City, I always used to advise people not to bring up those few years at Manchester United,' his brother Gareth says. 'It was a no-go zone.'

'I only really had one conversation with him about it afterwards,' his cousin Sean Ferry says. 'That was around the time he left Derry. He talked briefly about the injury and he said, "If only they had got to the bottom of it and sorted it earlier on," that sort of thing. But there was, honestly, no bitterness. He would just drip-feed the odd wee thing into a conversation and then he would be talking about something different.'

'You couldn't say he clammed up about it,' Brian McGillion says, 'because the fact is he barely talked about it even when things were going well. And if he didn't talk about it when things were going well, why would he want to talk about it afterwards? I always felt it was a part of his life he had shut off and had moved on.'

But how do you move on when, as Giuliano Maiorana says, there is no escape from the sociocultural behemoth that football has become? In Doherty's case, you move to a new town, where nobody knows your background, and you immerse yourself in other pursuits – reading, writing, playing the guitar – and you try to purge your mind of all the negative emotions that might otherwise deny you the opportunity to get on with your life.

Doherty was still reading, writing, strumming away on his guitar, whether at open-mic nights, in the privacy of his flat or in front of the Saturday afternoon shoppers on Fishergate. It all helped. So did gnosis. Now free of football commitments, he would sometimes go to meet-ups with gnostic groups at weekends. 'Every few months we would meet with other centres around the country,' Alison Jones says. 'I attended a group in London. He had attended a group in Manchester. At certain points we would all meet together. I would imagine it was in Manchester that we met.'

What would they do on those weekend gatherings? 'Normal things,' she says. 'Relaxation practices, walks, listening to music, listening to lectures. The aim was to learn meditation and self-observation, to slow down and get in touch with who you are rather than losing yourself in the superficial aspects of life. It really was about slowing down.'

That seems to have struck a chord with Adrian Doherty. There were certainly periods when he would let his hair down, whether in Preston or visiting friends elsewhere, but there were also spells when he was content to wind down to the slower pace of life that Alison Jones is talking about. Jimmy Doherty remembers his son telling him how, at times, a big night out in Preston would involve a long evening stroll, finishing off with a couple of pints of Guinness in an 'old timers' pub', where he would listen intently as the locals regaled him with wartime stories. Jimmy adds, 'He used to joke about Preston, saying he had "finally found a place more boring than Strabane", but he was happy there for a good while.'

'I always find it funny when I hear of Adrian being described as a loner or detached,' Gareth Doherty says. 'He was more comfortable in his own company than anyone I've ever met, but he could also strike up a conversation with anybody in any situation. He made friends wherever he went in the world. I know it sounds strange, and it's hard to explain to people who didn't know him, but he just got on with life and he enjoyed it. I know if it had been me in that position I would have struggled to deal with what Adrian went through, but it just didn't interest him what Ryan Giggs was doing or what David Beckham was doing. He had no ego whatsoever. The lifestyle in Preston suited him. He used to tell us he didn't mind that things were quiet and humdrum. In the four years he was in Manchester, he had had enough highs and lows to last him a lifetime.'

Thoughts on Tick Tock

The clock struck one
The clock struck two
Man, that last hour
Sure really flew
The day wears on
Soon it is through
Another day dawns
The sky is blue
Tick tock tick tock, the clock keeps moving on
Tick tock tick tock, soon another day is gone

Adrian Doherty spent two and a half years in Preston and, among family and friends alike, there are gaps in what they know about his life there. It is not altogether surprising. His friends from Strabane, having previously been scattered across the north of England, had dispersed in search of employment. Doherty was out on a limb in Preston and it certainly crossed the minds of some of his friends that, for a time, this was just the way he wanted it.

'We didn't lose touch, but we definitely weren't in contact as regularly for a couple of years,' Niall Dunphy says. 'This was before email and mobile phones. We certainly met up in Manchester a few times, but around this time it was mostly when we were back in Strabane for Christmas or whatever.'

Separate enquiries are made via the *Lancashire Evening Post*, Facebook and Twitter, calling out to anyone in the Preston area who might remember an Adrian (or Aidan) Doherty who lived there in the mid-1990s. John Gillmore, the presenter of BBC Radio Lancashire's popular afternoon show, makes room for a telephone interview in which we ask anybody who knew Doherty to come forward. Mention is made of Beech's and another known place of work, Silcock's Fresh Foods and Flowers, which closed down years ago, as well as the fact that Doherty belonged to at least two guitar groups. In the social media age, remarkably, nobody comes forward.

The discovery of an old handwritten greetings card throws up a couple of leads, mentioning a few details of one of the guitar groups in which Doherty played in Preston – at the New Britannia on Wednesday nights. The card is from a Keith 'Moggie' Morgan, who mentions Doherty co-writing a song about a chip shop.

The search is renewed and then narrowed. Fresh appeals are posted on Facebook pages for the Preston Arts Festival and then for another guitar group in Chipping, ten miles outside Preston.

Finally, Keith 'Moggie' Morgan is tracked down, but he has been unwell and cannot stay long on the phone. 'I didn't know the guy well at all, but he turned up on these acoustic nights and singing nights that various people were running at the time,' he says. 'But it was a long time ago and we would all have had a lot to drink. I don't remember much more than that, I'm sorry – except for his wonderful renditions of "Gotta Kill a Chicken by Tuesday", something like that. I knew next to nothing about the guy. I'm sorry I can't help more.'

Did Morgan and his fellow guitarists know Doherty had been a professional footballer at Manchester United, on the verge of the first team until injury cruelly intervened? 'No,' he says. 'I didn't know that. I didn't know that at all.'

Neither did Neil Hunt. He is nonplussed at first when asked, via Facebook, whether he remembers Adrian Doherty, a former United footballer who used to belong to the same guitar group. He is sent a picture to try to jog his mind. 'My god, Aidan!' he says. 'I don't remember too much about him, but he used to make everybody laugh in the music sessions because he sang a song about chickens and killing them by Tuesday.'

Finally, Keith Mitchell, a veteran of the live music scene in Preston, comes forward to reveal that he too knew Doherty – although he too remembers him as Aidan, not Adrian. 'I used to run the open-mic night on a Monday night at the Lamb, which was the main music pub in Preston,' he says. 'I remember the first time he came along, this wiry little Irishman, and you were wondering what he was going to be like, but he did all these songs, like "Gotta Kill a Chicken by Tuesday", with this big loud voice. He was very popular with the punters.'

Did he mention football? 'Vaguely,' Mitchell says, 'but only that he had played a bit. He didn't make anything of it. He certainly didn't mention Manchester United. I didn't have a clue about that. We talked briefly about him working at Beech's chocolate factory, which I had done thirty years earlier, but I didn't know anything more about him. He would just turn up, play his music, hang around a bit afterwards, maybe have a couple of drinks, and then we would see him again the next week – unless we saw him at another open-mic night during the week. He was just a nice guy.'

The Preston Blues (incomplete)

. . . With nought to lose
But clothes and shoes
If someone takes it on themselves
To myself abuse
I go to the job centre
To peruse
Then back to my room
To muse

Preston blues
O, the Preston blues
Living by a hotel
They call 'The Moose'

On Stanley Terrace
God keep and spare us
Don't let no ghosts come out
Of the night and scare us
Proudness the proud
Prestonians ooze

They claim: 'None could
Lace Tom Finney's shoes'

Preston blues
O, the Preston blues
Living where Tom
Finney's still news
O, the Preston blues
O, the Preston blues

And I walk up Fishergate Hill
See young lasses hanging around
I say: 'Hey, is this downtown?'
'Yes, straight ahead tae Preston Guild'

O, the Preston blues
O, the Preston blues

There were times when Adrian Doherty would go to visit Leo Cussons in London and, later, in Enschede, Holland. Cussons recalls that Doherty enjoyed his trips to Holland, but he also says he was never quite sure what to expect when they met up. On one visit, it would be all philosophical discussions. On the next, Doherty would be dismissive of all of that, gnosis included, and would be wanting to turn the clock back to those wild nights playing to the crowds in New York's East Village in the summer of 1992. Was his outgoing, extroverted musical persona consistent with his quest for introspective self-observation? Probably not, but there must have been times when he wanted to be eighteen again – not because he missed football (which it seems he genuinely did not) but perhaps more because, back then, anything and everything had seemed possible.

On one visit to Preston, Cussons recalled Doherty excitedly introducing him to a new girlfriend, but by the next time they met up, she was no longer on the scene. 'As brilliant and talented as he was, I don't think he ever had a steady relationship with a girl in the time I knew him,' Cussons says. 'And it wasn't for want of trying. He definitely wanted to.'

Doherty and Cussons spent much of their time showing each other their latest compositions or strumming away in search of inspiration for new ones. When they put their guitars down, it was to chew over their quest for the meaning of life. 'He had read so much, by such a young age, and he was always wanting to read more and learn more, always wanting to find out more than had ever been found out before,' Cussons says. 'A lot of people might end up in great positions, professionally, as they get older, but there's an element to suggest that if you don't keep progressing mentally, expanding your mind, challenging yourself, you end up in mental poverty. In our society, we're not really encouraged to think that way and to challenge ourselves mentally. But, in some ways, isn't that what life is about?'

Philosophying

So you dream of philosophying
Want to tell the world where it's going wrong
Don't want to join some phoney organisation
Write for them a few corny songs

You really want the world to know your heart
I mean, come off it
Do you want civilisation to fall apart
And you to be the cause of it

So if you're gonna philosophise there ain't no easy way out
You gotta examine all points of view, find out what it's really
about
You know this is the truth, you know I'm not lying
But it ain't an easy life philosophying

It was Ciara Doherty's eighteenth birthday. 'I had a few friends around and we were sitting here, having a few drinks, about to go out, when suddenly Adrian appeared at the door,' she recalls. 'I couldn't believe it. He had got the bus over and he hadn't told anyone he was coming home. It's one of the best memories I have, him coming home that night. We went into town – the Blue Parrot, as it was then – and my friends were in awe of him. One of my friends was saying, "I can't believe it. Adrian Doherty. I'm going to challenge him to a race." It was just lovely that night because Adrian had hardly been home for years and it was a chance not just for us to see him but for my friends to get to know him. And he was just Adrian, the same as always.'

After two and a half years in Preston, on top of four years in Manchester, Adrian was home. Work had dried up over there and he felt it was time for something new. He warned he was likely to be off again sooner rather than later – where, he did not know – but he was going to stick around long enough to get some work in Strabane. He tried the local factories. Adria Ltd, the hosiery factory where his mother had worked, were always looking for casual workers. He told them he could begin immediately, so he did. And for a couple of months at the start of 1996, with a regular income and without the burden of paying rent on a one-bedroom flat, back in the bosom of his family, with Ciara and Peter growing up fast, and with some of his old friends still around, as well as aunts, uncles and cousins, it seemed that Adrian Doherty had come home at last.

There was always something in the background, though. 'It was hard for him when he was back here,' his brother Gareth says. 'He would go out walking or running – if his knee was up to it – and he would play a lot of pitch and putt, but the majority of the time, away from work, he would stay in. It was hard for him to go out in Strabane. That's not a reflection on Strabane. It's just that it's a small, football-mad town and there would have been people bombarding him with questions, not realising he wanted to put the whole football experience behind him. There was always that innuendo about what happened at United because people didn't want to believe it was as straightforward as him getting a terrible injury. Like any small town, there would be some cynics who would be convinced there was more to it and wouldn't be shy of telling him so.'

'If he had gone into town, he would have been plagued by people asking him about United,' Brian McGillion says. 'Half of Strabane supported United and the other half supported Liverpool. Everyone would want a piece of him if he went out. A lot of people didn't realise he wanted to put football behind him.'

It is something with which Giuliano Maiorana can identify, having moved back to his home town, Cambridge, after seeing his dreams shattered at United. 'That's exactly it,' Maiorana says. 'That [pointing to his knee] is what screwed me, just like it did Doc, but people don't want to believe that. People want to believe there must be something more. There's 120,000 people in Cambridge, but it still feels like a village at times, with rumours flying around. In a small town, like where Doc was from, I expect you would get even more of that. That can drag you down. You haven't just got to put up with being injured, being unlucky and then retiring. You go home and people are talking behind your back and, even if they're not saying anything wrong, that's not nice. It's another thing to deal with.'

Gareth Doherty and those friends who were back in Strabane would urge Adrian to ignore the noise and join them in town. 'He would come out for a few pints every now and then, but usually he would stay at home, sitting in the kitchen with his guitar,' Gareth says. 'When we got back he would still be there, strumming Leonard Cohen or whatever, or he would be sitting there, listening to music, and you would just see the light on the end of his cigarette as he sat there smiling. It was great to have him home, but I think we all knew he was going to be off again soon.'

CHAPTER 26

Dublin was calling. Ever since his return from England, Adrian Doherty had been pondering his next stopping point. Strabane just wasn't going to cut it. Quite apart from the idea of facing the small-town music every time he left the house, he wanted something different – a different place, a different scene, different people, different sounds, a different vibe. He had wondered about Galway, down on the west coast, but he had settled on Dublin, a city with fine literary and musical traditions. He had nowhere to stay, no job to go to, but he had made up his mind. He was looking forward to this.

'We were sitting around that morning and he was all ready to go, bags packed,' Gareth Doherty says. 'It was just before St Paddy's Day, so I said to him, "Do you not think you should wait a couple of days to travel? Because it's St Paddy's Day on Sunday, all the buses will be packed, there'll be nowhere to stay and everything will be crazy over the weekend." He stood there and said, "You could be right, aye . . . ." He thought about it for a few seconds and then said, "Right. Well I'll go to Galway then." He got the bus to Galway the next day and he stayed for four years.'

To find the Latin Quarter in Galway, you only have to follow your senses. It is full of life, full of colour, full of music, full of smiles. It has a seductive quality, which just lifts the mood. In the heart of the Latin Quarter is the House Hotel or, as it was known back then, Brennan's Yard. It was there that Adrian Doherty, having found his bearings and somewhere to spend his first couple of nights in Galway, knocked on the door one spring morning in 1996 in the hope of finding work.

'He walked in off the street and asked if there were any jobs going,' John O'Connell, who ran the hotel, says. 'He was very polite and it probably helped that he was from Strabane, because I'm from Derry. I gave him a job as a day porter. He also needed a place to live because he was staying in some dirty wee hostel at the time, so I said he could come and live with me, which he did for about four or five months.

'He was very popular with all the staff. They loved him. He was a good worker. When people arrived, he would take their bags to the room. He would fetch their keys, take them their room service. He would be out sweeping, helping in the bar. We were all very fond of him. In the evenings, back at the house, he would sit up in his room, doing wee bits of poetry and songwriting or strumming on his guitar. They were the only real interests he seemed to have. I used to try to get him out on a Monday night to watch the football on Sky – it was around the time Manchester United and Newcastle were competing for the title – but he never showed any interest in football. He told me he had been a postman before, living in Preston, and I didn't think anything more of it.'

Adrian Doherty did not want to be known as an ex-footballer. He wanted a fresh start, a clean slate. 'It's the type of place where he would just blend in,' Sean Fitzgerald, who met him in Galway, says. 'He didn't stand out. You're surrounded by music and culture there, which was what he liked. You're allowed to be sort of a vagabond, really, just writing poetry and music and having conversations about philosophy or whatever. He just blended in, playing his music, writing his songs.'

Thomas Veale, who shared a flat with Doherty in Galway, agrees. 'The lifestyle suited him,' he says. 'It was quite bohemian, quite hippyish, quite special. It was laissez-faire. It had that sort of village-that-is-a-city demeanour.'

'It's a bizarre place in a way,' Fitzgerald says. 'It's one of those places where you can't tell if it's Saturday or Monday; particularly in the summer, the weekend just extends. You would get people coming from all over Europe – and this was during the "Celtic Tiger" boom. It's a magnet for all kinds of people, people who are into Irish culture, poetry, music or all sorts.'

Fitzgerald was another music buff who was teaching business studies in Galway. He casts his mind back to his first encounter with Doherty. 'It's not there now, but there was this French wine bar called Biquets, where they had an open-mic night on a Monday,' he says. 'We used to call it the graveyard of aspiration. It was poets going on about lost childhoods or the death of a tree, that sort of thing. Then suddenly this bright spark of a guy, in a baggy jumper, popped up with some song he had written. Musically it was nothing spectacular, but lyrically it was witty and original, really clever, some sort of quirky observation on society. He brought the house down. A few acts later, everyone insisted on him going up to play another, which he did. I remember laughing out loud watching him that night.

'I thought to myself, "I've got to go and speak to this guy. He's too good to ignore." He was almost bashful when I went over to speak to him. I told him he was really good. Some talented people do the reverse-psychology thing of pretending they don't think they're any good, but Adrian seemed genuinely flattered.'

John O'Connell's father was down from Derry for the weekend. As the three of them chatted over breakfast, he scrutinised the lodger from Strabane suspiciously. Afterwards, once they had all left the table, he said to his son: 'I'm sure that's the wee lad who went to Manchester United, you know.'

At first, O'Connell assumed his father must have been mistaken. After all, this 'wee lad' had not shown the slightest interest in watching the football with him. But a few weeks later there was a story about Keith Gillespie – by now at Newcastle United – in one of the Sunday papers and O'Connell saw Doherty craning his neck to read it across the breakfast table without being noticed. 'I sort of sussed it,' he says. 'I said, "You're the Adrian Doherty who was at Manchester United, aren't you?" He owned up.

'I never got much information out of him. He never really wanted to talk about it. I then let slip to one of the neighbours that Adrian used to play at Manchester United. The next Sunday morning these wee lads of thirteen/fourteen knocked on the door, all in Manchester United shirts, to ask him if he would play with them. Adrian was a bit annoyed with me. He didn't want the publicity.'

*

Adrian Doherty was smitten. There was a local girl, Kathy Maloney, who worked on reception at the hotel. 'We were like kindred spirits,' she says. 'We couldn't be separated when we worked at Brennan's Yard. We used to go out and do things. He taught me how to juggle. I think I became better than him in the end.

'He told me he had been a footballer. He wasn't bragging about it. It was the opposite, if anything. He didn't go into it in much detail, but he said Manchester was the worst period of his life. I remember him talking about Ryan Giggs once – "Oh he's a top man, he's good" – but that's about all. I probably asked him about David Beckham too. But he was just happy doing what he was doing in Galway, the poetry and what have you.'

Jimmy and Geraldine Doherty were introduced to Kathy on their trips to Galway. They, just like the staff at Brennan's Yard, were sure the pair were an item. 'I know they must have thought we were boyfriend and girlfriend,' she says. 'We didn't say we weren't because we pretty much were. But it was a very platonic friendship.'

> *A madwoman, Maloney*
> *You're a madwoman*
> *You really are a bit mad*
> *It's not a complaint*
> *But I would become a saint*
> *If I can't become your madman*

'He did tell me he was interested in me,' she says, 'and I really loved him, but it was platonic. Everyone would have thought we were girlfriend and boyfriend, but I put up a bit of a block in terms of that. I was thinking, "Adrian is lovely, and we're great friends, but I need someone who can provide for me." He was never really interested in making a living. He didn't want money at all. He would see how long he could live on IR£5. We used to live in the same house for a while, sharing with a few other people, and I would go out and get us a T-bone steak or something. He would enjoy it but he would never really realise or appreciate that it cost money. Money just didn't interest him at all.

'He wasn't motivated by a career in the same way most people would see a career. He wasn't interested in material gain or getting recognition. But whatever he did, he would take great pleasure from it and he liked to master it. The main mission in his life was to achieve enlightenment. He liked to meditate sometimes, but he would keep that to himself. Even when he was cleaning the windows at the hotel, he would try to do it very mindfully. I think that was his ambition: enlightenment. That's what it was really about for him.'

Connie Fennell, who was the general manager at Brennan's Yard, remembers Adrian Doherty as being 'completely reliable'. 'He was a bit different from your typical hotel porter, but he worked hard and he was very good at his job,' she says. 'I knew I could rely on him.'

Gareth Doherty recalls that there were limits to his brother's skills. 'One time the chef didn't turn up and he stood in and helped them make breakfast, but it was a disaster,' he says with a laugh. 'Everything was burnt.'

Despite that mishap, Fennell was disappointed when

the day porter handed in his notice in the summer of 1997. 'I can't remember why he left,' she says. 'He was very reserved and very private but still sociable, that kind of character. He was very popular with the other staff, but he was his own man. I wonder if maybe he wasn't long for this world. I don't know why I say that. I just think he had lived before. He had his own presence, his own path. Nobody else was setting him goals. He was doing his own thing.'

Upon leaving Brennan's Yard, Adrian Doherty discovered that not every potential employer would be as happy to trust their gut feeling as John O'Connell had been. Enquiries to employment agencies in Galway invariably led to a request for a CV.

. Writing was his great pleasure in life, but he needed Alison Jones's help when it came to putting together a CV that would not make potential employers raise an eyebrow in suspicion when they saw Manchester United juxtaposed with Beech's Fine Chocolates, Silcock's Fresh Foods and Flowers and now Brennan's Yard. 'He had to put down his previous jobs,' she says. 'I remember him saying, "Previous jobs: professional footballer. Responsibilities: playing football." He said to me he was never going to get a job with a CV like that,' she says.

He did, though. From July to December 1997 Doherty worked in Galway for Grosvenor Services, a company specialising in cleaning, security and facilities management for businesses. His CV says he was a cleaning operative. It is not the job you would expect of an aspiring singer-songwriter who had been on the brink of a first-team debut

at Manchester United, but it was just about secure enough
to allow him to pay his rent and to leave time for his creative pursuits, such as those open-mic nights at Biquets,
Java's and Roísín Dubh, where emerging artists mixed
with established acts.

From time to time, when he had enough money,
Doherty would just get up and go. He visited friends in
London or he went to see Leo Cussons, now a father, in
Enschede. These trips were nothing like so riotous as their
days in Manchester and New York. Cussons remembers
his friend trying to go for a run one morning and being
unable to move without encountering pain in his knee.

It was one of these trips to Holland that led Doherty to
move out of John O'Connell's house. He would find a
new living arrangement on his return. On the day he left,
O'Connell gave him an IR£50 note, along with his wages
from Brennan's Yard, to help him on his way. 'He thanked
me but gave the money back and said he couldn't possibly
take it,' O'Connell says. 'Eventually I persuaded him to
take it. A week later I had a letter from him in Holland:
"Dear John, thank you for everything you've done for me.
You've really looked after me." And in the letter was the
same IR£50 note.'

On another occasion Kathy Maloney remembers
Doherty abruptly deciding to go back to England for a
visit. 'We waved him off at the bus, myself and my brother
Martin,' she says. 'All my family loved him. You couldn't
help but love him. And then I didn't hear from him for
weeks.

'When he got back, it was as if nothing had happened. I
was saying, "Adrian, where did you go? Why didn't you tell

me where you were?" But you couldn't stay angry with him for any length of time. He was that type of person. Whatever anger you had or threw at him, he would just dispel it. You couldn't help but love him.'

'I had known him before, but I got a much more rounded view of Adrian when we moved to Ireland,' Alison Jones says. 'I would describe him as mild, humble, very shy and very funny. He liked a good joke. He would laugh until he cried. He would be tickled pink by things. He would laugh along with my little boy Thomas. The pair of them wouldn't stop laughing. He would be singing, writing songs, writing poems, playing chess with my husband. When Rob and I got married in 1997, Adrian sang at our wedding reception. There was another pair of singers and they didn't generate anything like as much attention. He was getting requests: "Sing again, sing again," "Not yet, not yet. Soon." Then he would sing and people would gather around to enjoy it. He was a show-stopper. It was all his own songs. They were all quirky, clever. He was one of life's little geniuses.'

Rob and Alison Jones helped to run a gnostic study group in Galway, which Adrian Doherty joined. 'He would come along for an hour, maybe a couple of times a week,' Alison says. 'It was run as a school, really. We had lectures and studies. We had certain days when we would look at certain principles. Monday might be meditation. Wednesday might be relaxation. He would listen very intently. He did have a grasp of it.'

Some of the intellectual, philosophical aspects of these gnostic study sessions fascinated him. But other fundamentals of gnosis were hard for him to embrace. The teachings urged him to distinguish between personality (the aspects of a person that are derived from and exhibited in his environment) and essence (the inner, spiritual aspect) – and for his development to work around essence at the expense of personality. Realistically, all the meditation in the world was not going to dampen Doherty's personality.

'He was a bit of a contradiction,' Rob Jones says, 'in that he was a shy, reserved sort of fella and yet another side of him would go into this bar, recite his poetry, play his guitar, sing his songs and enjoy that side of life. The personality side of life meant putting yourself out there, showing yourself to the world. The inner side of life would be about who you are and who you could be if your personality didn't dominate. I don't think Adrian ever came to that conclusion.'

For a while, he lodged with the Joneses – an arrangement that was revived on a couple of occasions when he was between rentals – and it was on evenings like this, whether at the dinner table or over a chessboard, that Doherty might just drip-feed the odd reflection, direct or implied, on his football career.

'I don't think he had been particularly happy in Manchester,' Rob Jones says. 'He loved playing football, but not necessarily on such a large scale as that. He thought he might have preferred to play for Derry or someone of that nature. It wasn't so much what he said. It was more the lack of enthusiasm he had when he talked about it. It wasn't such a big deal for him not to be playing for Manchester United. He wasn't devastated about it. I don't think he was hugely bothered about it, which is a good thing.'

Rob Jones remembers Doherty saying Ryan Giggs and David Beckham were both 'nice fellas' as well as talented footballers, but he did not go much further. 'He didn't make a song and dance about any of it, though,' Jones says. 'He had the sense that there was more to life – more depth.'

The Soul of a Poet

This soul of a poet:
Can one grow it?
And those who have it
Must they always show it?

The days of a poet
Do you know what?
On ode and sonnet
Musing, they're eroded

And many's a poet
Fallen low, yet
Whose words, from habit
Remain sugar-coated

Each soul of a poet
Needs to glow, it
Spews forth but vomit
Growing sick or bloated

CHAPTER 27

Whatever happened to Adrian Doherty? The question had nagged away at Michael Walker for years. This time the journalist's curiosity had been piqued and heightened by an interview he had read in Manchester United's official magazine, in which Chris Casper was asked to name the most skilful player he had ever seen. 'An Irish lad called Adrian Doherty,' Casper, who was now a member of United's first-team squad, replied. 'He had to be the most unlucky lad ever. He got a really bad injury and his career was finished. But what a player.'

The man from the *Irish Times* decided it was time to hunt for Doherty. Why? 'Because,' Walker says, 'whenever people used that term "Fergie's Fledglings" and talked about all the kids who broke through at United – Giggs, Beckham, Scholes, Butt, the Nevilles, Gillespie and so on – it always struck me that Adrian should have been the first. People talked about Ryan Giggs being the first of that generation, but there should have been one before that. The first "Fergie Fledgling". And that interview with Chris Casper reignited my interest in trying to find what Adrian was up to – if he was still playing, where he was living, where he was working, that sort of thing.'

Walker started making enquiries and finally, after what

had at times felt like a wild-goose chase, managed to track Doherty down to a flat at the back of a pub in Galway. He rang the pub a few times and was told Doherty was not there. He asked when he was likely to catch the tenant at home. He was given a certain time and said he would call back.

'I remember someone else answered and then they went to get him to come to the phone,' Walker says. 'Adrian came on, I told him who I was and what I was thinking of writing and . . . he just wasn't interested. I can't remember the exact phrase he used, but he said football was over for him. No matter how I tried to keep him going, that wasn't what interested him any more.'

It was, Brian McGillion says, 'the most incongruous thing you could think of'. He and his girlfriend – now his wife – were down in Galway for a short break, driving out to the coastal resort of Salthill one morning, when they spotted a young man walking down the road, oblivious to the rain and the traffic.

'We were driving past this guy, walking down the road on his own, and I just looked and I suddenly said, "Oh my god, it's Adrian!"' he recalls. 'I couldn't believe my eyes because I hadn't seen him for a good while. I stopped the car and wound down the window and said, "What are you at, sir?" "Yes, Peedge. What's the *craic*?" I asked him what he was up to. "Ah, bit of this, bit of that, bit of busking."'

Most of the lads from St Colman's offer a decent impersonation of Adrian Doherty. Judging by that grainy camcorder footage from the Manchester days, none has mastered it quite like McGillion ('What d'you mean, sir? What d'you mean?'). It is somehow soft and staccato at the same time. It is certainly upbeat. It is unmistakably Strabane and it is applied as readily to the eleven-year-old Doherty as to the figure McGillion saw standing in the rain on the way to Salthill that morning. McGillion was delighted to see his friend was the same as ever.

'I probably would have picked the fella up no matter who it had been,' McGillion says, 'but I literally couldn't believe it was him. We gave him a lift to Salthill and he was still talking about his poems and his songwriting. He was never concerned about money and things like that. He was on great form. Whenever I think of Adrian, I think of his amazing smile. It was infectious. He was smiling that day.'

Jimmy and Geraldine Doherty used to worry when they heard their son talk about his long strolls in Galway. It was not just to and from work. He would walk all over, enjoying the coastal air and taking the opportunity to clear his head. He would think nothing of walking in winter on roads that had no lights and no pavements. Walking in the dark did not bother him, but it bothered his parents.

Adrian Doherty rarely stayed long enough in one house or flat to bother sorting out a telephone. That worried his parents too if they had not heard from him for a few days. They would ring Rob and Alison Jones to ask if they had seen him. They would ring Kathy Maloney, who would at times have to stop herself telling them she had the same worries.

After Brennan's Yard and the house share, Maloney lost track of where Adrian was living. 'Then for a while he moved into this place that I used to call his treehouse,' she says. 'It was an apartment at the back of a pub or a guest-house and there was a tree going through it and a fantastic view looking out over Lough Corrib. There was no plaster on the walls when he moved in, but he did it up nicely. He got real satisfaction out of that.'

Still, moving further from the centre of Galway meant more walking, more cycling and more worrying for his parents, who knew that, with his earphones in and singing along, in a daydream, he was quite capable of drifting off into a world of his own.

Christian Pauls is one of those Germans whose command of English would put many a native speaker to shame. In a typical Galway arrangement, the German gap-year student was living with a Scottish writer named Rab Fulton. They were ideal additions to the polyglot mix among the Monday night crowd at Galway's premier French wine bar.

Pauls was not as bowled over as others were by Adrian Doherty's poetry recitals at Biquets. 'I think that was less to do with his poetry and more to do with the fact that I was a wannabe intellectual and a bit snobbish,' he says. 'His poetry scanned and rhymed, whereas I was into this modernist poetry – the more complicated, the better in my twenty-year-old mind. I liked his poetry, but I remember saying to Rab I thought some of Adrian's poems were very simple. Rab said, "No, you're taking them liter-ally. They are clever. You have to read between the lines." Then I realised there was something more to Adrian's poetry.'

Hungover Plant

A hungover plant
Hung over an aisle
In a bar, that has been hungover for a while

Abandoned restraint
And so wild has grown
All the roughs in the bar it makes feel at home

It's spent too much time in the bar
And went just too far

Though its branches groan
Yet seems improper;
To cut it down to size no one does offer

Tourists in raptures
And novelty seekers
On coming across it like to take pictures

It's hung round too long in the bar
And gone now too far

This hungover plant
Sympathy no one
Offers, but its hapless flight of, just make fun

From time to time, when struggling to find work in Galway, Adrian Doherty would seek employment back in Strabane. In early 1998 he spent two months on the

Ballycolman industrial estate, working on the factory floor at Moldall Ltd, which manufactured lingerie. He became one of the many Strabane men who, as the local joke used to have it, worked in women's underwear.

He spent time at the family home, but often it was weekend shifts, which allowed him to spend the week in Galway before escaping when the crowds came in on Saturdays and Sundays. It was an arrangement that suited him and his family back in Strabane. 'It was always a massive deal for me when Gareth or Adrian came back, even if only for a few days at a time, because I would always end up playing football in the garden or playing pool with them,' their younger brother Peter says.

Music, increasingly, was another bond. 'When I first started learning guitar, Adrian used to show me things,' Peter says. 'Then he went away and came back and I had got really into it. He would come back and play songs he had written and we would record them on the four-track we had. He would write stuff off the top of his head in no time. He wasn't trying to write big hit songs. It was just quirky stuff. He loved doing it. He used to say how he loved going around playing open-mic nights in Galway.'

Ciara Doherty enjoyed spending more time with her brother too. 'We always had a bond when we were growing up, but I hadn't seen much of him over the years when he was in Manchester and Preston, so I think it was more around this time that I got to know him better,' she says. 'The house was always transformed when he was home. We would all look forward to it. But I always remember Adrian saying he got itchy feet whenever he was home longer than a week. He wanted to get away again.'

*

It was, says James Allison, 'a dirty job – not a nice job'. He is talking about the work at Galway Plating, where he employed Adrian Doherty as a general operative, electro-plating metal, between April and October in 1998. 'We had quite a rough bunch of lads working there, some of them from the wrong side of the tracks,' Allison says. 'We had the police around one morning because one of the guys was caught up in a bit of bother.

'I didn't know much about Adrian at all; he was just a lad who came to work in an Aran sweater and big pair of black boots, did his work and went home. But there was something more to him than the others. I didn't know he had played football and, to be honest, that surprises me, but music, yes, you could sense he was a musician, even though I don't think he ever mentioned it. He just had that musician thing about him.

'He was a good worker, one of the few I could rely on. I thought maybe I could train him up, pay him a bit extra and get him to stay on a bit longer. I trained about six of them up to drive a fork-lift truck. The other five left as soon as I had trained them. He was the only who stayed, which I think was out of loyalty, but he didn't stay all that long and I couldn't blame him for that. To be honest, I didn't stay there long either. It wasn't a nice place to work.'

Doherty's next job in Galway, from December 1998 to May 1999, was rather more sedate. 'It was at my house, a home bakery,' Joan O'Dea says. 'He worked for a few hours in the mornings. I used to make the doughnuts and we would work together until 9.30, when I would go on deliveries and he would clean up afterwards. He would be gone by the time I got home. The only qualification he needed was honesty. He was certainly honest. He was a nice guy.'

Did she know he had been a footballer? 'No, I had no idea,' she says. 'He did mention writing poetry, but I didn't give it much credence at the time. I regarded him as a kid because he was similar in age to my kids. I remember he was living in an apartment on his own somewhere and I thought that sounded like a very solitary existence for a young fellow.'

'Oh, he definitely wasn't a recluse or anything like that,' Alison Jones says. 'Far from it. He had a busy life in Galway. He worked. He went to open-mic nights, singing, playing music, writing poetry. He was in competitions every week. They would vote for the winner. He had friends. We saw a lot of him right up until he left. He would come out for dinner with us or he would come to ours and play chess or entertain our little boy. He did live quietly – he might have lived on his own in a single-room flat at one point – but he was definitely not a recluse.'

One of his flats in Galway met with disapproval from the Joneses. 'It was like a garage flat and it was damp,' Rob Jones says. 'I went round there once to see him in cold weather and the place was freezing. I said to him, "Adrian, why haven't you got your fire on?" I got the fire going and he was delighted. But he would just ignore those unpleasantnesses. Luxuries, even something like warmth, did not interest him.'

As winter approached in 1999, Adrian Doherty moved into a flat with Thomas Veale, who recalls it as 'the downstairs part of a big semi-detached house in a nondescript estate in west Galway'.

Doherty would head back to Strabane to do factory work at weekends, at Adria Ltd, and Veale remembers that his flatmate 'always had a chuckle to himself because he would have his work done for the week just as other people were going off to work'. 'It was an arrangement that suited him and suited his lifestyle,' Veale says. 'He was working at weekends and was free in the week to pursue his interests. I think he had found his equilibrium.'

Veale admits that Doherty's big revelation, about his previous career as a professional footballer, was probably wasted on him. 'It was just something he mentioned once or twice in the course of conversations,' Veale says. 'Apart from that, he didn't mention it at all. He certainly wouldn't be bragging to anyone that he had been at Manchester United. Nor did he want to be looking back and regretting. He felt there wasn't much point in regrets. He had moved on and was doing his own thing.'

It seems telling that Doherty mentioned the United experience to Veale, who was not interested in football, but not to Sean Fitzgerald, who was. 'There's no way he ever mentioned it to me,' Fitzgerald says. 'If he had done, I would have been desperate for him to tell me more. Maybe that's why he didn't tell me.'

'I'm not saying life was a bed of roses for Adrian,' Veale says. 'He wasn't sitting in the sun, smiling with a girlfriend. But he was just there to do what he was doing. He did meditation now and again. He read. He was doing something productive, something artistic. He was performing. Manchester United wasn't on his mind at all. He had moved on.'

*

It was December 1999 and Michael Walker was in the Manchester United manager's office at the Cliff. The man from the *Irish Times* had scooped a rare one-on-one interview with Sir Alex Ferguson, newly knighted in recognition of United's historic treble success earlier that year. The interview was going perfectly to plan. Unusually relaxed, with a journalist he respected and trusted, Ferguson had opened up about potential changes to the club's ownership, his plans beyond his proposed retirement in 2002 (just the eleven years earlier than it transpired) and his disappointment that United had been forced to withdraw from that season's FA Cup.

It was all going so swimmingly that Walker decided it was time to drop in the question that intrigued him more than any other: whatever happened to Adrian Doherty? Since that part of the interview has remained unpublished, Walker uses his own words, rather than Ferguson's, to paint the picture.

'Ferguson's office had a floor-to-ceiling window, overlooking the training pitch,' Walker says, 'and when I asked him about Adrian, he got up from his desk, looked out of the window, onto the training pitch. He said, "I can see the game now where he did his cruciate" – or whatever the initial injury was. He proceeded to talk absolutely glowingly about Adrian. He talked about his physical courage, but he said other things that were equally praiseworthy, if not more so.'

Did Ferguson give the impression Doherty could – or would – have made it but for the injury he suffered as a seventeen-year-old? 'Oh yes,' Walker says. 'And it wasn't "could have". It was "would have". He was due to make his debut against Everton when Ryan Giggs did. He was an absolute certainty. It wasn't typical for a manager to talk about a player like that.'

Was there any caveat to Ferguson's lavish praise? 'He did say Adrian wasn't a typical footballer in terms of either talent or temperament,' Walker says. 'He had other interests and perhaps Ferguson had difficulties understanding what his motivation was and what got him going. But there was absolutely no vagueness about his ability.

'What he really talked about and really loved, as well as the speed and the ability, was Adrian's physical courage. Speed, courage, ability – Giggs and Doherty, two wingers with the same qualities. He was very graphic about it. For him to get out of his seat in his office, looking out of that window, looking down on the pitch where the injury happened, was quite striking.'

Walker kept those quotes from Ferguson on his tape and then transcribed them for use at a later date. But for reasons we shall return to, the contents of that part of the interview have yet to see the light of day.

They met at Roísín Dubh, another of those Galway music venues where Adrian Doherty had made an impression on locals and tourists alike. 'He hadn't changed a bit,' Dee Devenney says of their overdue catch-up towards the end of the 1990s. 'Jumper, jeans and a pair of trainers. Hadn't brushed his hair. He said he was playing the guitar, writing poems, doing loads of reading, playing pitch and putt. He was on good form. He liked Galway, that sort of bohemian vibe they have down there – much more low-key than Manchester, a few pints of Guinness, good live music.

'He was working – a menial job, stress-free. A job, to him, was just a means of getting money and he was never interested in money anyway. I remember saying to him, "Why don't you go back to college? Do your A-levels. We've all been through college and you're smarter than any of us. Do English literature or anything." Because he could have done anything, you know. He said he would think about it, but, to me, he seemed happy drifting. It was great to see him. We said goodbye at the end of the night. He went back to wherever he was living. I was only there for the night and I headed off the next morning.'

One day – he thinks it was while they were out walking in Galway – Christian Pauls asked Adrian Doherty about his childhood. 'He said something about the role football played in his past and about having been really good at it,' Pauls says. 'He mentioned an injury and how it changed his plans for the future and he had to change everything. But I had no idea the level of football that he reached. There was a note of regret, but, from where I stood, I think he was OK with how things were. He wasn't angry about what happened – not at all – and just told it in a neutral way, which must be why I didn't think more of it at the time. I'm sure it would have come out more if it had been weighing heavily on him.'

How would he describe Doherty? 'Exceptional,' Pauls says. 'Yes, I would endorse that. He touched a lot of people's lives in a very positive way by dint of his character and by being, in the truest sense of the word, good-natured. The Adrian Doherty I knew had a very good essence, nature, soul. Whatever you would want to call it, a lot of people liked it.'

Did Doherty give an indication of any long-term plan? 'I don't think any of us in this group in Galway had a plan at the time,' Pauls says. 'That's probably why we all seemed to fit into this loose group of people – people who had all come from somewhere else, all of us expats in one way or another. What we were all looking for, I don't know. I felt he would probably go somewhere else when the mood took him. That was the same with many people in Galway.'

It was January 2000, a new millennium, and time for Adrian Doherty to try something different. He had been in Galway nearly four years – almost as long as he was in Manchester – and was going to head back to Strabane while weighing up his next move. He said his goodbyes. Kathy Maloney recalls that, for want of a pen, they failed to exchange up-to-date contact details when they met for the last time, for a pizza at Monroe's; Sean Fitzgerald found himself the lucky recipient of a Leonard Cohen book, which Doherty said he did not want any more; Alison Jones says he told her he was planning to get a job abroad, perhaps for the summer, perhaps longer term.

Was there a plan? 'I don't think he had one,' Rob Jones says. 'He was being blown by the wind a bit.'

If, as Bob Dylan suggested, the answer was blowing in the wind, Adrian Doherty took a strangely proactive approach to finding it. Back in Strabane, he wrote to employment agencies enquiring about summer jobs abroad. He talked to his family and friends of going somewhere else to work for a couple of months – France, Belgium, Holland, Germany – and then perhaps heading to Denmark later in the summer. It was all rather vague, but there was far more of a long-term plan than preceded his moves to Preston and Galway.

In the meantime Adrian spent afternoons playing pitch and putt with Peter and then went to watch his younger brother's band if they were playing. 'He was very encouraging with my music,' Peter says. 'Just before he left, they released these new eight-tracks and we were going to go halves on one.'

Adrian would still go for an occasional kickabout with his brothers. 'I remember chatting to him not long before he left, up on the playing fields where he always used to train as a youngster,' his former schoolmate and Moorfield teammate John Tinney says. 'Gareth was there and I think possibly Peter too. There were three or four of us and we played a game. I remember thinking, "All right, it didn't work out for Adrian at United, but it's great just seeing him kicking a football." We were in our mid-twenties and we were running around like we were youngsters.'

In May 2000, an employment agency came up with a job working for Dekker Hout, a Dutch furniture company based in Warmond, not far from The Hague. It seemed to meet Adrian Doherty's basic requirements. His brother Gareth disapproved, citing his own joyless experience doing agency work in Holland the previous year. 'I told Adrian I didn't know if it was a good move,' Gareth says. 'He said, "I'm just going to go there for a few weeks and I'll catch up with Leo and then I'll move on."

He was talking about this job as a stopgap and then fruit-picking and maybe going up to Denmark later in the summer.'

It is strange, the details people recollect. Peter Doherty knows exactly what was on television when he said good-bye to his brother. 'I just remember sitting there,' Peter says, 'watching *The Count of Monte Cristo*, of all things, and Adrian put his head around the door and said, "I'm head-ing off. I've got a job in Holland." To me, it all seemed really sudden.'

'Yes, it was sudden,' his sister, Ciara, confirms, 'but he had been home for a while and I think the opportunity just came up. I've often thought about this, going over it in my head, thinking, "Why there?" because it wasn't as if he had always said, "I've got to go to Holland." But he had signed up with an employment agency, got a phone call and he was off. He was like that. Whereas maybe I would have been more, "Let's think about this," Adrian was impulsive. He would get the opportunity and he would just go and see what it was like.'

'We just thought it would be the same routine as when he went to the other places,' Peter says. 'You never got the impression he would stay in one place for a long time.'

They said their goodbyes and, with that, Adrian Doherty was off again. 'I remember thinking at the time, "Will Adrian ever settle down?"' Ciara says. 'He was only twenty-six, but because he was my big brother, I probably thought of him as being much older. I really thought he would stay in Holland for a while and then be back again before long. That was just Adrian.'

CHAPTER 28

The patient in the coma had not been carrying any identification when he was pulled out of the canal near The Hague's main station at 9.15 a.m. He was unconscious, in a critical condition in the intensive care unit at Westeinde hospital, and nobody, including the local police, had the slightest idea who he was. He was the patient with no name.

Josette Morrison, an Irish nurse who had worked at the hospital for nine years, was coming to the end of her night shift when the patient was rushed in on a trolley. 'He hadn't been identified, but I saw him and thought, "Dark hair, pale complexion, freckles. That looks like an Irish or Scottish guy,"' she says, recalling the morning of 7 May 2000.

He still had not been identified when she returned for her night shift that evening. Again she told colleagues she thought he must be Irish or Scottish. Does he have any distinguishing marks, she asked? Yes, a huge scar on his right knee.

Jimmy and Geraldine Doherty were anxious. They had asked Adrian to keep in regular touch, but it was nearly a week since he had called. On that occasion, a few days

339

after his arrival in Holland, he rang from a phone box in the Dutch coastal town of Katwijk, telling them how nice it was. He told them his accommodation in nearby Warmond was extremely basic (no telephone) and the work – making, moving and packing wooden furniture – was boring, but he was sure he could save enough money to enable him to move on somewhere else in Europe for the rest of the summer. He liked Holland, he told them. He was going to go to The Hague soon. He had not been in touch with Leo Cussons yet, but he planned to visit him in Enschede, possibly via Amsterdam, once he was finished with Dekker Hout. From there he might head up through Germany into Denmark or go south through Belgium and into France. He had not decided yet. How was he going to get around? He would catch trains or buses or maybe hitchhike, he told them. 'Oh, Adrian,' they said. 'Please be careful, won't you?'

As the days went by, they told their eldest son, Gareth, they were worried. What if something had happened? 'I just said, "Don't worry. It's Adrian. He'll be in touch,"' Gareth recalls. Another day passed. They got the same message of reassurance from their daughter, Ciara, back in Strabane as she sought somewhere quiet to revise for her university finals. 'I told them, "You know what he's like. He's just being Adrian,"' Ciara says.

Jimmy Doherty was not reassured. He rang the employment agency and got a number for the furniture company in Holland. He told them who he was and asked whether it would be possible to speak to his son. He was informed Adrian had not been seen all week. He rang Cussons, who said Adrian had not been in touch. That was when the sound of alarm bells became deafening for Jimmy Doherty. He still clung on to the hope that Adrian had upped and left, moving to another town like a wandering minstrel, but something felt very wrong. He contacted UK police to inform them he feared his son was missing abroad. From there his appeal was passed on to the emergency services in Holland, who were asked whether they had any record of a British citizen named Adrian John Doherty, twenty-six years old, dark hair, 5ft 9in. Any distinguishing marks? Yes, a huge scar on his right knee.

The picture that various members of the Doherty family paint of Friday, 12 May 2000, once the news filtered through from Holland to their home in Strabane, is a harrowing one. Gareth Doherty returned from work in Derry that evening to find a scene of distress and devastation. Some of his nearest and dearest were in stunned silence. Others were wailing. He was told his brother Adrian had fallen into a canal in The Hague on the Sunday morning and had spent the past five days in hospital, in a critical condition. 'It was just awful, a complete nightmare,' Gareth says. 'Everyone was in pieces.'

Peter O'Brien, a cousin, took charge of arrangements to get the family to Holland as a matter of urgency. He came back with flights from Belfast the next morning. Adrian's younger brother, Peter, would not be able to go because he did not have a passport. He would stay with an aunt while Jimmy, Geraldine, Gareth and Ciara flew to Amsterdam the next morning to be at Adrian's bedside in The Hague.

When the news came in, Ciara had been revising for

her exams. Hours later, when she went back upstairs, she saw the books were still laid out as they had been before. 'I just thought how my life had totally changed in those hours since I had last looked at them,' she says. 'It was your biggest nightmare. From that moment, life has just never been the same.'

The only good news awaiting the Doherty family on arrival at Westeinde hospital, following a traumatic journey, was that Adrian was still alive. They were allowed to visit him in the intensive care unit, where the doctors spelt out that they had tried to stabilise him over the previous days, but his condition was life-threatening. From what little that could be ascertained, he had fallen into the canal and, unable to swim, had been drowning, unconscious, the oxygen to his brain cut off. He was being kept alive by a ventilator. Even if he were to pull through over the next days and weeks, he could be left with severe brain damage.

They had a million questions to ask about his recovery prospects, his injuries and of course the circumstances leading up to what had happened. Police were still carrying out their investigation, they were told, but there was no evidence so far to suggest, judging by their tests and enquiries, that it was anything other than a freak accident. There were hundreds of canal accidents across the Netherlands each year. The vast majority of them were precisely that – accidents – and this looked like another. As for his condition and his recovery prospects, there was nothing positive the doctors could tell them.

Josette Morrison stayed on at the hospital after her shifts to offer support. She and Catherine Couinhan, another Irish nurse at Westeinde, vowed to do whatever they could to make life more bearable for the Dohertys at this awful time. As well as supporting them with tea and sympathy, they helped the hospital to sort out an apartment for the family to stay in nearby once it became clear that they would not be rushing home. The nurses also helped with translations to ensure there was a regular flow of information, delivered as compassionately as possible.

'As a nurse, of course you do go the extra mile – that goes without saying – but it didn't feel like it was going the extra mile,' Morrison says. 'You just do what's right to help a family in a very difficult time. And when it's a family from the same background as you, coming to the Netherlands, not knowing anyone, in a situation like this, you do whatever you can.'

The other friendly face awaiting the Dohertys when they arrived at Westeinde that Saturday was Leo Cussons, who had hot-footed it over from Enschede. He remembers stumbling around the hospital in a state somewhere between trauma and disbelief. On one hand, the reports on the news were telling him of a huge explosion that afternoon at a fireworks factory in his adopted home town of Enschede – a disaster that would leave twenty-three people dead and 947 injured. On the other, he was standing in a hospital in The Hague, seeing his friend looking lifeless. 'Everything got very blurred, like a dream,' he says. Whatever was going on back in Enschede, it just seemed so, so wrong to see the life being extinguished from the 'fireball' he remembered from their days together in Manchester and New York.

*

For nearly four weeks, Jimmy and Geraldine Doherty went through every parent's worst nightmare, conducting a vigil as the life ebbed away from their beloved son. They prayed and prayed for him to recover. Long, desolate mornings, afternoons and evenings were spent at Adrian's bedside, occasionally taking a walk to the hospital café or just a little further. 'That's how we spent our days,' Gareth Doherty says, 'at the bedside, taking turns to sit with Adrian, or sometimes one or two of us would go for a walk. Ciara and I would go for a walk into town and have a coffee. We would try to talk about normal things, but it was impossible. There was always a hope against hope that a miracle would happen and he would be OK, but, as the days went by, Adrian's condition was getting worse, not better.'

At one point Gareth and Ciara went back to Strabane for a few days to see their younger brother Peter and ask whether he might want to come back with them if they could organise a passport. The nurses advised Gareth and Ciara to say their goodbyes to Adrian just in case. The situation was that bleak.

The Irish nurses, Josette Morrison and Catherine Counihan, continued to go the extra mile for a family in distress. They talked to Jimmy and Geraldine for hours, trying at some times to help them focus on fonder memories of their son – and at other times to focus on anything but the tragedy that was unfolding.

'It would have been unusual to find Irish nurses in a hospital in the Netherlands,' Josette says. 'We were in a group of twenty-five who had moved out there in 1991, when the hospital was looking for nurses and they advertised in Ireland. We had gone there as student nurses and it was nice in this situation to think we were able to help out an Irish family at such a hard time.'

By now, the nurses knew all about Adrian. Both of them – but particularly Catherine, a big fan of both Gaelic and association football – had been astounded to hear of his pedigree as a footballer at Manchester United. They had also heard about his upbringing in Strabane, his poetry and songwriting, his time in Preston and Galway and the characteristic impulsiveness with which he had left for Holland just a week before he ended up in hospital.

The nurses came back to the apartment to keep the Dohertys company in the evenings. Sometimes they would watch television together. At other times they would bring food so Adrian's parents did not have to think about cooking or going out for dinner. 'As time went on, and they were staying for a longer period, we grew closer to them,' Josette says. 'They were lovely, such a nice family. They were going from hour to hour, from day to day, from week to week. And then unfortunately an end came to it.'

News reached Gareth, Ciara and Peter Doherty, back in Strabane, that their brother's condition was deteriorating by the day. It was time to fly back to The Hague. They talked about the practicalities of trying to fix up Peter with a passport. 'I've thought about this,' Peter told his brother and sister, 'and I've decided I'm going to stay here. I want to remember Adrian as the last time I saw him, smiling and joking.'

Gareth and Ciara flew back to Holland. They got to the hospital to find their father and mother in tears. 'That second, I knew that was it,' Ciara says. 'All along, I had been hoping and praying and thinking, "This can't happen. This can't happen." Until then, the whole thing had felt very surreal being out there, so far away from home. There was a dream-like quality to it. And that was the moment when suddenly it felt real.'

Yes, Adrian was still alive, but it was only a matter of time now. They did not leave his bedside. Adrian John Doherty passed away on the morning of 9 June 2000, a day short of his twenty-seventh birthday. 'We watched him take his last few breaths,' his brother Gareth says. 'And that was it.'

The moment the car pulled up outside, Peter Doherty knew. His parents had wanted to keep the news from him until they got home, so they could be with him, to comfort him, when they told him, but he worked it out before they reached the threshold, before they even got out of the car.

They told the fifteen-year-old that his big brother, whom he worshipped, had died, peacefully, that morning. They told him they were so, so sorry. They wept and he surprised them all, and himself, by responding stoically. 'It will sound weird, because I know I was absolutely devastated, but at first, I couldn't feel that,' Peter recalls.

For all of the others, the feelings were overwhelming, particularly for Geraldine. A doctor was called to see if he could do anything for her. There was not. She had lost her son. She was inconsolable.

Peter's reaction sounds like what psychologists call denial, with the mind building up a barrier to defend it from the brutal reality of bereavement. That barrier is only ever superficial. For Peter, the trigger was the sight of the coffin after his brother's body was flown home from

Holland five days later. He walked into a room and saw some of Adrian's friends, lads he had not seen for years, standing next to the coffin, paying their respects. He broke down. Reality – the worst imaginable reality – had just bitten hard.

Since that horrible night when they first heard the news of Adrian Doherty's accident, his friends had been in daily contact, trying to find out the latest news and what, if anything, they could do to help. The hardest thing, in some ways, had been trying to work out precisely what was going on when the rumour mill back home in Strabane was going wild.

As far as Niall Dunphy had been aware, there was a rumour that Adrian's condition had been improving, however slowly, however unpromisingly. Dunphy and his friends had clutched that straw tightly, daring to believe the worst might be over. And then he took a call from his mother, telling him – or warning him – of an awful rumour that was beginning to spread around Strabane.

'My mother said she had heard someone say that Aidy might have died,' Niall recalls. 'I panicked. I phoned Kevin [Doherty]. He said he hadn't heard that. We tried to convince each other it was just a Strabane rumour, but we weren't reassured. We decided we would call Father Doherty, the priest. He would know. I phoned him and I said: "Hi, it's Niall Dunphy here. Listen, I'm sorry to bother you, but I'm hearing a really bad rumour and . . ."'

Even before Father Doherty could say the words, his tone was enough to tell Dunphy what he had dreaded. 'I'm so sorry, Niall,' Father Doherty said. They spoke for a few moments. Dunphy was in tears. 'I phoned Kev back and said, "It's true, man."'

For Kevin Doherty, it was 'a knock-out blow'. Dunphy says it was 'devastating, absolutely devastating'. Dee Devenney says he was in 'utter shock' when the news reached him in Berlin. He had assumed, like they all had, that their mate would pull through.

Dunphy tracked down Gerard Mullan at work in Nottingham. 'I couldn't believe what Niall was saying,' Mullan recalls. 'I was just totally shell-shocked. "What am I going to do now?" I couldn't concentrate at all.'

They were all in pieces, all feeling the same emotions in different towns, unfamiliar towns where they barely knew a soul. The isolation of their new-found grown-up existence had just hit home: in Berlin, in Leeds, in Nottingham, in London. They decided to seek strength in numbers. Dunphy, Mullan and Kevin Doherty met up at King's Cross the next day and spent a couple of days together. It helped them, being able to share their grief with each other. But it also spelt out a terrible, inescapable truth: things would never be the same again.

Adrian Doherty's family knew they had to talk about the practicalities. What kind of funeral would it be? They agreed it was important, amid the grief, to celebrate his life. That meant music. Maybe they could play one of his favourite songs or even one of those he had written. Someone proposed Bob Dylan's 'Forever Young'. That was perfect, they said. Peter volunteered to play it, but it was initially felt this might be too big a burden for a grieving younger brother. Michael Ferry, Adrian's cousin, offered to play and sing. There was talk of one of Peter's friends joining Michael, but Peter insisted he would like to play too. 'Are you sure you're OK with this, Peter? Are sure you're OK?' 'Yes, I'll do it. Adrian would like that.'

They talked about readings. Gareth said he would read something from the Bible. Would Ciara like to do a reading? Someone mentioned a poem she had written about Adrian while at school years earlier. This would lend some much-needed warmth to proceedings. Would Ciara be happy to do this? She thought about it. She was not sure she would be able to compose herself to get through it. She asked if Father Doherty might read it out. They agreed on this but told her she was welcome to change her mind and do it herself if she wished.

Thoughts turned to other matters: flowers, the wake. Would they have pall-bearers? Yes, they agreed, it would be nice if Adrian's friends would carry the coffin, but they would have to check with the lads first. Of course, they said. Nothing was too much trouble. Everyone was going along with whatever had to be done. Playing 'Forever Young'? Of course. A reading? Yes. Carrying the coffin to the graveside? It's what Adrian would have wanted. For a short time, these practicalities were all anyone was able to talk about. Inside, everyone was feeling the same thing: total devastation.

The sun had the temerity to shine on Strabane on the morning of the funeral. 'I remember getting up and it being a bright day,' Ciara says. 'That whole week was sunny and it just didn't seem right, considering what was going on.'

Niall Dunphy's eyes turn red when he recalls the funeral. He is remembering how, again seeking strength in numbers, he arranged with Kevin Doherty and Dee Devenney for the three of them to walk down together to the church for their pall-bearing duties. As soon as they turned the corner to see the mourners gathering, it suddenly struck them how wrong it would look for Adrian Doherty's parents to see the three of them without their fourth *amigo*. 'It had always been the four of us when we were kids – me, Kev, Dee, Aidy,' Dunphy says. 'We just didn't think. I still feel awful about that now.'

Inside the packed chapel, Gareth Doherty was set off by the sight of his younger brother struggling to hold back the tears as he played 'Forever Young'. 'I thought I would be OK to do it,' Peter says. 'Then when I started to play, the first few chords, I was definitely very emotional. It was a very strange experience, but I was glad I did it because, to me, playing the guitar, playing Bob Dylan, was one of the things Adrian and I did together.'

Peter strummed along and his cousin Michael Ferry sang. Dylan's lyrics about the innocence of youth carried a haunting quality, particularly the last line of the chorus:

May you stay forever young.

Ciara Doherty decided she would, after all, read the wonderfully poignant poem she had written about Adrian years earlier as part of her GCSE English coursework. The poem reflects on his personal journey, likening him to a bird venturing out into the world for the first time, spreading its wings and finding beauty and humour even in the harsher aspects of life. It perfectly captures Ciara's heartfelt admiration for the way in which her brother dealt with and moved on from whatever cruelties he encountered.

They stepped outside, all of them, into the sunshine – the horrible, unwelcome, totally incongruous sunshine – and crossed the road to the cemetery, where Adrian was buried. From there, they went back to Belldoo, back to the house with the empty chair, for the wake. 'We were still in shock,' Gareth says. 'We were trying to have conversations about normal things, but nothing was ever going to be the same again.'

'I think you're kind of carried along with it, especially in Ireland,' Ciara says. 'I don't know if it's just Ireland, but it was that Irish wake thing. The house was just packed, people everywhere, and it just doesn't feel real.'

'And then everyone went away again,' Peter says, 'and it was just the five of us sitting there. And it was then that I just thought, "Jesus. This is . . ."'

'We were all mentally exhausted from everything and hadn't slept all week,' Ciara says. 'I slept for what seemed like hours. And then I woke up and Kathy was there.'

Kathy Maloney had been on holiday in France with friends when she heard the news. Jimmy Doherty had called her parents in Galway to tell them after finding their telephone number on a scrap of paper in Adrian's Bible. She was devastated. She flew back to Dublin the next day, too late to get to Strabane that evening. She spent the night at the airport, got the first train to Belfast the next morning and then caught a bus to Strabane. 'It was late in the afternoon when I got to the house,' she says. 'By then he had been buried.

'I had met Jimmy and Geraldine before, but that was the first time I met the rest of the family. We all sat around and talked about Adrian. It was nice to be able to do that. I didn't have anywhere to stay – I had just got there as soon as I could – so they said I could stay over. I wouldn't have wanted to be anywhere else.'

At a loss, a group of Adrian Doherty's friends had decided to stray into the town centre to drown their sorrows and celebrate his life. 'Ridiculous as it might sound, we had a really good time just reminiscing about old times with Adrian and some of the things he had said and done over the years,' Kevin Doherty says. 'Someone said: "What do you think he would say if he could see us here now or if he had seen us in tears at the church earlier?" We all agreed he would have said: "Catch yourself on," which basically is a Northern Irish way of saying, "Get a grip." So for two or three hours we had a right laugh, reminiscing and seeking solace in each other. That sticks out as a nice memory at a horrible, horrible time.'

They went through all their favourite memories of Adrian: the uncontrollable laughing fits, the 'Battle of Marathon' drawing, the infamous chemistry exam at St Colman's, the holidays at Downings and Bunbeg, the Egyptian mummy routine, the Drunken Louts and his brilliance with a football, whether it was dribbling the length of the Gaelic pitch, running rings around defenders from the next school, the next town, the next district, or indeed starring alongside Ryan Giggs in the Manchester

United youth team. They joked about how Adrian would have been the first Premier League superstar to spend his afternoons busking outside the Arndale Centre wearing second-hand clothes and that pair of steel-toecapped boots. But then the laughter died down again and, as Dee Devenney reiterates, it just seemed unreal.

Back at the Parochial House, Father Michael Doherty was left to reflect on one of the saddest days in all his time as a parish priest. During the funeral he had told the mourners how he used to 'watch in great admiration' as Adrian Doherty would train alone for hours on the adjoining playing fields and how 'in my first months here, I used to notice the boy who came to evening Mass almost every day and who sat over on the organ side of the church'.

'His coming to Mass was part of his personal search for truth,' Father Doherty told the mourners. 'What he wanted in his life, what he needed in his life, what he had in his life, was authenticity. He was true to himself.'

CHAPTER 29

We are sitting in Giuliano Maiorana's kitchen. He has been answering questions for an hour and a half, speaking at length about his own experience of damaged ligaments and shattered dreams at Manchester United, the difficulties of adjusting to life after football and about how his own case compares and contrasts with that of his former team-mate Adrian Doherty. He has enjoyed unburdening himself, but he has not found it easy.

This time he poses the question. 'So what did happen then?' he asks. 'What happened to Doc?'

'What do you think happened?'

'All I heard is . . . he was in Amsterdam one night and he fell in a canal. And . . . you hear that and you don't know what to think.'

'Well if I told you it wasn't in Amsterdam and it wasn't at night, would that make a difference?'

'To be fair, it does make a difference. Where was it?'

'It was in The Hague and it was in the morning. Why does that make a difference to you?'

'Because as soon as you hear Amsterdam, at night, you think . . . you know . . . seedy. If you heard it was somewhere else, you wouldn't jump to the same conclusion. And then it's the human brain putting two and two together and that's a horrible shame, especially for the ones he has left behind. Has he got brothers and sisters? Because that would be hard for them and even harder for his poor parents.'

Adrian Doherty's brothers, Gareth and Peter, and sister, Ciara (now McAnenny), still live and work near the family home in Strabane. They have all moved away at times but have found their way back. They are now settled down with kids of their own – all boys, at the time of writing. Jimmy and Geraldine Doherty, the most doting of grand-parents, joke that they will soon have enough boys for an eleven-a-side team at what they call their 'crèche'.

Fifteen years have passed since they lost Adrian – 'a beloved son and brother,' as the inscription on his head-stone reads. The sense of loss will never leave them, but over time little things come along (children and grand-children, for instance) to make life more pleasant and help them look both back and forward with happiness.

The thing that causes most hurt is the innuendo that has continued to surround Adrian's death. It is not just the time and the place that people have got wrong. It is the whis-pers, the speculation and the bold-as-brass declarations the family keep hearing about how he must have ended up in the water. When you are talking about such an enigma as Adrian Doherty – the kid who saw his dreams shattered at Manchester United by injury and then ended up writing poems in a one-bedroom flat in Galway before taking a summer job in a furniture warehouse in provincial Holland – there is no shortage of people willing to specu-late it must have been drugs, excessive alcohol or suicide.

'I've had someone come up to me and say something

directly, to my face, not realising they were saying any-thing wrong,' Ciara says. 'They thought it was fact.'

'I've had that too,' Peter says.

'They're not necessarily being nasty, but they were mak-ing a comment about Adrian as if it was true – and it wasn't,' Ciara says. 'But they believe it because they've been told it and they've never heard otherwise.'

'What a lot of people don't realise is that the years from twenty to twenty-six, after he left football, were the happi-est of Adrian's life,' his brother Gareth says. 'Instead they see, "Footballer, released by Manchester United, fell into a canal in Amsterdam" – which isn't true – and they jump to conclusions. They speculate and come up with their own theories. Over fifteen years those theories have just taken hold in people's minds and there has been nothing said or written to put that right.'

The report into Adrian Doherty's death has been retrieved from a vault in The Hague by Simon Daw, an Englishman who serves as a *wijkagent* (community police officer) in the Stationsbuurt area of the Dutch capital. On the morning of 7 May 2000 he was an *agent* (constable) on street-patrol duties with a colleague in the city centre when they were alerted to an incident near Zwarteweg, the road that runs parallel to the canal near The Hague's central station.

There are restrictions to what he can disclose about the contents of the report – including specific details of offi-cers and witnesses named in the file – but, with authority given by the family of the deceased, Daw is able to shed some light on the events surrounding and the subsequent investigation into Adrian's death.

Shortly after 9 a.m. that Sunday, Daw and his police colleague were on patrol on Zwarteweg when they were alerted by an Asian man gesturing that someone had fallen into the canal near the intersection with Herengracht. Upon seeing a body in the canal, they called for assistance. The fire brigade sent a diving team, who retrieved the unconscious man from the water. Resuscitation attempts began at the waterside before he was rushed by ambulance to the Westeinde hospital, just over a mile away.

That was the last Daw ever saw of Adrian Doherty. He and his colleague returned to the police station at Jan Hendrikstraat to report the incident. The case was then passed on to the detectives at the station.

On arrival at Westeinde, Adrian was examined by doctors. The doctor's report at 9.59 a.m. said the patient was unconscious but his heart was still beating. It also stated there was no evidence of violence or drug use. Tests revealed there was some alcohol in his blood, but the relatively small quantity involved led police to conclude this was from the previous evening. 'We're not talking about a rolling-around-in-the-street quantity of alcohol, or anything like that,' Daw says.

Daw says that, in a statement to police, the Asian man said he had heard a splash made by someone either falling into or struggling in the water. Adrian – as several of his friends have noted – never learned to swim and was, in fact, terrified of water.

At this stage we, like the police, can discount drugs or excessive alcohol consumption as the reason for Adrian's fall into the canal. To judge by the Asian man's statement, we can discount the possibility that Adrian had been in

there for hours as a result of any excesses the previous
night.

Adrian Doherty had been due at work at Dekker Hout,
back in Warmond, that morning. The location where he
was found – and, according to Daw's description of the
Asian man's testimony, heard – in the canal by the intersection of Zwarteweg and Herengracht was 400 metres from
The Hague's central station, from where six trains leave for
Warmond every hour, even on a Sunday morning. So far as
anyone can assume anything about what happened that
morning, every last bit of evidence indicates he was either
walking or running to catch a train back to Warmond to
work and somehow fell into the canal.

Once the unknown patient at Westeinde had been identified –
with the missing-person appeal from Strabane helping
to bring together those two separate police inquiries in
The Hague and Katwijk – the investigation gathered pace.
Detectives were sent to Warmond in order to try to find
out more about Adrian Doherty and the sequence of
events that had left him fighting for his life back at
Westeinde.

Several of those interviewed at Dekker Hout's head-
quarters on 17 May were Irish; the company appeared to
have recruited extensively by using the same employment
agency that contacted Adrian barely a fortnight earlier.
Police also interviewed a cleaner at the firm's living quarters. The detectives wanted to find out what these Irish
lads knew about Adrian and whether he had said anything
about his plans for his visit to The Hague. They also asked
whether he drank, heavily or otherwise, whether he had

shown any signs of taking drugs, whether there was any hint of depression.

The answers the detectives were given were all similar. The Irish workers had only met Adrian in the days prior to his disappearance, but the words they used to describe him included quiet, naive, innocent, calm; one of them referred to him being like a 'hippy', walking around, playing his guitar; he had shown no interest in drugs when the subject cropped up in conversations about the far more permissive Dutch laws; after his visit to The Hague on 3 May he had enthused about the quality of the Guinness at an Irish bar, saying it was better than back home; he had told the cleaner and one of his co-workers he had made some friends in the capital on the Wednesday night and was returning on the Saturday for a night out with them.

Police then enquired at Irish pubs in The Hague, showing photographs of Adrian, asking if staff or punters recognised him. At one pub, a barmaid said she vaguely recognised his face from a recent visit, but she did not remember anything more than that. After that, the trail ran cold and the police were left to inform the Doherty family – at this point still fretting at Adrian's bedside at Westeinde – that they had found no evidence of any suspicious circumstances regarding the incident. Their investigation led them to the firm conclusion that it was a freakish accident.

Simon Daw is unable to make any official comment on the matter but, flicking through the police report for the first time in many years, he makes the casual observation that Adrian Doherty sounds like a guy who was looking forward to a few pints of Guinness on that Saturday night and who was heading back to work the next morning when he fell into the canal.

It is not quite enough, though. It could do with an official clarification. Under Dutch law, this can only be sought with the permission of the bereaved family. The Doherty family are persuaded that the only way to dispel the innuendo is by requesting an official statement from the Dutch authorities. They write a letter to accompany mine, in which the public prosecution service is asked whether it is able to reveal its findings in order to help establish the truth about Adrian Doherty.

Clarification arrives on 23 July 2015 in the form of an email sent initially to Jimmy Doherty from Giel Franssen, the assistant public prosecutor, at the Palace of Justice in The Hague:

Dear Mister Doherty

With reference to your letter and Mister Kay's of the 25th and the 22nd of June 2015, I hereby can state the following.

As I was not familiar with this case, I got in touch with Mister Simon Daw of our Police. He explained to me what had occurred that particular day with your son.

Intensive investigations have never shown any proof that the way your son got in the canal was in any way due to or could be linked to criminal behaviour. Also for foul play, as you mentioned it, [there] were no indications at all.

In the blood of your son, no signs of drugs were found. There was, however, alcohol in his blood detected, although the level of it was not considered dangerous or very high.

The conclusion that could therefore be taken here was that this must have been an accident with, unfortunately, a very tragic outcome.

I hope this letter answers your questions and I am deeply sorry for your loss.

The public prosecutor
On his behalf
G. T. M. Franssen, Master of Laws
Assistant Public Prosecutor/International Legal Assistance

Still not clear enough? Mr Franssen is questioned about his use of that word 'could' – the conclusion that *could* therefore be taken here. Does this raise some small degree of doubt about the 'accident' verdict?

He writes back:

There was no reason to believe that anything else [other] than an unfortunate accident had taken place that day. So therefore the conclusion here was the one taken by us, as it must have been an unfortunate accident.

When Adrian Doherty died on 9 June 2000, national media coverage on the British mainland was restricted to a single ten-paragraph story in the *Sunday Mirror*, filed by Maeve Quigley on the newspaper's Irish desk. Six of those paragraphs consisted of quotes from Father Michael Doherty, who spoke of the shock and sorrow felt in Strabane. Beyond that, Quigley simply reported the facts: that the 26-year-old former Manchester United footballer had been working in Holland and, after falling into a canal, he was in a coma for a month before passing away in hospital in The Hague that Friday.

The story was also reported in the twice-weekly *Derry Journal*, which at the earliest opportunity, on 13 June 2000, published an article under the headline 'Tributes flow for tragic soccer "gem"'. The main tribute in the article came from United's assistant secretary Ken Ramsden, who spoke warmly of Adrian's talent and good nature, saying that everyone at Old Trafford was 'very shocked and very very upset'. The *Journal* published a little more information on the circumstances, saying that Adrian 'was returning from spending the first weekend of his stay with friends in The Hague when the accident happened. He was on his way to catch an early-morning train when a passer-by saw [sic] him trip and fall into one of the many canals in the area. He was recovered from the water by police and emergency services, who were on the scene within minutes, but he never regained consciousness.'

Somehow, though, 'Amsterdam' stuck. It is astounding how many of the former United players brought up that word in the course of interviews for this book. And it was alarming that, seemingly on the basis of an incorrect link with Amsterdam and all the connotations that go with it, the United old-boy network was full of wild theories about what had happened to 'Doc':

'Didn't he fall off a boat in Amsterdam or something?'
No, he did not.

'He drank himself to death, didn't he?'
No, he did not.

'I heard he died in Amsterdam and it was drug-related.'
No, he did not. No, it was not.

'I just heard he was found in a canal in Amsterdam, so you just
    think either he fell in and he couldn't swim or . . . he took
    his life.'
It wasn't Amsterdam. But yes, that is true, he couldn't swim.

'I heard it was suicide.'
From whom? The authorities in The Hague?
'No, just on the grapevine.'

That last one summed up how the gossip takes on a life of its own. The ex-player in question was, like so many others, extremely helpful and indeed warm in sharing his memories of and insights into Adrian's four seasons at United, but he knew nothing of his former team-mate's movements from 1993 onwards. Only a handful of them knew he had briefly played for Derry City and moved to Preston to make a fresh start in life. None knew he had moved to Galway and none had heard a single thing about him for years until learning of his death. The same goes for many people back in Strabane, where he rarely ventured out in later years. And yet despite knowing so little about his post-football life – or perhaps precisely *because* they knew so little about his post-football life – some believed and passed on the gossip that inevitably filled up the information vacuum where the death of the mysterious, enigmatic Adrian Doherty is concerned.

For his family, it has been painful enough to deal with the grief without having to contend with the untruths that have followed. So if the truth as laid out by the Dutch police and by the public prosecutor's office in The Hague is still not enough to satisfy you, and you feel the need to embellish it with some details of your own, might I propose the simplest, most straightforward version whereby this wonderful guy who happily stumbled through life, ignoring its pitfalls, was daydreaming away, composing his next poem or song, singing away to himself on his way to the station, when he took a fateful wrong step. What sort of person would do something like that? A dreamer, with his head in the clouds, like Adrian Doherty.

CHAPTER 30

Life goes on. Football certainly does. By August 2000 a new season had dawned as Manchester United played host to their highest attendance since the war as 67,477 filed into a newly expanded Old Trafford for the opening game of their latest Premier League title defence. Sir Alex Ferguson was still on the touchline, a rather more imperious figure these days, and the United starting XI contained no fewer than five players who had learned their trade under Eric Harrison and Brian Kidd at the Cliff and Littleton Road: Gary Neville, Phil Neville, David Beckham, Paul Scholes and Ryan Giggs, all of them established internationals, all of them Champions League winners in 1999, some of them genuine global superstars. So far, so familiar, but United had grown into a different institution over the past decade. Manchester United plc was becoming a global success story, a latent fanbase across the world now being actively targeted as the club entered the digital era and, aided by a smattering of home-grown superstars, sought to increase and exploit its burgeoning popularity. The changes in the football business, with United at the vanguard, were reflected in the day's match programme, with full-page adverts for the new kit, the Megastore, MUTV, manutd.com, manUmobile, the new credit card and, perhaps most notably, the handover of the entire back page (previously the sacred home of the team line-ups) to a banner listing the club's twelve official sponsors, including a new e-betting partner, e-business partner, technology partner, sports retailer and so on.

Less conspicuous in the programme was a short item halfway down page 14, telling the more eagle-eyed readers of a death in the Manchester United family. 'News of the death of Adrian Doherty was received with great disbelief,' it said. 'He was 26.' Adrian was described as a 'precociously talented youngster . . . tipped for the top by many observers', but the five-paragraph item went on to say that 'despite his early promise he failed to make the breakthrough into the first team and was given a free transfer in June 1993'. It added that 'his tragic and untimely death . . . came as a numbing and distressing shock to everyone who knew and remembered him'. Belated, sincere condolences were offered to his family. And with that, the club moved on – matches to win, trophies to chase, markets to target, money to make. Life goes on. Football certainly does.

Grateful as they were for the condolences offered, the wording of that article did nothing to ease the Doherty family's deep anguish. 'Despite his early promise he failed to make the breakthrough into the first team'? That was clumsy at best. It did not sit comfortably with them. But at a time of intense grief, the wording of a tribute from Manchester United was not at the forefront of their minds.

Over time, as the years passed, the Doherty family found themselves starting to wonder as if Adrian had been airbrushed from Manchester United history. He might only have been a small footnote in any case, but, at a club so eager to embrace and indeed market the nostalgia for the generation of players who came and went through their youth system in the early 1990s (which includes many of those who did not make it, as well as those who did), it felt increasingly strange that his name was never brought up when the club's many official media outlets took their supporters on their frequent trips down memory lane. Robbie Savage and Keith Gillespie, who flew the Old Trafford nest at a young age, both referred to him briefly but glowingly in their autobiographies, but those whose words about the youth set-up carried most weight within the United family, such as Sir Alex Ferguson, Eric Harrison, Ryan Giggs and Gary Neville, never mentioned him. When the journalist Michael Walker went back to United on a couple of occasions to ask if it would be possible to resurrect and update those unpublished Ferguson quotes about Adrian from his December 1999 interview, for an article that would now be about a precocious talent whose career and life had ended tragically, he was told it was not a suitable time.

The family's suspicions were so deeply held that years later they were pleasantly surprised – astounded in some cases – to be told that Ferguson, Harrison, Giggs, Neville and so many others had agreed to help in the course of researching this book.

Earlier, Giggs spoke with great warmth, fondness and admiration about Adrian Doherty as a footballer. Now the questions come with a harsher focus on the stark contrast between the superstar – Ryan Giggs, OBE, Freeman of the City of Salford, assistant manager of the club where he made 963 appearances, winning thirteen Premier League titles, four FA Cups, three League Cups, two Champions Leagues, the European Super Cup, the Intercontinental Cup and the Club World Cup – and the similarly gifted team-mate whose career and life took such a different turn after their days starring together in the United youth team.

How did Giggs learn that Doherty had died in June 2000? 'I don't remember how I heard,' he says solemnly. 'I just remember it was one of those where you think, "Is that true? It can't be true. It must be a mistake." It was one of those bits of news you get that you just can't believe. As a footballer, you share a dressing room with someone for four or five years, seeing them every day, and then perhaps you don't see them for years because you go off on different paths. But then to hear that he had died was such a blow and such a shock because he was so young. It was just so sad.'

Did Giggs ever consider how differently things might have turned out had he, rather than Doherty, experienced that *Sliding Doors* moment, struck down by injury when the pair of them were on the verge of a first-team call-up in early 1991? 'As a young player, you're so caught up in what you're doing, you don't really think about that at the time,' Giggs says. 'But yes, that could easily have been me. I would have been playing in an A-team game a couple of weeks before. We were at the same level at that time. But then the injury happened, which I think was the first cruciate injury I'd ever known, and he was never the same again after that. It was tough for him.'

There is one particular question that Doherty's family want answering, if only for their own peace of mind. Why has Doherty never previously been mentioned in any of the books or interviews in which Giggs and other team-mates have reeled off the names of talented players (Giuliano Maiorana, Raphael Burke, Ben Thornley, Chris Casper, George Switzer, John O'Kane) who were not quite lucky enough to have made the big time at United? Was it out of awkwardness at what happened? Was it some-thing else? 'Maybe an awkwardness, yes, because nobody knew the full details,' Giggs says. 'Doc was never really close to anyone at the club. Within the dressing rooms he was fine, a really lovely lad, but away from the football, you wouldn't see him or hear from him. None of us could really say we knew him. We just knew him as a lovely lad and an incredible talent.'

Adrian Doherty's family always suspected there was another reason for the silence from Old Trafford. For more than a decade, a dispute rumbled with Manchester United over the standard of care – both medical and welfare – that Adrian received during his four years at the club.

Jimmy Doherty was not seeking financial gain when he requested a meeting with United in February 2002. Wrest-ling with his grief, he had found himself looking for answers – the answers that had not been forthcoming when he travelled to Manchester following Adrian's release by the club almost nine years earlier. In one sense those questions were irrelevant now, but Jimmy, wanting to know more about his son's life, felt it was time to ask about the care that Adrian had received, medical and otherwise, at United. And the more Jimmy thought about it, the more he wanted something else – an article in which the club would pay tribute to Adrian and help to set the record straight regarding both his departure from Old Trafford in 1993 and his death seven years later. Such a move, Jimmy believed, would go some way towards silencing the hurtful slurs and innuendo the family had already begun to hear.

Over the years that followed, Jimmy travelled to Manchester for a series of meetings with Sir Alex Ferguson and successive United chief executives (Peter Kenyon and David Gill), as well as Maurice Watkins, the club's solicitor at the time. The more pointed the questions that Jimmy asked, the more adversarial the situation became. Some of the meetings ended with handshakes, others with Jimmy infuriated by what he considered a dismissive, condescending attitude to his complaints about the treatment of his late son. Jimmy felt humanity and empathy from Ferguson and Gill when he was in a room with them, but then things would turn corporate and legal and the shutters would go up. It was not the Manchester United he had known and loved since his days growing up in Derry, devoted to the Busby Babes. He had loved the family feel of Old Trafford in the days of Adrian's apprenticeship, but now it was like dealing with a big, faceless corporate machine. Any time he left a meeting feeling that progress had been made and some common ground reached, the follow-up correspondence, in which both parties gave their reflections, would result in the two sides further apart than ever.

Jimmy Doherty was not interested in legal action or a compensation claim, but as he broadened his enquiries about both the medical treatment and the welfare aspect of his son's time in Manchester, and as the tone of the

discussions with the club became colder, he became convinced that United owed the family an apology – whether
public or private – and should help to set the record straight
with a statement or article about Adrian.

Letters continued to be sent back and forth, with Jimmy
approaching the PFA, whom he imagined would be keen
to support the family of a footballer who died at a tragically young age, and the FA, in the hope of mediation. He
was left with the feeling that United, the PFA and the FA
closed ranks. The FA spoke to United at executive level,
sought assurances and closed their investigation. An FA
spokesman declined to make an official comment on the
matter but said that the investigation had been closed.

At one point Gary Neville, as club captain, was roped
in to try to help with the mediation process. Jimmy
Doherty's recollection of that telephone conversation is
that Neville, after speaking so fondly and admiringly of
Adrian, advised him, in friendly terms, that it would be
pointless trying to take on the might of Manchester United.
Neville sympathised with the family and the feeling was
mutual; what was a player expected to say or do when
somehow dragged into the middle of a dispute between
his club and the grieving father of a player with whom he
had shared a dressing room? Besides, everything Jimmy
encountered from the football authorities – not least the
dead ends that greeted him when he tried to take the matter to the FA, the Premier League and the PFA – told him
that Neville was probably right.

After an awful lot of deliberation, Jimmy, Geraldine and
the rest of the Doherty family decided against airing their

grievances in this book. They do not want a book about their beloved Adrian to end with a 'slanging match'.

Yet those grievances persist and are deeply held. They boil down to three issues. First, how and when did Adrian sustain the cruciate ligament damage that effectively ended his career? Did the injury evolve over time or was it sustained, as both Sir Alex Ferguson and the club's former physiotherapist have suggested in this book, in that A-team match against Carlisle United reserves in February 1991? If the latter, why was it not diagnosed for five months and not operated on for almost a year, by which time he had suffered a reoccurrence and his prospects of a recovery looked extremely bleak? Second, why was Adrian simply released when his contract expired at the end of the 1992/3 season rather than being given time to regain his fitness and his sharpness after almost two years out with a career-threatening injury? The club told Jimmy Doherty at one stage that Adrian 'left of his own accord', but that was not consistent with anything they had suggested previously or since. Third, why – seemingly – was little done to protect Adrian and his fellow apprentices from the culture of intimidation and humiliation described in these pages as well as in books written by other players of that generation? Adrian's parents were assured prior to his move to Manchester shortly after his sixteenth birthday that the club would offer him a 'home from home', yet the testimonies of several of his contemporaries in this book and others only heighten the impression of a dressing-room culture that at times lurched between the inane and the sinister. Was enough done to protect the club's young players, particularly those in digs?

Long before his retirement in 2013, Ferguson used to cite the expansion of the medical department as one of the greatest illustrations of how things had changed over the course of his tenure at United. Expertise has grown enormously where both prevention and treatment of injuries are concerned. Joe McClelland, who carried out Adrian's knee operation in February 1992, says the success rate for cruciate ligament reconstruction improved dramatically over the course of that decade, to the extent that surgery could soon be approached confidently rather than as a last resort. It seems beyond question that Adrian Doherty would have had a far better chance of making a full recovery – or any kind of recovery – had such an injury occurred three or four years later, let alone now. His family's question will always be about whether the damage could and should have been treated better at the time and, in view of all that had happened, whether more could have been done to help a brilliant young player who was left so disillusioned by the injury and its grim aftermath.

Likewise, it is clear that some of the issues that Adrian encountered upon moving to Manchester as a sixteen-year-old – isolation, homesickness, vulnerability, disaffection – would be identified and addressed now with an expertise that was sorely lacking in the football industry in 1989. While being interviewed for this book, Brian Kidd, who back then was a youth-team coach at United, draws the distinction between the psychological expertise that exists in football now and 'the old-fashioned way, which, as we've said, was like "Get on with it." Which is wrong. Which is wrong.'

Other aspects of English football's dressing-room culture in the 1980s and early 1990s were considerably more wrong. Those 'initiation' trials – and they went on far longer than just the first week for the apprentices who joined in 1989 and the couple of years that followed – might have been mythologised by some of those who graduated from the school of hard knocks, but if Adrian Doherty felt intimidated, degraded or humiliated by some of the antics detailed earlier in this book, he would not have been the only one. Whether it was placing apprentices in tumble dryers, kicking balls in their face, stripping them and daubing them with a dubbin-smeared wire brush, forcing them to simulate sex on a treatment table, let alone the even more sinister stuff mentioned by Lee Sharpe about schoolboys in digs being lined up in front of a porno-graphic film and 'made to watch it', fearing a flurry of punches if they dared to get aroused, it says an awful lot about standards at the time – in English football as a whole, not just at United – if it was regarded as anything other than appalling.

Some will claim this kind of stuff makes aspiring profes-sional sportsmen and sportswomen stronger. Maybe in a few cases it did. But, among the 1989 intake at United, Mar-cus Brameld says that 'some of them crumbled a little bit'; Les Potts says the second-year apprentices 'probably made my life hell'; Jonathan Stanger feels he 'wasn't mentally strong enough to survive in that environment'. And before any old-school types suggest that a professional sportsman should have the mental strength to grin and bear it when subjected to that kind of culture – particularly that described by Sharpe – we are talking in some cases about boys, aged sixteen and younger, going away from home and being sub-jected to various levels of what most people would term abuse.

In common with most clubs, United now have in place a rigorous 'safeguarding policy' which includes strict guidelines to protect children, which in this instance is defined as anyone up to the age of eighteen. It prohibits the type of dressing-room culture that was so commonplace in English football in the late 1980s and early 1990s – not least at United until, as Paul Scholes says, a parent caught wind of it and complained.

One man well placed to discuss the improvement in standards is Chris Casper, the former United and England Under-21 defender who now works for the Premier League as a club support manager, ensuring that youth academies meet the required standards of coaching, facilities, education and welfare. 'There is so much more support now,' Casper says. 'The Premier League have put a really big emphasis on making sure young players have the right support around them to give them the best chance of making a career in football – and, if not in football, then the best chance of making a career elsewhere.'

Do young players still find themselves in the kind of chaotic living arrangements that several former United players have described in digs in the early 1990s? 'No,' Casper says. 'It's very rare now to have more than two players to a house parent. I know what you mean. I lived at Brenda's for a week and I couldn't stand it. I had to move back home again. That was no reflection at all on Brenda. It's just that I found nothing worse than training day in, day out with players and then going back to digs with six or seven of you under one roof. That doesn't happen now.'

When approached prior to publication of this book, Manchester United declined to comment on the issues raised with regard to Adrian Doherty and to medical and welfare standards at the club in the late 1980s and early 1990s. Jonathan Noble, United's former orthopaedic surgeon, also declined to comment, saying he would never discuss the case of any patient, alive or dead. The club's position can be best summed up by the sentiments expressed by David Gill, then the chief executive, in a letter to Jimmy Doherty on 17 September 2012. Gill told Adrian's father that, having studied the file again, along with the notes from the many meetings held over the previous decade, he felt they would have to agree to disagree. Gill said he firmly believed that 'the club, both at the time and subsequently, acted fairly and appropriately'. 'It is a situation that is clearly unfortunate and sad,' he added, 'but for which I don't believe that the club is culpable.'

As far as any kind of peace offering is concerned, United proposed to dedicate a trophy in Adrian's name, to be awarded at the Northern Ireland Milk Cup each July, but the Doherty family felt such a gesture would be hollow unless accompanied by some acknowledgement – private or public – of mistakes the club made with regard to both his injury and his welfare. Eventually, they reached an agreement that saw the club publish an article about Adrian Doherty 'The star we never saw' in their official magazine, *Inside United*, in February 2007. A single-page item, towards the back, it contained brief quotes from Ryan Giggs, Gary Neville, Brian McClair and Eric Harrison, but it left various loose ends, raising almost as many questions as those it answered. Moreover, there was no input from Sir Alex Ferguson apart from the 'greased lightning' quotes the club had recycled from a match programme almost twenty years earlier. The family felt it was half-hearted, an opportunity wasted.

There were further meetings with Ferguson and Maurice Watkins in Manchester in March 2011 and with Gill in Belfast in September 2012, but the stalemate remained. What has followed has been a cooling-off period. The Dohertys still feel Adrian was badly let down during his four years at Manchester United – not just with regard to the handling of his injury and its aftermath but also the failure to deliver the 'home from home' environment that was promised. They cannot help feeling that, for a boy so dedicated to become so disillusioned that he fled Manchester in the first months of the apprenticeship and then rejected the offer of a five-year contract, with the door to the first team opening, there must have been something badly amiss. Essentially it comes down to the family's belief that with better care and supervision from Manchester, United, Adrian Doherty's experience of professional football – like that of countless other young players lost to the game in that era – could and should have been very different.

CHAPTER 31

It is springtime once more in Strabane, 'that happy-go-lucky town at the confluence of two tumbling rivers', and another mid-morning walk beckons. The bluebells are out on the riverbanks and on the canal towpath, where there is a steady flow of walkers, some of them coming back from ASDA, weighed down with their shopping bags, and others returning with mud-spattered boots from a ramble in the Sperrins. Elsewhere, people are going about their business, the nature of which continues to change. These days, following the decline of the manufacturing industry, the town's largest employer is the call centre for an outsourcing business. Unemployment is still a problem in Strabane, more than double the rate across the rest of Northern Ireland, but the Troubles are a distant memory, as if from another lifetime. Strabane knows its place, a remote and largely ignored outpost of the United Kingdom, but the locals are used to that by now. They have learned to live with and embrace it. Catch yourself on. The walk follows a now-familiar path, through the town centre, over the River Mourne, past the gleaming Melvin Sports Complex, down through the Ballycolman estate, past the golf club and into Melmount Cemetery.

Within a few hundred yards of Adrian Doherty's resting

place are the spots his life revolved around while growing up in Strabane. Around the corner is the quiet cul-de-sac where his parents still live, where neighbours recall looking out to see him performing impossible tricks with a tennis ball in the garden. Next to the main road is St Mary's Boys' R.C. Primary School. Across the road is the impressive new Holy Cross College – on the site of the old St Colman's High School – and coming back down the road again there is Melmount parish church, where he went to Mass every night during his early teens. Beyond the church are the playing fields, where he would venture every evening, armed with a football, a collection of empty Coke cans and a stopwatch, and put himself through a solo training regime so rigorous and so impressive that it even captured the attention of the visiting servicemen during the Troubles.

The inscription on Adrian's headstone remembers 'a beloved son and brother'. 'Died 9th June 2000,' it says, 'Aged 26 years.' To a passer-by, it might look like the grave of a typical provincial boy who was born in Strabane, raised in Strabane and died in Strabane before he had a chance to broaden his horizons. It happens.

Adrian Doherty's story is not like that. His was a life well lived. He travelled to Manchester, New York, Preston and Galway, and then came that fateful decision to go to Holland and, as he saw it, wherever the wind would take him after that. There were times, over the course of five years researching and investigating his life, when the tale that was unfolding felt more like something from the pages of *Roy of the Rovers*. In the era of pampered football prodigies, whose agents secure them their first multi-million-pound contract long before they have kicked a ball in the

Premier League, Adrian's story – the boy wonder who had the world at his feet but suffered a terrible injury and retreated into obscurity, finding solace in music and poetry – seemed less like a throwback and more like the stuff of fiction.

It was at times like this, though, standing at his grave-side or looking into the eyes of his parents, brothers, sister, cousins or friends, that I found myself bitten by reality, reminded that, for all the joy that the lighter aspects of his story might bring, there would be no happy ending. There is no escape from the grip of the tragedy and its aftermath, which have left a grieving family and a group of close friends to treasure and protect the memory of a unique individual who touched them in ways that went far beyond his extraordinary ability on a football pitch.

In the lounge of their home, just around the corner, Jimmy and Geraldine Doherty are sitting together on the sofa once more, looking across to the mantelpiece and the por-trait of Adrian as they remember him – happy, smiling, forever young. They would prefer not to talk about his accident or the awful years that have followed. The emo-tions remain too raw. Geraldine wishes to leave the talking to her husband. Normally an easy-going, talkative man, Jimmy warns that this is going to be hard for him.

'It's devastating,' he says. 'As any parent who has lost a child will say, nothing could ever prepare any human being for the scale of that shock. You can never get over it. It's impossible to describe the pain or the sense of loss. We find it hard to talk about, particularly Geraldine.

'All parents believe their child is special – and they're right. We sincerely believe Adrian was special. Anyone who knew him would probably say there was something unique about him. He had an aura. In some ways he might have seemed shy or introverted, but he actually had a great strength of character and was incredibly focused. I've heard him described as bohemian, happy-go-lucky and laid-back. And yes, he was all of those things, but that didn't stop him being extremely tough and focused on being the best he could possibly be as a footballer. When he was fifteen he told me he wanted to be the best footballer in the world by the time he was twenty-one. Lots of boys of that age might say that kind of thing, but Adrian really believed it could be achieved. He trained obsessively on his own for hours and hours in all conditions. That's why I believe in some ways Adrian's story is an inspirational one about how a boy from a small town like Strabane could get to Manchester United and reach the verge of the first team at sixteen/seventeen. That tells you a lot not just about his talent but also about his fierce determination.

'He was doing brilliantly at United. Who knows how far he could have gone if he hadn't suffered a terrible injury at the worst possible time? Who knows how far he could have gone if they had got to the bottom of the injury? Then, just as it seemed he was starting to get fit again after nearly two years of intense rehabilitation, the club released him. Even hardened pros will tell you that recovering from a long-term injury is soul-destroying, mentally as well as physically, and has wrecked players' careers and in some cases lives. One year out of the game through injury can be a distressing time for even the most experienced professional footballers, but for a teenager living away from home, in digs, with little moral support, suffering setback after setback, those two years must have been like an absolute nightmare at times for Adrian. We try not to dwell on that these days.

'Some people suggest that Adrian chose music and poetry over football. He didn't. He was writing songs and poetry before he got injured, when he was on the verge of his first-team debut. It was something he always enjoyed and it helped him to deal with the pressures of football. If it hadn't been for the injury, he would have been in United's first team – as Sir Alex Ferguson has said to me and others – but I'm sure he would still have kept up his outside interests. He definitely wouldn't have been your typical footballer. As it turned out, it was important that he had those things in his life, especially after the injury. Without his other interests and his friends outside football, I don't know how he would have come through that life-changing experience.

'As parents, we sometimes used to think, "Why is he going to Preston? Why is he going to Galway? Why is he going to Europe to travel? Is that the right job for him to be doing? What will he do next? Does he have a plan?" But that was Adrian. He was his own man and he didn't sit around feeling sorry for himself when his football career ended. He was just finding his own path and when we look back, we're just so proud of everything he did in his relatively short life – not only his football achievements, but also his music and his writing and how he was able to move on with his life. Above all, we're so proud of him for the person he was. He didn't worry what others thought about him. He always remained true to himself. I'm confident that very few, if any, people who met Adrian, in any walk of life, would have a bad word to say about him. I don't want to make Adrian out to be some kind of saint. He wasn't. He knew how to enjoy himself and I'm sure his mates will tell you he had his own sense of humour. He definitely didn't take himself too seriously. But he really was a one-off, so talented, but also humble and with such strong morals. We always have been and always will be incredibly proud of him.'

Several of his former team-mates have ventured that, but for the injury, Adrian Doherty would have established himself in Manchester United's first team. Sadly we will never know, but there is a widespread belief, expressed by Gary Neville, Ryan Giggs and many others, that he would have coped, mentally and physically, with the pressures of playing first-team football for United in front of a huge crowd. 'If it hadn't been for the injury,' Neville says, 'he would have had a very good career. How good? You can never say for sure, but he was a terrifically talented, skilful footballer who would have had a really good career. He wasn't soft by any means. He was the opposite. On the pitch, he was was a tough little sod. He was certainly tough enough.'

There was, though, another side to Doherty's particular brand of toughness; it meant he was capable of walking away. Some might feel it was weakness that led him to turn his back on football at various points, at first temporarily and then later for good. Others regard it as a strength. This is just a hypothesis, by no means universally accepted, but the more I learned of Adrian Doherty, the more I felt inclined to believe that even had he established himself in

United's first team, no matter how much success he was enjoying, he might have walked away from professional football sooner rather than later. Not because he lacked mental fortitude, but, on the contrary, because he had the strength, single-mindedness and depth to see there was more to life and to follow his own path.

'His outlook on life was so different to that of a typical footballer,' his friend Kevin Doherty says. 'I've no doubt at all that, but for the injury, his star would have continued to rise at United. But with his love for music and writing, that might have opened other horizons and given him opportunities to do other things he wanted to do, perhaps more than the football. Would he have wanted the career Ryan Giggs had? I'm not so sure he would.'

Adrian Doherty would be in his forties now. His brother Gareth allows himself a chuckle when asked what Adrian would be doing had it not been for what happened on that fateful morning in The Hague. 'Nothing would have surprised me with Adrian,' Gareth says. 'It could be anything. Literally anything at all.'

Dee Devenney suggests that Adrian would ultimately have gone back to college to continue his education. Leo Cussons imagines Adrian being 'one of those guys who would sing at festivals and make a lot of people laugh. He would be a wow at festivals actually. People would love him.' Colin Telford, his former team-mate at Manchester United, says: 'If you had told me he was a musician now, or a roadie, in Europe or in America, I would have said he had found his vocation. He was someone you could imagine sitting on a fence in the middle of nowhere, playing his guitar, happily watching the world go by. Or sitting in a bar, having a pint, his guitar at his feet, and then after a few drinks he would get his guitar out and start busking away.'

The next generation of the Doherty family never got the chance to meet Uncle Adrian, but, one by one, they are learning about him. 'My oldest boy, Thomas, is always asking me to tell stories about when I was young,' Gareth says. 'He asks what Adrian and I got up to. If I tell him I played in a football match and I scored two goals, Thomas will say, "I bet Uncle Adrian scored ten goals, didn't he?" Which he probably did. His name is Thomas James Adrian Doherty. He tells people, "Adrian is after my uncle. He played football, but he got hurt in an accident and he's up in heaven now." I think that's nice.'

'One of the saddest things is that they'll never know Adrian,' Ciara McAnenny says of her sons and her nephews. 'You don't want them to grow up hearing the kind of stuff that people have made up about Adrian. You want them to know the truth about what a special person he was.'

How special? One former United team-mate, Marcus Brameld, calls him 'the nicest lad in the world'. Another, Craig Lawton, says he was 'one in a million'. Christian Pauls, his friend in Galway, describes him as 'exceptional.' John Tinney, who played football with him for St Colman's and for Moorfield, says, 'No matter what I do in my life, if I died tomorrow, I would be proud to have been one of those who knew Adrian Doherty first-hand. He was unique.' Another former United team-mate, Sean McAuley, puts it beautifully: 'He played football like Ryan Giggs and played guitar like Bob Dylan.'

As an epitaph, that last one is rather difficult to beat. It would certainly have met with Adrian Doherty's approval, his cheeks reddening, his smile insuppressible. But he never aspired to be like Ryan Giggs. He never even aspired to be like his great idol Bob Dylan. He just wanted to be himself. He was happiest as a busker, an artist, a musician, a poet. He was, after all, a complete unknown, a rolling stone. He liked it that way.

An Oblivious History (abridged)

Socrates was a wise guy – diddle diddle do
Knew about everything under the sky – diddle diddle do
All day long he could reason and chatter – diddle diddle do
But nothing he ever said ever really did matter – diddle diddle
  do
Yeah, Socrates he don't matter
He was just an ancient Greek
Socrates he was just a smart ancient freak

John the Baptist lived in the wild
Prepared the way for the man to be crucified
Had his head brought in on a silver platter
Just shows how much John the Baptist really mattered
Yeah John the Baptist, he don't matter
I know it might sound surprising
But John the Baptist, he did far too much baptising

Moving on now to the Middle Ages
And old Mickey Beth, who was outrageous
Killed his king with a silver dagger
And had hands that could not be washed by water
But old Mickey Beth, he don't matter
Him, his story and his deeds
Old Mickey Beth and his wife were two lousy creeps

Young boy called Arthur before he was fully grown
Pulled a sword out from a stone

Helped by sorcery to rise in rank and stature
But King Arthur slightly never ever mattered
Yeah, King Arthur, he don't really matter
Him, his knights and his round table
It was all just a fable

Moving on now to more modern times
And Arthur Rimbaud, who wrote a lot of rhymes
Read his stuff, man. Just left me staggered
But I'd just like to say that that Rimbaud, he don't really matter
Yeah, Rimbaud, he don't matter
As a young man he was quite stunning
Rimbaud, he soon went gun-running

Friedrich Nietzsche had a marvellous plan
For a while he thought he was Superman
Always was mad but soon went even madder
Yeah, Friedrich Nietzsche, he never mattered
Yeah, Nietzsche, he don't matter
He was just a German crackpot
Yeah, Nietzsche don't matter a lot

Now Muhammad Ali and Bob Dylan
From showbusiness they've made a shilling
Everywhere they go they're treated preferential and flattered
But none of them really matter
Yeah, them showbiz talents, they don't matter
They all only got fingers and thumbs
They all only got cardiovascular systems and lungs

Me myself I'm only a young lad
Sometimes I'm good and sometimes I'm bad
Sometimes I'm happy and sometimes sadder
And me, myself, I don't matter
Yes, me, myself, I don't matter
But I don't have no complaints
Matter of fact I find the anonymity just great

Acknowledgements

The obsession behind the publication of this book began in early 2011. I was researching an article on the 20th anniversary of Ryan Giggs's Manchester United debut, speaking to those who had played with him in the youth team, when one of them asked if I was familiar with the name of Adrian Doherty. It rang the most distant of bells, reminding me of forgotten names on the pages of match programmes and an old *Rothman's Football Yearbook* – Tonge, Costa, Lawton, Toal, Smyth, Doherty – and of informed whispers, two decades earlier, that there was a brilliant young winger who was just as good as Giggs and would join him in United's first team just as soon as he got over an injury.

Telling Adrian's story, from Strabane to Manchester, Preston, Galway and finally Holland, has been an enormous honour, privilege and pleasure, but it would not have been possible without the generosity and support shown to me by so many people.

I would like to start by thanking my two special girls: my wife, Emma, and our daughter, Esmé, who is already, at seven, telling us how much she is looking forward to when she too is a published author. After all those evenings, weekends and indeed holidays that I spent working on the book, thank you both from the bottom of my heart for your patience, your support and your love, which is an inspiration. Thank you to all my family for encouraging and indulging me over the years, particularly my parents for their constant offers of help, whether it was proofreading, transcribing or anything else. Naturally, I rejected every single one of those offers – not out of ingratitude, but simply because, as I've told them many times over the past forty years, 'I want to do it myself . . .'

Thank you to all of my colleagues at *The Times*, present and recently departed, for your support – conscious or otherwise – and particularly to Matt Dickinson, Michael Walker, Danny Taylor, Sam Wallace, Steve Bates, Paul Hetherington and Martin Leach for the various forms of help (and in your case, Danny, just the odd hindrance – wink, wink). A special thank-you goes to literary agent extraordinaire David Luxton, who showed just why he has become the go-to man for any sports hack who aspires to write something a little more enduring than the fish-and-chip paper in which we specialise. David's insight, enthusiasm and unswerving support helped me enormously. David also introduced me to the team at Quercus, led by Richard Milner, who has been everything I would want an editor to be. Thank you also to Richard's Quercus colleagues Elizabeth Masters, Fiona Murphy, Ella Pocock and in particular Ed Griffiths. I am also grateful to Mark Swift, who copy-edited the text, and to Meryl Evans for her legal (and, as it happened, geographical) expertise. Thank you also to Alan Miller on the picture desk at *The Times*, Steve Baker in the News UK archives department, the ever-helpful staff at the British Library and Callie Gladman at Special Rider Music.

As for those who helped me piece together Adrian's story, I'll start in Strabane with an enormous thank-you to Sean Ferry and the boys from St Colman's High School – Kevin Doherty, Dee Devenney, Niall Dunphy, Gerard Mullan, Brian McGillion, Mick Winters and John Tinney – for the depth and warmth they were able to bring with their memories of their great friend, whom they all miss terribly. Those trips down memory lane brought a few tears of laughter as well as tears of sadness. An extra thank-you to Mick for sharing his photographs, including the splendid image on the front cover, and to Ryan McAnenny for his multimedia expertise. Thank you to Sean Davis, Matt Bradley, Brendan Rodgers, Michael Nash, Bob Nesbitt, Marshall Gillespie, Mark Kinsella, Neil Lennon and Liam O'Kane for their insights into youth football in Northern Ireland. Many thanks also to Bob Crilly, Mick Crilly, Johnny Kelly (for putting me up at the Fir Trees on my regular visits), John Farrell, Jim Hunter, Paul Vaughan, Stephen Devenney and Galvin Early, and also to Father Michael Doherty, who made my initial introduction to the Doherty family. Thanks also to the Strabane History Society, the Northern Ireland Statistics and Research Agency and Erin Craig at the Department for Finance and Personnel in Belfast. I am equally appreciative of the many others in Strabane whose offers of help I was unable to take up due to time constraints.

In the early stages of this project I feared I might encounter obstruction from within the Manchester United old-boy network. I was heartened and delighted to find the opposite. It says everything about the esteem and affection in which Adrian was held that so many former players and staff were willing to spare so much time to share their memories of him. A huge thank-you to (in alphabetical order) Viv Anderson, Mark Bosnich, Marcus Brameld, Derek Brazil, Steve Bruce, Wayne Bullimore, Raphael Burke, Chris Casper, Lee Costa, Sir Alex Ferguson (to whom it felt strange to refer without the usual prefix for much of the book), Ryan Giggs, Keith Gillespie, Deiniol Graham, Michael Gray, Eric Harrison, David Johnson, Brian Kidd, Archie Knox, Craig Lawton, Jim Leighton, Jason Lydiate, Sean McAuley, Pat McGibbon, Jim McGregor, Jules Maiorana, Gary Neville, Phil Neville, Gary Pallister, Kevin Pilkington, Mike Pollitt, Les Potts, Mark Robins, Bryan Robson, Bryan 'Pop' Robson, Robbie Savage, Paul Scholes, Jimmy Shields, John Shotton, Peter Smyth, Jonathan Stanger, Colin Telford, Ben Thornley, Kieran Toal, Alan Tonge, Ian Wilkinson and to those others who spoke on condition of confidentiality. Thank you to United youth-team aficionados Tony Park, Ian Brunton and Steve Hobin; to Phil Townsend, Diana Law, Cliff Butler, David Meek, Mark Wylie, Tim Glynne-Jones, Joe McClelland, Brenda Gosling and to those others whom Adrian encountered in Manchester, such as Frank and Geraldine Manning, Francie McCauley, Gerard Kehoe, David Furey, Gary McHugh, Paul Chi, Chas Rigby and particularly Leo Cussons.

Thank you to Karen Ferry, Paleface and Mo Samalot for helping, along with Leo, to piece together the details of Adrian's trip of a lifetime to New York in the summer of 1992; to Roy Coyle, Liam Coyle, Peter Hutton, Eddie Mahon and Kevin Morrison for their help regarding

Adrian's time at Derry City and to Arthur Duffy and Keiron Tourish, who were invaluable in sharing their experiences of reporting on Adrian during different times of his football career; to Thomas Woodward and unnamed others for their insights into gnosis; to Cliff Kellett, Marilyn (I'm sorry, I never caught your surname), Keith Morgan, Neil Hunt, Keith Mitchell, Leah Bamford, John Gillmore and Stef Hall for their help with the Preston years; likewise to Rob Jones, Alison Jones, Kathy Maloney, John O'Connell, Connie Fennell, Pascal Boucaumont, Christian Pauls, Noel Bridgeman, Sean Fitzgerald, Thomas Veale, Joan O'Dea and James Allison for their help with the Galway years; to Catherine Counihan, Josette Morrison, Simon Daw, Giel Franssen and unnamed others for their help in shedding some much-needed light on the saddest part of this story.

All of which brings me finally to the Doherty family – 'the nicest folk you could wish to meet', as I was told on my first visit to Strabane. For Jimmy and Geraldine Doherty, their sons, Gareth and Peter, and their daughter, Ciara McAnenny, this has been a long process and at times a painful one, but I hope this book lives up to their hopes and expectations as a tribute to Adrian. I thank them not just for their time and their memories but for the trust they showed in allowing me first of all to take on this project and then to do it my way, without interference. My overriding hope is that this book helps them – not by bringing any kind of 'closure' but by opening up Adrian's story to a wider audience, thus leading to a greater appreciation of his wonderful talent and personality. I told them that some of the stories I had heard about Adrian reminded me of myself, but deep down I know I was flattering myself. From an early stage, I realised I was writing about an extraordinary individual.

Adrian, we never met, but I like to think we would have got on. This book is dedicated to you and your ever-loving family. I know you would be as proud of them as they are of you.

Bibliography

Baker, Joe, *The Troubles: A Chronology of the Northern Ireland Conflict*, Glenravel Publications, 2011

Beckham, David, *My Side*, Willow, 2004

Ericsson, K. Anders, Krampe, Ralf Th. and Tesch-Romer, Clemens, 'The Role of Deliberate Practice in the Acquisition of Expert Performance', *Psychological Review*, Vol. 100, No. 3, 1993, pp. 363–406

Ferguson, Alex, *Just Champion!*, Manchester United Football Club, 1993

Ferguson, Alex, with David Meek, *Six Years at United*, Mainstream Publishing, 1992

Giggs, Ryan, *Giggs: The Autobiography*, Penguin, 2006

Gillespie, Keith, *How Not to be a Football Millionaire*, Trinity Mirror, 2013

Harrison, Eric, *The View from the Dugout: The Autobiography of Eric Harrison*, Parrs Wood Press, 2001

Heylin, Clinton, *Bob Dylan: Behind the Shades Revisited*, Harper Entertainment, 2003

Hobin, Steve and Park, Tony, *Sons of United: A Chronicle of the Manchester United Youth Team*, Popular Side Publications, 2012

Lake, Paul, *I'm Not Really Here: A Life of Two Halves*, Century, 2011

Lennon, Neil, *Man and Bhoy*, Harper Sport, 2006

McKittrick, David and McVea, David, *Making Sense of the Troubles: The Story of Conflict in Northern Ireland*, New Amsterdam Books, 2002

Margotin, Philippe, *Bob Dylan: All the Songs – the Story Behind Every Track*, Black Dog & Leventhal, 2015

Neville, Gary, *Red: My Autobiography*, Transworld, 2011

Robson, Bryan, *Robbo: My Autobiography*, Hodder & Stoughton, 2006

Savage, Robbie, *Savage!*, Mainstream Publishing, 2010

Sharpe, Lee, *My Idea of Fun: The Autobiography*, Orion, 2005

Also:

Belfast Telegraph, City Life, Daily Express, Derry Journal, Inside United, Manchester Evening News, News of the World, Strabane Chronicle, Sunday Mirror, The Shankill Skinhead, United Review

Credits

399

Index